CHOICE THEORY

T0115860

CHOICE THEORY

THEORY

A New Psychology
of Personal Freedom

William Glasser, M.D.

HARPER

NEW YORK · LONDON · TORONTO · SYDNEY

HARPER

A hardcover edition of this book was published in 1998 by HarperCollins Publishers.

CHOICE THEORY. Copyright © 1998 by William Glasser. All rights reserved. Printed in the United States of America. No part of this book may be used or reproduced in any manner whatsoever without written permission except in the case of brief quotations embodied in critical articles and reviews. For information address HarperCollins Publishers, 195 Broadway, New York, NY 10007.

HarperCollins books may be purchased for educational, business, or sales promotional use. For information, please e-mail the Special Markets Department at SPsales@harpercollins.com.

First HarperPerennial edition published 1999.

Designed by Elliott Beard

To my wife, Carleen

This book is as much hers as mine. I wrote it, and she gave input to every page, literally to every word. I love her very much and wish I had the words to describe our marriage. But in *Far from the Madding Crowd*, Thomas Hardy had the words, and I quote to describe what we have together:

> This good fellowship—camaraderie—usually occurring through the similarity of pursuits is unfortunately seldom super-added to love between the sexes, because men and women associate, not in their labours but in their pleasures merely. Where, however, happy circumstances permit its development, the compounded feeling proves itself to be the only love which is strong as death—that love which many waters cannot quench, nor the floods drown, besides which the passion usually called by the name is as evanescent as steam.

CONTENTS

Preface

THIS BOOK IS ABOUT how important good relationships are to a successful life. In it I state that, if we are not sick, poverty stricken, or suffering the ravages of old age, the major human problems we struggle with—violence, crime, child abuse, spousal abuse, alcohol and drug addiction, the proliferation of premature and unloving sex and emotional distress—are caused by unsatisfying relationships. This whole book is both an explanation of why this happens and what to do to get along better with one another.

I focus on four major relationships, all of which are in obvious need of improvement. These are husband-wife, parent-child, teacher-student, and manager-worker. I make the claim that if we do not improve these relationships, we will have little success in reducing any of the problems in the previous paragraph.

For me to make such a broad claim may be considered presumptuous but, just before this book went to press, I was pleased to find recent research that strongly supports my thesis that adolescents, especially, need good parent-child and teacher-student relationships if they are to avoid self-destructive behaviors.

The September 10, 1997, issue of the *Journal of the American Medical Association (JAMA)* includes an article entitled "Protecting Adolescents from Harm," which describes the first findings from the National Longitudinal Study on Adolescent Health. The most significant finding was: "Parent-family connectedness and perceived school connectedness were protective of every health risk behavior measure except history of pregnancy."

The research does not as yet go into how to improve these two important relationships, but it does show clearly that this is the direction in which to go—and that is the subject of this book. I would suggest that the researchers also focus on how husbands and wives can achieve more marital satisfaction, which I think is a vital factor in achieving child-parent connectedness. Years ago, a priest I knew in Chicago, by the name of Father John, said something I have never forgotten: "The best thing parents can do for their children is love each other."

As you read this book you will note that I do not use the word "connectedness." Although I use "satisfying relationships," I can see no difference in the terms. I encourage you to read the *JAMA* article if you want to see for yourself how strongly it supports what I say in this book.

Acknowledgments

WHEN I GOT STARTED on the wrong track, Bob Sullo did a lot of thinking and helped me straighten out. I probably would have gotten there eventually, but I appreciate very much what he did. His book, *Inspiring Quality in Your School* (NEA Professional Library, 1997), discusses how a lot of choice theory is put to practical use in a school.

Bob Wubbolding, a colleague of twenty-five years, made some good suggestions throughout. His expertise is reality therapy, and he is in the process of writing a new book, *Reality Therapy for the 21st Century*. Among the things he'll do in this book is answer all the people who question whether there is a research base for this therapy. There is.

Kay Mentley, mentioned in depth in chapter 10, is the principal of the first quality elementary school, Huntington Woods, that is choice theory from floor to ceiling. Put together every fantasy about what a school should be; Kay and her staff have brought them to life. Her book, *Quality Is the Key: Stories from Huntington Woods,* is available from the William Glasser Institute. Linda Harshman, the director of the William Glasser Institute, made it possible for me to have the time to write this book. She is a lead manager; talk to any of our staff and you will quickly see why. To me, she is indispensable.

If you found that the book reads easily and clearly, I thank Cynthia Merman, my editor. When I sent her the manuscript, I said, "Work your magic." She did.

Brian Lennon, from Skerries near Dublin, Ireland, gave me the support I needed when my editor faxed me while I was in Slovenia to tell me that the book was great, but that it needed a new subtitle. He helped to steer me in the right direction, but my many Slovenian and Croatian colleagues also did their part. When we asked, "What does choice theory mean to you?" they said, "Freedom." Recently at a conference in Acapulco, I had the pleasure of meeting a caring brain researcher, S. Paul Rossby, who presented a paper on the neurophysiology of violence. When my wife and I talked to him afterward, tears came to his eyes when we told him we believe that violence is not irreversibly imprinted into the brains of many young people who seem so callous and hard to reach. With caring and choice theory, their violence can be reversed. We look forward to sharing ideas with him again.

If you want to reach any of these people for any reason, and they are well worth reaching, contact the William Glasser Institute for their addresses. They helped me, and I'm sure they would not hesitate to help you.

I have to stop here. If I went on, I might not be able to stop short of the hundreds of people teaching choice theory who are joining me in the task of driving the plague of external control psychology from the Earth.

PART I
The Theory

CHAPTER 1
We Need a New Psychology

SUPPOSE YOU COULD ask all the people in the world who are not hungry, sick, or poor, people who seem to have a lot to live for, to give you an honest answer to the question, "How are you?" Millions would say, "I'm miserable." If asked why, almost all of them would blame someone else for their misery—lovers, wives, husbands, exes, children, parents, teachers, students, or people they work with. There is hardly a person alive who hasn't been heard saying, "You're driving me crazy. . . . That really upsets me. . . . Don't you have any consideration for how I feel? . . . You make me so mad, I can't see straight." It never crosses their minds that they are choosing the misery they are complaining about.

Choice theory explains that, for all practical purposes, we choose *everything* we do, including the misery we feel. Other people can neither make us miserable nor make us happy. All we can get from them or give to them is information. But by itself, information cannot make us do or feel anything. It goes into our brains, where we process it and then decide what to do. As I explain in great detail in this book, we choose all our actions and thoughts and, indirectly, almost all our feelings and much of our physiology. As bad as you may feel, much of what goes on in your body when you are in pain or sick is the indirect result of the actions and thoughts you choose or have chosen every day of your life.

I also show how and why we make these painful, even crazy, choices and how we can make better ones. Choice theory teaches that we are much more in control of our lives than we realize. Unfortunately, much of that control is not effective. For example, you choose to feel upset with your child, then you choose to yell and threaten, and things get worse, not better. Taking more effective control means making better choices as you relate to your children and everyone else. You can learn through choice theory how people actually function: how we combine what is written in our genes with what we learn as we live our lives.

The best way to learn choice theory is to focus on why we choose the common miseries that we believe just happen to us. When we are depressed, we believe that we have no control over our suffering, that we are victims of an imbalance in our neurochemistry and hence that we need brain drugs, such as Prozac, to get our chemistry back into balance. Little of this belief is true. We have a lot of control over our suffering. We are rarely the victims of what happened to us in the past, and, as will be explained in chapter 4, our brain chemistry is normal for what we are choosing to do. Brain drugs may make us feel better, but they do not solve the problems that led us to choose to feel miserable.

The seeds of almost all our unhappiness are planted early in our lives when we begin to encounter people who have discovered not only what is right for them—but also, unfortunately, what is right for us. Armed with this discovery and following a destructive tradition that has dominated our thinking for thousands of years, these people feel obligated to try to force us to do what *they know* is right. Our choice of how we resist that force is, by far, the greatest source of human misery. Choice theory challenges this ancient I-know-what's-right-for-you tradition. This entire book is an attempt to answer the all-important question that almost all of us continually ask ourselves when we are unhappy: How can I figure out how to be free to live my life the way I want to live it and still get along well with the people I need?

From the perspective of forty years of psychiatric practice, it has become apparent to me that all unhappy people have the same problem: They are unable to get along well with the people they want to get along well with. I have had many counseling successes, but I keep hearing my mentor, Dr. G. L. Harrington, the most skillful psychiatrist I've ever known, saying, "If all the professionals in our field suddenly disappeared, the world would hardly note their absence." He was not disparaging what we do. He was saying that if the goal of psychiatrists is to reduce the misery rampant in the world and to help human beings get along with each other, their efforts have hardly scratched the surface.

To begin to approach that goal, we need a *new psychology* that can help us get closer to each other than most of us are able to do now. The psychology must be easy to understand, so it can be taught to anyone who wants to learn it. And it must be easy to use once we understand it. Our present psychology has failed. We do not know how to get along with each other any better than we ever have. Indeed, the psychology we have embraced tends to drive us apart. In the area of marriage alone, it is clear that the use of this traditional psychology has failed.

I call this universal psychology that destroys relationships because it destroys personal freedom external control psychology. The control can be as slight as a disapproving glance or as forceful as a threat to our lives. But whatever it is, it is an attempt to force us to do what we may not want to do. We end up believing that other people can actually make us feel the way we feel or do the things we do. This belief takes away the personal freedom we all need and want.

The simple operational premise of the external control psychology the world uses is: Punish the people who are doing wrong, so they will do what we say is right; then reward them, so they keep doing what we want them to do. This premise dominates the thinking of most people on earth. What makes this psychology so prevalent is that those who have the power—agents of government, parents, teachers, business managers, and religious leaders, who also define what's right or wrong—totally support it. And the people they control, having so little control over their own lives, find some security in accepting the control of these powerful people. It is unfortunate that almost no one is aware that this controlling, coercing, or forcing psychology is creating the widespread misery that, as much as we have tried, we have not yet been able to reduce.

This misery continues unabated not because we have thought it over and decided that controlling others is best. It continues because when people do not do what we want them to do, coercion and control are all we think of using. It is the psychology of our ancestors, our parents and grandparents, of our teachers and leaders, of almost all the people we know or know about. Coercion, to try to get our way, has been with us so long that it is considered common sense, and we use it without thinking about it. We neither care where it came from nor question its validity.

If external control is the source of so much misery, why is it the choice of almost all people, even powerless people who suffer so much from it? The answer is simple: It works. It works for the powerful because it often gets them what they want. It works for the powerless because they experience it working on them and live in hope that they will eventually be able to use it on someone else. The lowest people on the totem pole look up more than they look down. But even more so, the powerless accept it because as miserable as they may be, they believe that they are not free to choose otherwise. They further believe, usually correctly, that to resist would be worse.

So one way or another, most people are doing many things they don't want to do. For example, many women stay in abusive marriages because they think leaving would be worse. Alone, they fear they would be unable to support themselves, lose their children, might still suffer abuse, and maybe risk their lives. Many continually entertain the hope that if they stick it out, things will get better. But this book is about much more than why people stay and accept external control. It is about the fact that the belief in and use of external control harms *everyone*, both the controllers and the controlled. For example, the abusive husband also suffers (though not as much as his wife and family). He, too, is a victim of external control psychology. In choosing to do what he does, he loses any chance for happiness. This psychology is a terrible plague that invades every part of our lives. It destroys our happiness, our health, our marriages, our families, our ability to get an education, and our willingness to do high-quality work. It is the cause of most of the violence, crime, drug abuse, and unloving sex that are pervasive in our society.

This book is all about this human toll and how it can be reduced by both learning why external control is so harmful and how a new, pro-relationship theory can replace it. Choice theory is an internal control psychology; it explains why and how we make the choices that determine the course of our lives. Choice theory is a complete change from what has been common sense to what I hope will become, in time, a new common sense. This change is not easy. It can happen only through learning what is wrong with external control psychology and the overwhelming reasons to replace it with choice theory as we deal with the people in our lives. As we attempt to do this, we will continually ask ourselves: Will what I am about to do bring me closer to these people or move us further apart? How we use this basic question and what would be possible if we did are the heart and soul of this book.

What I do in this book is question the basic psychology of the world, and I have no illusions that it is an easy task. To begin to realize the existence of this psychology and how harmful it is to our lives, we need to take a look at some of the misery we suffer because we depend on our common sense even when it becomes apparent that it isn't working. For example, using the only psychology you know, you punish your teenage son for not doing his schoolwork by grounding him on weekends. But after you ground him, he still doesn't do his homework, and to make matters worse, you have a sullen teenager hanging around the house all weekend. After a month, you begin to think: Why am I doing this over and over? There must be a better way.

It may take a while to come to this realization because punishing your son is so much a part of your common sense that it doesn't feel like a choice. It feels right. It's what a good parent does in this situation—it's probably what your parents did to you—and you are supported by everyone you ask. Giving you the benefit of an almost universal common sense, they say, *Punish him. Why are you asking me this stupid question? Do you want him to grow up to be a bum?* The only problem with this advice is that it rarely succeeds. As you continue to punish your son, he and you stop talking and listening to each other. You are both miserable, you blame each other for how you feel, and he does less schoolwork than before.

Still, for most people, the idea of going against common sense, especially in how they deal with their children, is a new and troubling idea. But assuming you would like to have less misery in your life, you may be open to learning why controlling and allowing yourself to be controlled are so destructive to the relationships you need to be happy. Then you may be willing to try choice theory in some situations in which attempting to control has been ineffective. If it works better—and my twenty years of experience with choice theory argue that it will—you may want to begin the difficult process of discarding external control and replacing it with choice theory. Psychologies, even common sense, ancient psychologies, should be discarded if they damage relationships.

To convince you that we should give up external control psychology, I have included a simple graph that compares two kinds of progress: technical progress and human progress. Such a comparison is unusual because when we think of progress, the progress that comes to mind is technical because, as the graph shows, this progress is so obvious. We rarely think of human progress, which is getting along with each other better than we have in the past, because we haven't seen or read about enough people getting along that much better with each other to begin to think there has been much progress in this area.

In the past hundred years, there has been considerable techni-

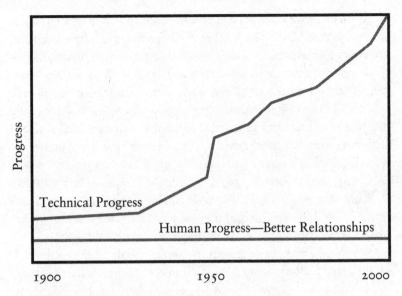

Technical progress as compared to human progress.

cal progress. We have moved from the first airplane to the supersonic jet to exploring Mars. Communication has gone from the turn-the-crank phone to the internet. The list is endless. Not so with human progress. Except for some improvements in civil rights in the 1960s and some recent movement toward better relationships between managers and workers since quality management surfaced in the 1970s, we are no more able to get along well with each other than we ever were.

Can anyone say that there has been any improvement in how husbands and wives get along with each other? Are families in better shape today than years ago? If they are, it's news to me. I work in schools, and I have yet to hear a teacher say that things are better now than when he or she started teaching. Actually, I hear more of the opposite—that the kids are tougher to teach than ever. And in these days of the sacred bottom line and the heartless downsizing it takes to raise it, no one is making much noise about how much better the workplace is than it was years ago. In fact, even bosses are experiencing less job satisfaction.

As much as we haven't been able to make any improvement in the way we get along with each other to nudge the graph upward, there are enough situations in which we do that there is no doubt that we could do so if more of us learned how. Here and there, we find marvelous schools, in which all the teachers and students care for each other and everyone is learning and happy. All of us know happily married couples, solid families, and people who are well satisfied with their jobs. But when asked to explain their happiness, many hesitate. They aren't sure. Some say, *We work hard to get along with each other*, but others shrug and say, *Maybe luck has a lot to do with it*. What they never say is, *We have given up trying to control each other*. They don't realize that they may be following a different theory, that inadvertently they have discovered choice theory.

When asked about technical progress, people occasionally talk about getting along better with each other. Many do see that there is a correlation between the two in some cases. But few people attribute major technical progress to luck. Technology has progressed in this area because we are willing to or have embraced a new theory or a new way to use an old one.

In almost all attempts to improve human progress, for example, to improve marriages, families, schools, or work, there has been no operational change in theory. External control is so firmly in the saddle that even when we make a little progress, we are blind to the fact that we have given up external control psychology and are starting to use what is, in essence, choice theory. What I am addressing is our need to become aware that there is another psychology.

I do not claim that there are no other psychologies that are similar to choice theory. Albert Ellis's* rational emotive behavior therapy is certainly one of them. In the area of work, W. Edwards Deming† has shown that high-quality work is dependent on driving out the

---

*Albert Ellis, *How to Stubbornly Refuse to Make Yourself Miserable About Anything—Yes Anything* (New York: Lyle Stuart, 1988).
†W. Edwards Deming, *Some Theory of Sampling* (New York: Dover, 1966).

fear that prevents people from getting along well with each other. He likens the manager in the workplace to the leader of a symphony orchestra in which everyone willingly follows the leader and contributes to the performance. No one is forced to make a contribution; they do so because they see that it is to their benefit.

Even though he is probably not aware of it, Herb Kelleher, the extremely successful CEO of Southwest Airlines, is practicing choice theory in how he runs his company. In a recent book, *Nuts! Southwest Airlines' Crazy Business Recipe for Both Business and Personal Success,** Kelleher said this about leadership: "It really signifies getting people, through both example and persuasion, to happily join together in pursuit of a worthwhile common cause." On downsizing, which he called a corporate blunder, he stated, "We haven't had any furloughs at Southwest, although obviously during the recession we could have made more money if we had. The disaffection it engenders, the angst. Once you do it [workers] don't forget about it for a long time." The people, not the bottom line, are sacred at Southwest.

But Southwest is an exception. If Kelleher sells out or retires, it is almost certain that the people who take over will downsize and become coercive to try to improve profits. And in the short run, they may be successful. Without Kelleher, however, the new owners are likely to revert to external control and fail in the long run.

We also do not see how widespread misery really is because, again guided by common sense, a lot of us think that misery is caused mainly by poverty, laziness, or how the powerful treat the powerless. But in the affluent Western world, there is no shortage of miserable people who are well off, hardworking, and powerful. I have noticed that there is a high rate of divorce among successful academics, with successful professionals and business leaders close behind. The failure of children and parents to get along well may be more extreme among the poor and powerless, but it is hardly exclusive to that group.

---

*Herb Kelleher, *Nuts! Southwest Airlines' Crazy Business Recipe for Both Business and Personal Success* (Austin, Tex.: Bard Press, 1997).

Although more students in poverty areas refuse to make the effort to learn than do students in affluent areas, this failure is related much more to how teachers and students get along with each other than to the fortunes of those who attend. Students from prosperous families, in which education is the main reason for the prosperity, are usually more motivated to learn than are students from families who have not been helped by education. Teachers appreciate this motivation and tend to make a greater effort to get along with the former students, which is another reason they learn more. But if teachers were offered choice theory and found how useful it was in their marriages and families, they could also begin to use it to get along better with students who seem to be unmotivated. This effort could go a long way to make up for the lack of support for education at home, and the previously unmotivated students would learn a lot more than they do now.

In chapter 10, on education, I explain how choice theory was used in a minority school that my wife and I worked in for a year. This is an area I know something about. The *common sense* that poor or minority students can't or won't learn is totally wrong. When they get along well with their teachers, they may learn more slowly because they start further back, but, in the end, they learn as well as any other students. Productive, high-quality work is assured in any organization in which workers and managers get along well together.

The name for what we usually do when we deal with each other is called *the system*. In an external control world, the system is naturally coercive. When it fails, as it is failing in marriages, families, schools, and workplaces, we use more coercion and focus on fixing the people. Many therapists stress the systems approach to counseling, in which they do not attempt to fix individuals as much as to help them figure out a way to make the family system work better for all involved. What I suggest is that we try to change to a choice theory system, which teaches everyone, not just unhappy people, how to get along better with each other. What makes external control doubly harmful is that not only does our belief in it create the problems we are trying to solve, but it is also used to deal with the problems. When punishment doesn't work, invariably we punish harder. It's no wonder there has been so little progress.

So far only a tiny fraction of the money spent to reduce misery has been spent on prevention, on teaching people how to get along better with each other before they get into the hard-core, adversarial relationships that are the result of too many attempts to control or manipulate. If we want to move the flat line of human progress up, prevention, which means changing from an external control to a choice theory system, is a way we can do so. Once any human problem occurs, for example, when marriages begin to fail, the couples rarely get back together. No matter how skilled the counselor, it is often impossible to save a marriage or a failing student. The answer lies in preventing these failures, not in looking for better ways to fix the people who are failing.

To substantiate my claim that vast numbers of seemingly unsolvable human problems are relationship problems, take a look at your life and the lives of the people you know. I'm sure that many of you are unable to get along with your spouses, parents, or children as well as you would like to. You may also admit that the longer you are with them, the harder it seems to get along.

Think about it. You were happy when you got married. Are you now miserable or divorced? Is there someone in your family you no longer speak to? Are your children as happy in middle school as they were in the early grades? Do you still find joy in the work you do?

If you experience any of the misery in the previous paragraph, you are involved in one or more of four variations of essentially the same attempting-to-control-someone-else situation.

1. You wanted someone else to do what he or she refused to do. Usually, in a variety of ways, some blatant, some devious, you were trying to force him or her to do what you wanted.

2. Someone else was trying to make you to do something you didn't want to do.

3. Both you and someone else were trying to make each other do what neither wanted to do.

4. You were trying to force yourself to do something you found very painful or even impossible to do.

The first three variations are obviously different aspects of the same situation. Although the fourth is somewhat different, it is in the same genre. In this instance, you may have been trying to force yourself to stop smoking, stay on a job you hated, lose weight when you didn't want to diet, or love someone you no longer even liked.

In the first three variations, you may be a wife complaining to your husband that you need more help with the children or a husband nagging your wife that her job has left her with no time for you. Or both complaining and nagging each other. You may be a parent or a teacher trying to motivate a child to do better in school. Or a boss coercing a worker to do something he doesn't think is worth doing. As long as we continue to believe that we can control others or, conversely, that others can control us, the misery associated with common situations such as these will continue unabated. These variations are as old as history, and the resistance to this coercion is the reason we are making so little progress in our relationships.

One of the most puzzling exceptions to this widespread use of external control psychology is that we rarely use it with our best friends, people who have been with us through thick and thin for many years. With them, even though few of us are aware of it, we use choice theory. But whether or not we know the theory, most of us are well aware that we often treat our good friends differently from our mates, children, students, and employees.

We recognize that good friends are our most reliable source of long-term happiness. We seem to know we could lose them, and the happiness that goes with them, if we tried to force them to do what they don't want to do. I believe this reluctance to try to force a friend, when we have few qualms about trying to force almost everyone else, may be a good way to define close friendship. If we practiced choice theory with everyone, we would make—and keep—many more friends, and our happiness would be substantially increased.

What may also be involved here is ownership. Most of us believe that we should or do own our husbands, wives, children, students, and employees. I have the right to control my wife and kids because they belong to me. This is my classroom, and my students had better do what I say. I own this company and I own you, so do what you are told or look for another place to work—are all examples of ownership thinking. As long as we believe that we own people, we don't hesitate to force them when they don't do what we want them to do. We feel differently with our friends; we accept that we don't own them and they don't own us. Caring for but never trying to own may be a further way to define friendship.

Without really thinking about ownership, most of us divide the world into two groups. The first group, those we own or try to own, is made up of lovers, wives, husbands, children, students, and employees. The second group, those we don't own or try to own, usually a large group, consists of good friends; acquaintances; people who have some power over us, such as bosses; and, of course, strangers.

A good way to learn choice theory is to take a close look at how you treat your best friend, your boss, and most strangers compared to how you treat the rest of the people in your life. You know why you don't try to force your boss or your friend. You rarely force acquaintances, and, if you have any sense at all, you never force strangers because you may get hurt or even killed. Why don't we live and let live? Why don't we practice the golden rule when most of us give lip service to it? Why do we keep trying to make other people do what they don't want to do when, most of the time, we have so little success in this effort? Earlier in this chapter, I began to answer these questions. In the next chapter, in which I introduce the basic needs, I add some new choice theory ideas to this explanation.

But first I want to describe the three beliefs of external control psychology in some detail, so you can understand what most people actually believe. You will easily see that it is the second and third beliefs that are so harmful to human relationships. The easiest way to understand this traditional psychology is to think of how almost all of us use it in our lives.

FIRST BELIEF: I answer a ringing phone, open the door to a doorbell, stop at a red light, or do countless other things because I am responding to a simple external signal.

SECOND BELIEF: I can make other people do what I want them to do even if they do not want to do it. And other people can control how I think, act, and feel.

THIRD BELIEF: It is right, it is even my moral obligation, to ridicule, threaten, or punish those who don't do what I tell them to do or even reward them if it will get them to do what I want.

These three commonsense beliefs are the foundation of the external control psychology that essentially rules the world.

In the first belief, the ring of the phone or any other mechanical signal is the external control that most people think makes them answer. In the second, extrapolating from the first, the control is always someone outside the behaving person, for example, a parent telling a child, "Mow the lawn"; a teacher telling a student, "Stop talking in class"; or a husband saying to his wife, "You made me mad." Following the third and most destructive belief, husbands, wives, parents, teachers, and bosses believe it is their right, their duty, and even their moral obligation to threaten, punish, or bribe children or adults who choose to disobey them because it is in these children's or adults' best interest to do what they are told.

The foundation of these beliefs, that we are externally motivated, is wrong. Just as the world was flat until someone began to question that belief, answering a phone because it rings seems right until we begin to question it. Once any external control belief is questioned, it becomes clear that what was right is actually wrong. For example, we do not answer a phone because it rings; we answer it because we want to. Instantaneous as our response may be, every time we answer a phone, we have decided that this is the best choice. If we didn't think so, we wouldn't answer it.

You may argue, "If I don't answer the phone because it rings, then what's the purpose of the ring? I certainly don't go around answering phones that aren't ringing." The ring does have a purpose, but it is not to make you answer. It is to give you information, to tell you that someone out there wants to talk to someone here. The ringing of the phone, and all else we perceive from the outside world, including what we perceive from our own bodies, is information. But information is not control. Choice theory explains that stimuli, in the sense that they can consistently *control* a human being to make a specific choice, do not exist.

Since information does not make us do anything, we can choose to ignore it or act on it any way we see fit. We are not machines. We are not, as machines are, designed to respond in a specific way to an external control. When we do as we are told, it is because we choose to do it on the basis of the information we have. In the case of the phone, if we don't want to answer it, we can let it ring, let a machine answer it, pull the clip out of the wall to disconnect it, or yell to someone else to answer it.

Whatever behavior we choose is generated inside our brains. Choice theory explains that we are, as all living creatures are, internally motivated. You may ask, "What difference does it make why I answer the phone or do anything else I do? I've done it, so what?" For simple mechanical information like the ringing of a phone or a red traffic light, it doesn't make any difference. It is not until we go from the first belief to the next, much more complicated second belief—trying to make someone do what he or she does not want to do or believing someone else can control our behavior—that you can begin to appreciate the enormous difference between external control and choice theory.

For example, if I know choice theory, you cannot make me feel guilty by telling me that you wish you had a house as nice as mine. If I had done something to deprive you of a nice house, I probably should choose to feel guilty, but if I haven't, why should I choose to feel guilty? Freedom from the undeserved guilt that floods the external control world we live in is a huge benefit of learning to use choice theory in your life. Many mothers rely on external control psychology to *make* their children feel guilty. But choosing to feel guilty because you don't do what your mother expects of you is a choice. When you learn this lesson—and if you have a skilled guilt-tripping mother it is not an easy one to learn—you will find that it frees both you and your mother to make better choices.

A striking example of the freedom to choose is best illustrated by the behavior of a good friend of mine, a criminologist, who didn't think that this theoretical difference between external control psychology and choice theory was important. He may owe his life to the fact that when he made what most of us would consider a poor choice, external control psychology was threatened but not used.

My friend went to Las Vegas on some academic business and was put up in a fancy hotel. Even though friends warned him to be careful and quickly lock, bolt, and chain the door every time he entered his room, he did not pay attention to this information. On one occasion, he forgot even to close the door securely, much less bolt it and chain it. A moment later a man, brandishing a gun, stepped in through the unlocked door. If you had been there, you would have witnessed a very unusual sight: a criminal and a criminologist face to face. The criminal, a seemingly firm believer in this traditional psychology, said, "Gimme your wallet." My friend, much to his surprise (he was surprised because he was practicing choice theory), told the thief, "You can't have my wallet. I'll give you money but not the wallet." The criminal took the few dollars that my friend put on the floor and left.

If the criminal had been a dedicated practitioner of external control psychology, my friend might not have lived to tell the story. A gun in the hands of a man who will use it is about as strong an external control as there is. At a crucial moment, just after my friend made the choice not to give the criminal the wallet, the criminal switched to choice theory and chose not to shoot him. Choices, even what may seem to be unusual choices, are what this book is all about. If even a dedicated criminal can give up external control when it seems better to do so, it should not be that hard for most of us.

But many times in life, when we are miserable it is because we continue to blame others for our misery or try to control others when it is against our best interest to do so. To explain, I'll continue the father-son example I started earlier. You grounded your son who didn't do his schoolwork, and now he has stopped working altogether. He is hanging around with the "wrong" kids and admits to smoking marijuana, and you have caught him sneaking out of the house on weekends.

You have spent a lot of time punishing and arguing, but your son is worse than he was before you started. You have now taken the step of grounding him during the week as well as on weekends. As time goes by, you begin to realize more and more that the punishment that may have worked when you and he had a better relationship is no longer working. He has stopped talking to you, and you have a note from school that he is cutting classes.

Punishment isn't working, but you firmly believe that what you are doing is right. Yet as you continue to keep him in, you notice that you no longer have any influence with him. When you try to talk with him, he just rolls his eyes as if to say, *Who would want to listen to you?*

As far as your son is concerned you are close to a nonentity. What little relationship you had with him before you grounded him seems to have disappeared. He is nothing like the son you had a few years ago, and you are at your wits' end. Your own child is treating you like an enemy. Even though you have no way of knowing what's actually wrong, you do know that what you are both doing is tearing the two of you apart.

Some variation of this scenario can be observed in much of the long-term misery many parents and teachers experience with teenagers. Marriage is also fertile soil for long-term misery, as is an unsatisfying job. But this current pain is controllable. It is different from the pain of uncontrollable tragic events, such as the loss of a loved one or the terrible disappointment that follows losing a good job through no fault of your own. It is controllable because you can choose to stop punishing the teenager you want to get along with and learn to deal with him so that disobedience rarely occurs. How to do so is covered in some detail in part 2 of this book.

In the case of your son, punishment—whether it's right or wrong—isn't working. Before you grounded him, he was doing some schoolwork; now he is choosing to do none. Before, you could at least talk to him; now he and you don't speak. From what was once a good relationship, you have become adversaries. Your choice to follow the second and third beliefs of external control psychology—that you can and should force your son to do what you want him to do—is the reason for your misery. If you can choose to stop controlling, even in a world based on external control, you can stop contributing to your own misery and to the misery of those you are using it with. Knowing that others need you as much as you need them, even if they are trying to control you, can help you to stop retaliating, and then things have a chance to get better.

But you can do more than stop. You can replace forcing and retaliation with negotiation. Tell your son why you are not going to punish him anymore—that your relationship is more important to you than his schoolwork and that you want to do some enjoyable things with him the way you used to. He knows you want him to do his schoolwork; you have more than made your point. Hammering away at it is totally unproductive. If he and you can get back to being close, the chances of his doing schoolwork and everything else you want him to do are much more likely than if you continue to be estranged.

We must realize that if we coerce anyone too long, there may be a point of no return. We and they may never be close again.

Lacking this closeness, some children begin to give up on relationships and, eventually, embark on a lifelong destructive search for pleasure. To achieve and maintain the relationships we need, we must stop choosing to coerce, force, compel, punish, reward, manipulate, boss, motivate, criticize, blame, complain, nag, badger, rank, rate, and withdraw. We must replace these destructive behaviors with choosing to care, listen, support, negotiate, encourage, love, befriend, trust, accept, welcome, and esteem. These words define the difference between external control psychology and choice theory.

When I checked my thesaurus for the words in the previous paragraph, I discovered that more of them were external control than choice theory. Since our language is a mirror of our culture, this is strong evidence that we live in a world that is attuned more to destroying relationships than to preserving them.

Despite the fact that we have had little success in improving relationships, as a nation we are concerned enough about this misery to spend a lot of money trying to reduce it. In just one area, public education, billions of dollars continue to be spent to improve school success, with no improvement no matter how success is measured. President Bill Clinton devoted ten minutes of his 1997 State of the Union address to education. He had some good suggestions and hinted that more federal money would be provided if it were needed.

But if there is a truth about people that no one can dispute, it is that success in any endeavor is directly proportional to how well the people who are involved in it get along with each other. Although this truth is self-evident in marriages and families, it is equally true in schools and workplaces. Students who get along well with their teachers and with each other are almost always successful, but, overall, less than half the students do. And the proportion of students who do so is less than 10 percent in schools in poverty neighborhoods, urban or rural. In these almost nonfunctional schools, most of the money and effort is not only wasted, some of it is used to purchase disciplinary programs that are harmful to the relationships that students need to succeed in school.

We need a national effort to run schools in which teachers and students are happy. But we have to go far beyond the schools and build a society in which husbands, wives, family members, workers, and managers are much happier than they are now. I will risk being called naive and say that ultimately this book is about happiness. Of all that we attempt, this seemingly modest goal is the most difficult to achieve.

To be happy, I believe we need to be close to other happy people. Therefore, the fewer happy people there are, the less chance any of us has for happiness. The world is filled with lonely, frustrated, angry, unhappy people who are not able to get close to anyone who is happy. Their main social skills are complaining about, blaming, and criticizing others, hardly the way to get along well with anyone.

What I would like to introduce here and explain much further in later chapters is that unhappiness can lead people in two directions. The first unhappy group tries to find the way back to happiness, which I define as pleasurable relationships with happy people. The second unhappy group has given up on finding happiness with happy people; they no longer even try to have pleasurable relationships. But like all of us, they do not give up on trying to feel good. They continually search for pleasure without relationships and find much of it by abusing food, alcohol, drugs, and by engaging in violence and unloving sex. If we cannot create a society in which more people are happy, we will never come close to reducing these destructive and self-destructive choices.

Recently a spokesperson for the Drug Enforcement Agency said on public radio that there are a half million heroin and cocaine addicts in New York City. Even if this figure is exaggerated, if we added alcoholics, who are also addicts, the number would be staggering. Almost all these unhappy people have abandoned good relationships for nonhuman pleasure. They find quick, intense pleasure easily in drugs because this pleasure requires nothing more than getting the drug into their bloodstream. Except for finding the drug, other people are not required.

Some of the unhappy people I am talking about are not necessarily poor or members of a minority. They are not necessarily involved with drugs, violence, or unloving sex. Many of them are responsible people who take care of themselves and do no harm to others. But because of the way they choose to behave, they are unable to sustain satisfying relationships with happy people, and as a result they are miserable. Misery is among the most democratic of all life experiences.

Because we don't understand the difference between seeking happiness in relationships and seeking pleasure without relationships, we don't understand why unhappy, pleasure-seeking people are so difficult to help. We assume that they are looking for the human relationships that helping professionals like psychiatrists, psychologists, social workers, and counselors ordinarily try to provide.

But with the second group of unhappy people, those who have given up on relationships and are looking for pleasure without them, this assumption is wrong. They may talk as if they are looking for relationships, but it's only talk. They don't make this attempt themselves, so the job of helping them is much harder than if they were still seeking happiness. Whether we like it or not, someone must reintroduce them to people who are seeking happiness.

Counselors and teachers are the most likely people to do so, but nonprofessional volunteers who know choice theory and have good people skills (such as successful retired people) are a source to be considered, which I discuss in the last part of this book. For alcoholics, Alcoholics Anonymous (AA) offers relationships they desperately need, and it is successful with about half who attend the meetings. If there is a defining characteristic of AA, it is that the organization uses much more choice theory than external control.

All of us, professional and nonprofessional alike, will have more success with this pleasure-seeking group (no matter how they behave) if we understand that what they are lacking is relationships. But to relate successfully to them, we must be scrupulous about not trying to control them. External control, their use of it and others' use of it on them, has led them to where they are. What also seems to work is to teach them choice theory, which can explain what they are doing to themselves. Choice theory education could be a part of every correctional and drug rehabilitation program because it is in these programs that these people are found in large numbers. Teaching them in small groups can be very effective because it offers them the opportunity to build relationships, in a sense by experiencing the theory as they learn it. As I begin to explain in the next chapter, we need each other; that need is in our genes.

CHAPTER 2

Basic Needs and Feelings

ECAUSE OUR PARENTS, aunts, uncles, brothers, sisters, and teachers—grandparents are often an exception—are all dedicated to trying to make us do things their way, we quickly learn to practice external control psychology. What we do not learn is the underlying motivation for all our behavior, for example, why long-term relationships are so much more important to us than to most other living creatures and why they are so hard to achieve. As I explain our motivation, which I believe is built into our genes, I will also explain that there are genetic reasons why we choose so many controlling behaviors.

When we are born, about all we can do is cry, fuss, suck, and thrash our arms and legs. This crying and fussing, an early expression of anger, is our way of trying to force our mothers to care for us, and most mothers choose to respond to these demands. Without this care, we would quickly die. This early crying, which is our attempt to satisfy a genetic need to survive, introduces us to what will be a lifelong practice of trying to control others. But this is only an introduction; we are not so strongly driven by our genes that we cannot learn to take care of ourselves.

The following story shows not only that the child's struggle for control is not genetic but that we can care for people we are not related to and don't even know. On a plane from Los Angeles to Minneapolis, a child, who looked to be around sixteen months old, screamed for the whole three-hour trip. The mother was at her wits' end. All of us felt for her and what she was trying to deal with. Some even tried to help, but the child was implacable. Fifteen minutes before landing, the mother shrieked, loudly enough to be heard all over the plane: *"This has been a flight from hell!"* The child was in pain; perhaps his ears were not adjusting to the change in pressure. His brain was programmed to interpret the pain as life threatening, and driven by his need to survive, he did what he could: He screamed. He knew what he was doing—he was trying to force his mother to help him. At that age, he knew no other choice.

But when these controlling behaviors stop working, as they will as the child grows older, the child can easily learn to take care of himself. Suppose the same child, ten years from now, still has some trouble with changing air pressure. On the same flight with his mother, he won't scream for three hours. He will understand that his mother can do nothing, that he is not in danger of dying, and that screaming does no good. He may even be concerned that, if he screams, she may get angry and give him even less comfort. He will pay no attention to his genes and will bear his pain as best he can.

But something else was going on during that plane ride. Almost all the passengers felt warmly toward the mother, and we would have put ourselves out to help her if we could. This is only one small example of the obvious fact that most of us care for people we don't know. We are also willing to pay taxes and donate to charity to care for strangers. This caring for those who are not related to us is a uniquely human behavior.

Since the long-term care of our children and lifelong concern for members of our species takes a lot of time, energy, and resources that could be devoted to our own and our children's survival, I believe that humans have additional genetic instructions, as strong as survival, that drive us to be closely involved with each other all our lives. In an affluent country such as the United States, where literal survival is not a major concern for most people, the vast majority of the misery we suffer or the happiness we enjoy is related to our ability to satisfy these nonsurvival instructions. To explain what I mean, I have to briefly discuss genetics.

When a sperm fertilizes an egg, each has contributed fifty thousand genes to this first cell. These hundred thousand genes carry the instructions for what each of us is to become. As the first cell divides and subdivides the billions of times it takes to create a person, a copy of these initial genes is duplicated in almost all the cells of the growing fetus. Every cell that carries a copy of these genes is instructed by one or more genes to become what is needed—skin, muscle, bone, bone marrow, heart, lungs, and brain.

Geneticists have discovered that these hundred thousand genes contain the total program that, when followed, causes each of us to become anatomically and physiologically what he or she is. If I have brown eyes and black hair, it is my genes that have provided these anatomical characteristics. If I have good digestion or musical talent, it is due to the physiology of my stomach, intestines, or brain, all derived from my genes. If I have cystic fibrosis, it is because some of the genes that deal with my lungs are not working anatomically or physiologically as they should.

Geneticists are continuing to try to discover the exact purpose of all hundred thousand genes—the human genome—but much is still unknown. They agree that thousands fewer than the hundred thousand genes are needed to produce a baby with a normal anatomy and physiology. This leaves a huge number of genes whose function is yet to be discovered. I believe that some of these unknown genes provide a basis for our psychology—how we behave and what we choose to do with our lives.

Therefore, besides survival, which depends a lot on our physiology, I believe we are genetically programmed to try to satisfy four psychological needs: love and belonging, power, freedom, and fun. All our behavior is always our best choice, at the time we make the choice, to satisfy one or more of these needs. All living organisms, plant and animal, have survival, including the ability to reproduce, programmed into their genes. Higher-order animals share some of our other needs. For example, dogs can love and can even be jealous, but they do not love with the intensity, complexity, and variety of human beings.

More than those of any other higher-order animals, our genes motivate us far beyond survival. Our need for love and belonging drives us not only to care for others to the point of caring for others we do not know, but also to seek satisfying relationships with special people, such as mates, family members, and friends all our lives. Other genes drive us to strive for power, freedom, and fun. Some large-brained animals, such as whales, porpoises, and primates, seem to have similar needs, but not enough is known to compare their needs with ours. My guess is that there are many similarities. Even though we do not know what these needs are and may never know them to the extent I explain in this chapter, we start to struggle to satisfy them as soon as we draw our first breath. We continue this struggle all our lives.

Our ability to start to satisfy our needs before we know what we are doing or why we are doing it is one of nature's strokes of genius. Evolution has provided humans and higher-order animals with genes that grant us the ability *to feel*. On the basis of this ability, the first thing we know and more than anything we will ever know is *how we feel*. Because we have the most diverse and complex needs of all living creatures, we have the widest range of feelings. But no matter how complex our feelings are, whether we feel good or bad, we also remember what we were doing when we felt very good or very bad. On the basis of these memories, we struggle to feel as good as we can and, as much as we are able, try to avoid feeling bad. Therefore, the tangible motivation for all our behaviors is to feel as good as possible as often as possible.

But as we grow from infancy to childhood and then to adulthood, we discover that feeling good becomes more and more difficult because our relationships with people grow much more complex. To the toddler on the airplane, things were simple: If it hurts, scream and try to get mother to solve the problem. To the twelve-year-old, things were more complicated: Bear the pain and don't try to get mother to do what she can't do; if I scream, I may endanger my relationship with her. So as much as we want to feel good and avoid pain, our relationships with the people we learn we need have a significant effect on what we choose to do.

To achieve a good relationship, most of us are willing to suffer pain, even a lot of pain, because the relationship is more important to us than the suffering. To gain, keep, and improve relationships, we are willing to engage in long-term unpleasant activities because we believe that in the end, we will feel better and get closer to the people we need. Even without the promise of a better relationship, most of us are willing to delay pleasure or suffer pain in the hope that we will feel better or suffer less later.

But even when we are unhappy, our genes do not limit our ability to feel good to a pleasurable relationship. To expand on what I began at the end of the last chapter, there are things we can do for pleasure that don't depend on anyone except ourselves. Beginning early in life, most people masturbate for pleasure. We may fantasize others while we do so, but the pleasure does not depend on them. We also get pleasure from hurting people—putting them down is a frequent way we do so—which may satisfy our need for power even though it frustrates our need for love and belonging in the process. We can satisfy our survival genes by engaging in nonloving sex, just using another person's body for pleasure. We can fool our brains with addictive drugs that provide feelings that are similar to how we feel when any need is satisfied.

Our society functions as well as it does because most of us never give up the search for happiness, never give up on the idea that even though people may not be easy to get along with, we need them. We struggle together to survive. It is easier, more efficient, and usually feels better than if we struggle by ourselves. Of course, we need others to satisfy our need for love and belonging. We discover that it feels good to use some of our power to help others and that we may gain more power in the process. When we seek freedom, we do so with the hope that someone will always welcome us back when we want to come back. We prefer learning and having fun with others. This is the ideal way to satisfy our basic needs—trying to get close and stay close to each other.

People who have no close relationships are almost always lonely and feel bad. They have no confidence that they will feel good tomorrow because tomorrow will be as lonely as today. Unlike happy people, they concentrate on short-term pleasure. The alcoholic lives for the immediate feeling provided by alcohol; that he may wrap his car around a tree does not cross his mind. Where pleasure is concerned, unhappy people may be totally irrational when they are seeking instant gratification.

Although the actual feelings that accompany pleasure without relationships may be similar to how we feel when we are enjoying relationships, the activities that lead to these similar feelings are different. Beware of getting involved with people who seem to be able to feel good but have no close friends. They may be witty and fun to be around, but their humor is all put-downs and hostility. If you marry such a person, you will soon be the recipient of that hostile humor and may regret it for the rest of your marriage. Look for someone who has good friends whom he or she treats well and whom you enjoy being with, too. Someone who does not have good friends does not know how to love.

Assuming that we feel good much of the time and keep close to others who feel the same, *how* we feel tells us with great accuracy how well we are satisfying our need for love and belonging (and how well the other needs are satisfied if we satisfy them with people we care about). Each of us has a unique level of need satisfaction that tells us that this or that need is satisfied and additional effort is not worthwhile. I explain this idea further in chapter 5 when I discuss the strength of individual needs.

If you get up in the morning and feel miserable, you can be

sure that one or more of the five basic needs is not satisfied to the extent you would like to satisfy that need or needs. For example, if you wake up with the flu, the *pain* tells you that your need to *survive* is being threatened by an infection. If you awaken *lonely* because your last child has just left for college, your need for *love and belonging* is acutely unsatisfied. If you are up for a promotion at work and you will get the news today, your edginess is your way of dealing with this possible *loss of power*. If you get the promotion, you will feel good; if not, you will feel worse than you feel right now. If you have been counting on being *free* to go on a family vacation and discover that the dog is missing, you are angry because you are not at liberty to leave until you find him. If you are scheduled to have *fun* playing tennis, but it's starting to rain, you don't have to wonder if your need for fun is frustrated; your disappointment tells you immediately that it is.

Once you learn about the needs, you can usually recognize which are frustrated when you feel bad and which are satisfied when you feel good. It may not be as obvious as in these clear-cut examples, but you can usually figure it out if you take the time.

SURVIVAL

All living creatures are genetically programmed to struggle to survive. The Spanish word *ganas* describes the strong desire to engage in this struggle better than any word I know. It means the desire to work hard, carry on, do whatever it takes to ensure survival, and go beyond survival to security. *Ganas* is a highly valuable trait; if you want a job done, hire someone with a lot of it. If you are looking for a mate you can count on to help build a family and a life with you, find one with *ganas* and treat him or her well. Try not to criticize this motivated mate; you don't want the *ganas* turned against you.

The other aspect of survival, the survival of the species, is based on sexual pleasure and, from a genetic standpoint, has been highly successful. There are few places where there is a shortage of people. Sex is, of course, involved with our other needs beyond survival; sex for pleasure is very often on the minds of many people. Whether or not love is combined with sex, birth control is an easy way to increase this pleasure, perhaps one of the best ways that human beings have figured out to eat their cake and have it, too.

One of the differences between human survival and the survival of animals is that early in life, humans become aware of the need to survive, both now and in the future. We make an effort to live our lives in ways that lead to longevity. Many people exercise, diet, and even buy bottled water in the hope of living healthier and longer lives. Unfortunately, fat, which is readily available but is harmful to survival, tastes good because our distant ancestors survived by eating it. Some of us give up our lives for cheeseburgers, but usually not until our children are well launched. So the genetic pleasure associated with eating fat is still with us and has to be overridden if we want to be healthy. But since we are conscious of the future, many of us are not comfortable eating fat, and this discomfort helps some of us avoid it.

I recognize that there are millions of people who suffer continually from hunger and disease because they do not have enough food or medical care. These people are not choosing to go hungry or without medical care. The pain of hunger is automatic, built into our need to survive, but this book does not deal directly with this kind of involuntary deprivation. I do, however, cover voluntary deprivation in some detail when I explain why so many teenage girls choose to starve themselves, a few even to death. Their doing so is an example of the ability to override one need, survival, for another, power. If survival was still the single basic need, there could be no anorexia and, of course, no suicide.

Choice theory can be applied to all human activities, including survival, but this book focuses on social activity: how giving up external control can help us to get along better with each other. However, it is interesting to note that in our violent society, getting along better with each other may have a lot to do with survival. For young men, gunshot wounds, not disease or accidents, are the leading cause of death. That many more would survive if they could get along better with each other is obvious. In our prehistoric past, survival was the single basic need, as it is with almost all animals today. But gradually, those who loved gained a survival advantage and, as this advantage continued, love began to separate from survival and became a basic need on its own. The same happened with power. As time went on, those who succeeded in achieving power had a much better chance of surviving than did those with little power, so the need for power also became a separate need.

To escape from the domination of others so we could more easily survive, we needed freedom; thus, it, too, became a separate need and served as a buffer against power. Fun, which is the genetic reward for learning, also became a separate need as we began to learn many things that were unrelated to survival but closely related to how to gain more love, power, and freedom. It is these additional lifelong needs beyond survival that make our lives so complicated, so different from those of animals. Next, I begin to take a closer look at the four *new, beyond survival,* needs, beginning with love and belonging, so you can better understand these complications. More will be explained about these psychological needs as I go further into the intricacies of choice theory, but what follows is a necessary beginning.

LOVE, LOVING SEX, AND BELONGING

Almost every great book, play, or opera tells the story of people who, seeking sexual love, often start out well but fail miserably later on as criticizing, blaming, complaining, and jealousy take their toll on the relationship. The beginning isn't so difficult. But our love and belonging genes demand that we keep love going for our whole lives, a demand that is hard to satisfy in an external control world. In time, many of what seemed in the beginning to be good relationships start to deteriorate. It is this deterioration that makes the trials and tribulations of love so interesting in literature.

If the love continued strong, there would be no story. Infidelity, murder, suicide, and mental illness are the common miseries associated with deteriorating love. The feelings of jealousy, abandonment, revenge, and despair often dominate the lovers' behavior.

But whether they kill, die, or suffer lesser degrees of misery, all people who are unhappy in love are involved in the first three variations of external control described in chapter 1, all variations of *You make me miserable, and I want you to change.* The books and plays, while often extreme in their portrayal of this misery, are accurate. Failure at love may top the list of human misery.

Love, as all of us know, is hard to define. But however we define it, all of us believe we know the difference between being in love, which feels ecstatic, and not being in love when we want to be, which feels miserable. Later in this book, using a choice theory concept that I will explain, I offer a definition of love that has worked for many people. But for now, use whatever definition of love you are comfortable with. For what I am going to explain here, we need not have the same definition.

Although we are driven to find both love and belonging, we rarely have difficulty with belonging or friendship. We make and keep friends easily. It is love, mainly sexual love, that is the most frustrating part of this need. Because infidelity is almost universally fantasized when sexual love is not satisfying, there is no evidence that we are genetically driven to find sexual love with the same person for our entire lives. Our genes want someone; they don't care whom. This truth is evident in the high divorce rate and the almost equally high remarriage rate, but, as I stated earlier, divorce is hardly the only indicator of an unhappy marriage. There are probably more unhappily married people who never divorce than those who do.

In most of our minds, satisfying sex and satisfying love go together. But when we get married and make a commitment to each other for life, we have no idea how difficult it will be to keep both sex and love going for anywhere near a lifetime. As the relationship continues and the coercion with which too many of us try to control each other starts to take its toll, the association between sex and love becomes tenuous to nonexistent. It is hard, if not impossible, to love someone who wants to control and change you or someone you want to control and change. Sex usually continues in the marriage, but it now becomes controlling. One or both partners practice external control and no longer finds love in the marriage. And each blames the other for how lonely they both now feel.

My guess is that the vast majority of people who engage in sex are not in love with each other, or one may be in love but the other is not. But many were once in love, and most would like to be in love if it were possible. To get sex, which can provide pleasure without love, many people are willing to act as if they are in love when they are not. But many don't even bother to act. Driven by survival hormones that care nothing about love, they have sex for pleasure with people they don't even like, much less love. The sex feels good for one or both, and that becomes sufficient reason to have it.

Sex is also very much involved with power, but that need not preclude love or friendship. This could be described as loving, or friendly, power sex. Henry Kissinger said that power is the ultimate aphrodisiac. Women are attracted to powerful men (men they wouldn't consider if they weren't powerful) for a host of obvious reasons, and vice-versa. Powerful men and women throughout history have indulged in the pleasures of sex with partners who want to fantasize they are sharing some of the power. In some cases, the fantasy becomes a reality, as it did for Wallis Warfield Simpson when Edward VIII gave up the British crown for her. Sex is also a way to share friendship and have fun. For one or both friendly partners, recreational sex, without the tensions of love and all its expectations, is enjoyable. It may be a pleasant way to learn about a new person.

Literature focuses on the beginning and end of love because that's when exciting things are happening. The more prosaic middle ground, the creative struggle to keep love going for the life of the relationship, which may be of great interest to those who read books, is missing. It is hard for a writer to make this part of a relationship dramatic. Yet lasting love is of vital interest to almost everyone.

To keep any love, sexual or not, going, we need to go back to the friendship discussed in the first chapter. Unlike lovers or even many family members, good friends can keep their friendship going for a lifetime because they do not indulge in the fantasies of ownership. To begin with, they do not become good friends if they have little or nothing in common. I discuss compatibility in detail later, but here, to test if your love is likely to last, ask yourself, How much do I have in common with the person I think I'm falling in love with and even beginning a sexual relationship with? Especially ask yourself, If I were not hormonally attracted to this person, would he or she be someone I would enjoy as a friend? If the answer is no, there is little chance for that love to succeed. Hormones get us together; they do not keep us together.

For a loving and sexual relationship to last, most of us also need a life of our own—not a sexual life but a social or recreational life separate from the relationship. Husbands and wives need to have their own interests, hobbies, and friends that each pursues separately. Can you indulge those interests without fear of criticism or complaint? We do so easily and naturally with good friends and among members of a caring family. Most of us need to learn to do so as easily in marriage. To try to stop a partner from enjoying these respites is destructive to the relationship. Depending on your mate for everything is asking more than what most relationships can provide.

When we think of love, we tend to think more of getting it than giving it. Do you love me? is the question we often ask the other when we are dissatisfied. Can love last when one partner gives a lot more than the other partner? Of course, anything can happen; you may find a giving person who asks little of you. But you can't depend on getting as much love as you want for very long without giving some back. Both love and friendship are two-way streets. Accepting love is also an art. To learn to receive it graciously is of great help to any relationship.

Difficulties also occur in nonsexual love. Members of families, especially children and parents, often want more than the other is willing to give. When they do, and one or both parties use external control, the family is often torn apart. There is no way to prevent this rupture as long as all parties involved try to control the others. Unfortunately, these are the behaviors that most family members use when they start to disagree. There is nothing I can suggest to solve family or any other difficulties that have to do with giving and getting love except giving up external control and starting to practice choice theory.

POWER

If there is a distinctive human need, it is power. As part of their need to survive, some higher-order animals want love; most want freedom; and, at least when they are young, most play and seem to be learning and having fun. But power in the sense that people want it—power for the sake of power—is unique to our species. Animals become aggressive when they are threatened, want sex, want food for themselves, or food for their young, but this behavior is for survival, not for power. When animals have enough food and are not driven by hormones or young to feed, they are not aggressive. We are the only power-driven species. It is this need for power that very early displaces survival and governs the lives most of us choose to live.

Many humans admit that they have enough of everything a person could possibly want but still want the pleasure associated with getting more even though getting more often means others get less. Even long-term friendships are vulnerable when one friend wants and tries to get much more power than the other. It's hard to stay friends with someone who is consumed with greed and status. For many people, the quest for this feeling is almost insatiable. We want to win; to run things; to have it our way; and to tell others what to do, see them do it, and have them do it the way we *know* is best. In the pursuit of power, many people have no qualms about doing whatever they believe is necessary to get it, even if it means sacrificing a marriage or a relationship with a child or parent or destroying a business competitor. Even murder is not beyond the pale for people obsessed by power.

In the external control society we live in, the powerful often define reality, even though this definition may be harmful to others. For example, teachers who believe it is right to fail students are common in all schools. Failing children, an abusive practice based on power, is a strong reason for the flat line of human progress graphed in the first chapter. By itself, power is neither good nor bad. It is how it is defined, acquired, and used that makes the difference.

As infants, once we get a taste of power through seeing our parents or others jump to attention to give us what we want, our need for more power starts to take over. By the time we are teenagers, power pushes us far beyond what we would do if our only motivation was to survive and get loving attention. Driven by power, we have created a pecking order in almost everything we do; social position, neighborhoods, dwellings, clothing, grades, winning, wealth, beauty, race, strength, physique, the size of our breasts or biceps, cars, food, furniture, television ratings, and almost anything else you can think of has been turned into a power struggle. Trying to get ahead even to the point of pushing others down is a way of life for some people in our society.

Of course, many people gain power working for the common good. We struggle to achieve things that give us a strong sense of power and may also help others in many ways. When one person raises his batting average or lowers her golf score, someone else's does not diminish. When a doctor saves a human life or develops a new treatment, he or she feels powerful and everyone benefits. The ranks of the teaching profession are filled with happy teachers who feel powerful when they see students succeed. I have written this book to try to help people, and if I succeed, I will feel very good and very powerful.

Fortunately, in an affluent, reasonably democratic society such as ours, almost everyone has some access to power, and many people are satisfied with the amount they have. We don't all aspire to as much power as do politicians or those rich people who have made their own money. But, at a minimum, we want someone to listen to what we have to say. If no one listens to us, we feel the pain of the powerless, the kind of pain you feel in a foreign country when you are trying to get information and no one speaks your language. In a choice theory world, many more people would enjoy the benefits of listening to each other without trying to get the last word.

In personal relations, coercion doesn't work any better for the powerful than it does for anyone else. Because the powerful tend to use it so much, it may actually work to their disadvantage in their marriages and with their families. Powerful men used to stay with their wives, but it was unusual for them to be faithful. Today many more of them divorce, rather than pretend that their marriages are successful. Because today the law protects wives who divorce much more than it did in the past, many more unhappy wives now divorce their powerful husbands. The powerful need choice theory for happiness as much as or more than other people. Because of their power, if they embraced this theory, the whole society could benefit.

In a choice theory society, where the emphasis is on getting along with one another, forcing others would be practiced less often. There would be little reason to judge each other, and more effort would be made to negotiate differences. The powerful would find that there is more power in getting along with people than in trying to dominate them. A characteristic of this society would be learning to deal with the need for power. Such a society is not beyond our grasp if we can change our psychology.

Freedom

Just as the power of others concerns us primarily when they use it to threaten what we want to do with our lives, freedom concerns us mainly when we perceive that it is threatened. I believe that the need for freedom is evolution's attempt to provide the correct balance between your need to try to force me to live my life the way you want and my need to be free of that force. This balance is best expressed by the golden rule: Do unto others as you would have others do unto you. External control, the child of power, is the enemy of freedom. Its bloody rule, use the power you have to kill the people who don't agree with you, is the leading cause of suffering around the world.

But more than suffering is at stake. Whenever we lose freedom, we reduce or lose what may be a defining human characteristic: our ability to be constructively creative. As I explain in great detail in chapter 7, our creativity is not necessarily good. When we don't feel free to express ourselves, or if we do and no one will listen to us, our creativity may cause us pain or even make us sick. The more we are free and able to satisfy our needs in a way that does not stop another person from satisfying his or hers—the golden rule again—the more we are able to use our creativity not only for our own benefit but for the benefit of everyone. Creative people who feel free to create are rarely selfish; they get a lot of pleasure from sharing their gift.

What made the United States one of the most creative, modern countries is that our Constitution protects our freedom, especially free speech. The Founding Fathers, many of whom were rich and powerful, were well aware of the dangers of an oppressive society when they wrote the Constitution. Most of them had fled England to find freedom and were generous enough to want to share it with many who were much less powerful. To be rich and powerful is not necessarily to be selfish.

But after so many years of the freedom we have, many people are still deeply suspicious of free speech, of allowing people to say things that they *know* are not *right*. Having enjoyed the benefits and suffered the problems of the Bill of Rights for so long, these people see only the problems and would vote against this protection today if they had a chance. *If you will do what I say, I will protect you against the forces of evil* is the working maxim of every tyrant who has ever lived.

Fun

Fun is the genetic reward for learning. We are descended from people who learned more or better than others. This learning gave these people a survival advantage, and the need for fun became built into our genes. With the possible exception of whales and porpoises, we are the only creatures who play all our lives. And because we do, we learn all our lives. The day we stop playing is the day we stop learning. Fun is best defined by laughter. People who fall in love are learning a lot about each other, and they find themselves laughing almost continually.

One of the first times infants laugh out loud is when someone plays peek-a-boo with them. I believe they laugh because that game teaches them a useful lesson: *I am I, and you are you.* Up to that time, they thought that I am I, and you are me, too— that they *owned* everyone who took care of them. Not being able to recognize that you are different from others and don't own them is not a problem when we are a few months old. But it is destructive to relationships if it continues into adulthood. It is important to find out early that we are different from others and that the only persons we own are ourselves.

It takes a lot of effort to get along well with each other, and the best way to begin to do so is to have some fun learning together. Laughing and learning are the foundation of all successful long-term relationships. When a marriage begins to go sour, fun is the first casualty. That's too bad because fun is the easiest need to satisfy. There are so many things you can do to have fun, and rarely does anyone stand in your way.

The Needs and Relationships

The answer to the all-important question posed in the first chapter, *How can I figure out how to be free to live my life the way I want to live it and still get along well with the people I need?* is that it is much more possible to find ways to do so with choice theory than with external control psychology. But if you want total freedom, you can't have it. None of us is free from what is written in his or her genes. As much as we may try to find love and belonging, we can't disregard the other needs, especially power and freedom.

Power destroys love. No one wants to be dominated, no matter how much those who dominate protest their love. Love also means working out how much to be together—there is less room for freedom in a good relationship than many of us want. Over time these amounts will change. If they cannot be successfully worked out, the relationship may fail.

The partners are the coleaders of a sextet of needs, his and her need for love, power, and freedom. Anytime there is tension in a marriage, it may be that the relationship among these six needs is no longer working. One or the other partner wants more power or more freedom if he or she is to give as much love to the marriage as the marriage needs.

Negotiation is necessary whenever there is a major change in the marriage. One or the other may need more power or freedom when a partner (or both partners) starts or stops working; children come; jobs change; they move to a new city; they buy an expensive home; and, especially, when one or both partners retire. For example, if the husband retires and is now around the house all day, the wife who had not worked or had retired earlier feels suffocated. He now begins to intrude in parts of her life where he had shown no interest before. If that marriage is to avoid a crisis, the couple must renegotiate the need for freedom.

The best time to negotiate this need is before the husband retires, but the wife should insist on it as soon as she feels uncomfortable. The longer she waits, the more difficult it becomes. If this couple had been familiar with the needs and had previously negotiated, there should be few problems. If this was the first time they attempted to negotiate, it would be very difficult. The way to do this negotiation is described in detail in chapter 5 in the discussion of the solving circle.

By now it is obvious that we are social beings, and to satisfy our needs we must have good relationships. Robinson Crusoe did not need Friday to survive, but he was a lot happier when Friday came along. Unless we are hermits, if we are doomed to a life by ourselves, even if we have all we need to survive and plenty of comfortable space to live in, life does not cease but it is miserably lonely. Misery is being without the people we want and need. When we are alone and want to be with others, we live in perpetual hope that someone will come along. That someone will be our friend and even possibly love us. He or she will listen to us, learn and laugh with us, not try to force us to do what we don't want to do, and maybe help us to survive.

In summary, power isn't worth much unless you can use it to influence people. It would be hard to satisfy your need for power if you were just appointed chief of sales in a tobacco company; selling access to the internet would be a lot more rewarding. Freedom is the freedom from others but never *all* others; our genes do not allow us to enjoy that much freedom. And what fun is it to learn anything or achieve anything if we can't share it with others? A friend of mine, a dedicated golfer, shot a hole in one playing by himself. Disaster.

CHAPTER 3
Your Quality World

ALL OF US ARE AWARE that we live in a world we can see, hear, touch, taste, and smell. We call it the real world or reality and tend to assume it's the same world for all of us. But as in the fable the Blind Men and the Elephant, no two of us perceive it the same. As difficult as this fact may be to accept, especially for those who pride themselves on their objectivity, we all perceive a great deal of reality the way we want to perceive it. Optimists and pessimists live in the same world, as do the sane and the crazy, but each sees it far differently. Much of what we see may be close to what others see or we couldn't get along at all, but it is not the same.

Choice theory explains that the reason we perceive much of reality so differently from others has to do with another important world, unique to each of us, called the quality world. This small, personal world, which each person starts to create in his or her memory shortly after birth and continues to create and re-create throughout life, is made up of a small group of specific pictures that portray, more than anything else we know, the best ways to satisfy one or more of our basic needs.

What these pictures portray falls into three categories: (1) the *people* we most want to be with, (2) the *things* we most want to own or experience, and (3) the *ideas or systems of belief* that govern much of our behavior. Anytime we feel very good, we are choosing to behave so that someone, something, or some belief in the real world has come close to matching a picture of that person, thing, or belief in our quality worlds. Throughout our lives, we will be in closer contact with our quality worlds than with anything else we know.

Most of us know nothing about our basic needs. What we know is how we feel, and we always want to feel as good as we can. Therefore, the overwhelming reason we chose to put these particular pictures into our quality worlds is that when we were with these people; when we owned, used, or experienced these things; and when we put these beliefs into action, they felt much better than did other people, things, or beliefs.

Our quality worlds contain the knowledge that is most important to us. As much as we may try to deny the importance of this knowledge, we cannot. When we say, *I don't care*, we are not telling the truth. If what we are talking about is in our quality worlds, we care deeply. All day long our minds drift back and forth to the images in our quality worlds; we can't get them off our minds. Examples of these pictures are the new homes we are saving for; the new jobs we want so much; the good grades that are so important to our future; the men or women we plan to marry; and our sick children, who are recovering their health. For alcoholics, the image is the alcohol they crave so much; for gamblers, the run at the crap table that is always on their minds; for revolutionaries, a new political system to replace the one they hate so much; and for religious people, the picture of heaven or paradise in which they hope to spend eternity.

For each of us, this world is our personal Shangri-la, the place where we would feel very good right now if we could move to it.

Anytime we are able to succeed in satisfying a picture in this world, it is enjoyable; anytime we fail, it is always painful. If we knew it existed and understood the vital role this world plays in each of our lives, we would be able to get along much better with each other than most of us do now.

For example, if Scarlett O'Hara knew that she was jeopardizing her place in Rhett Butler's quality world, she might have been much more careful how she treated him. If she had, he might never have spoken his famous line, "Frankly, my dear, I have just removed you from my quality world." (For skeptics, I admit that my copy of *Gone with the Wind** may be the only one in which this quote appears.)

It is a paradox that all of us know what's in our quality worlds to the minutest detail, but few of us know that these worlds exist. I may know nothing about my quality world, but I do know that my daughter, an actress, is very important to me. When I go to a play she's starring in, I perceive her as a great actress. If she has flaws, I don't see them. I tell anyone who'll listen how great she was, and I'm peeved if anyone disagrees with me. For me, her great performance is my reality no matter what others say. If the whole city raved about her acting, I'd be ecstatic because my reality would have been accepted as reality by a lot of people. So one way all of us tend to define reality, or the real world, is to base it on what a lot of people say it is as long as they agree with us. I see the one critic who tore her acting apart as crazy or detached from reality; that critic will never gain entrance to my quality world.

If the one critic who panned her was the greatest critic in the city—greatest because he was in the quality worlds of the city's theater lovers—what he said probably would be seen as reality by most people, especially in terms of her getting another part. It would hardly matter to the people reading his review that the lesser critics raved, since these critics are not in their quality worlds. Most people

---

*Margaret Mitchell, *Gone with the Wind* (New York: Simon & Schuster, 1936).

would base their opinions on what this popular critic said and not go to the play. It's hard to go against the beliefs of powerful people. Therefore, for each of us, as difficult as it may be to accept, reality has a lot to do with what a lot of us or some important or powerful people say it is.

But ultimately, whether people agree with us or not, we define reality in the way it works best for us. That is, I may never be able to agree with you about what is going on in the real world if what we are arguing about is pictured differently in our quality worlds. I watch the president on television and say he was marvelous; you look at me as if I was crazy. The president was what he was, but we do not have the ability to see him in the same way. To avoid controversy, many people tend to stay out of political and religious arguments and instead talk about the weather. Whatever weather is in our quality worlds, no one will fault that picture.

Because my daughter is in my quality world, I cannot see her as she actually is on the stage. But I, along with almost everyone else attending the play that night, tend to see the set the same way. We may admire it, but unless we designed it, the set is not in any of our quality worlds, so there is no need to see it any differently from the way it is. Total objectivity is a myth. It could exist only if we all had exactly the same quality worlds.

We see this discrepancy most clearly in jury trials. If the defendant is in the quality worlds of the jurors for a wide variety of reasons, they may pay little attention to the evidence and acquit him. If he is not the kind of person any of the jurors would put into their quality worlds, he is likely to be found guilty even on flimsy evidence. That is why defendants try to dress well for their trials and to be respectful to the judges. As much as we think we can, we cannot view a situation objectively unless it has nothing to do with what is in our quality worlds.

But in operation, there has to be such a thing as a real world. If we were not able to see huge parts of it in much the same way, we would be living in the equivalent of the Tower of Babel and be unable to deal with each other effectively enough to get anything done. For example, most of us agree on what time it is or there could be no concept of being on time. But time is not usually in our quality worlds; under ordinary circumstances, we get no great pleasure from knowing what time it is. If I am a dispatcher in a railroad yard, however, time is very much in my quality world because my not knowing the correct time can cause a severe accident. There is hardly anything that is not important to someone, but most of the time there is enough that is unimportant to almost all of us so that we can agree that what's out there is reality.

As we attempt to satisfy our needs, we are continually creating and re-creating our quality worlds. If I want a lot of power, I may put politics into my quality world. If survival is all I want, I may make Ebenezer Scrooge my role model. If freedom dominates the pictures in my quality world, I may buy a small sailboat and blissfully sail the sea alone. If I want a lot more sex, I may ignore my mate and look for a sexier partner who matches the one I picture in my quality world. If I spend a lot of money running for office and fail to get elected, I may eventually take politics out of my quality world. I tend to keep the pictures in as long as they have any chance of working for me.

But I still may keep these pictures too long because, frustrating as they may be, it is painful to take them out. It is giving up on something that was very satisfying to one or more of my needs in the past. So most of us keep pictures in our quality worlds long after we are no longer able to satisfy them to the extent we want. You may keep an ideal picture of your wife in your quality world for quite a while after you are no longer able to satisfy that picture in the real world. She has been there a long time, and you keep hoping she'll change. Also, if you take her out, you will be tempted to leave her, which could result in financial problems and unhappy children. You may be unhappy with your wife, but you'd be even unhappier if you took her out. No matter how good a reason you have to keep someone in your quality world, if you can't be with him or her the way you want to, you suffer. Romeo and Juliet might have been better off separating for a while until they got older, but their quality worlds did not give them that choice.

As I explained in the first two chapters, even feeling good is complicated because there are two different kinds of pleasure pictures. One pleasure I called happiness, which means that if you are unhappy, you keep trying to satisfy a picture of you and someone else being close. At a minimum, happy people have some people, usually loved ones, some family members, and at least one friend in their quality worlds.

But a lot of people have not found anyone they can trust and enjoy being with. They may have been rejected or abused, and they begin to give up on happiness, on feeling good in a relationship. In many instances, they discover that there are ways to find pleasure without relationships. To feel good, they begin to replace people pictures with nonpeople pleasure pictures—pictures of violence, drugs, and unloving sex—in their quality worlds. As they do so, they separate themselves further from people and happiness, compounding the urgency of their problem. The more lonely they get, the less they are able to accept that they have rejected people and the more they believe that people have rejected them. Many of them blame the government or people who are different from them.

If they are men, they often hate women and enjoy degrading them. They hate them because they need them sexually, and they like to see themselves as macho men who don't need anyone. *Hustler* magazine depends on the quality world fantasies of these men. And there must be a lot of them because that magazine has made millions for its creator.

A few years ago, my wife, Carleen, and I worked for a year in an inner-city middle school where most of the students did not have teachers, each other, or schoolwork in their quality worlds. The students felt no happiness in that school, but they did feel some pleasure talking about, and sometimes satisfying, the usual pleasure pictures of unhappy young people: drugs, violent clowning around, and nonloving sex. They were resigned to the fact that they would never be happy in school. It was apparent to us that because they had experienced so little pleasure in school, and what they had had been years ago in the primary grades, they couldn't even conceive that happiness in school was possible.

The more the teachers and the principal tried to force them, with threats and punishment, to do schoolwork, the more they resisted and the more they focused on what was in their quality worlds. I discuss all the things we did in that school to turn it around in chapter 10, on education. But from this much, you can see what we had to do if our goal was to convince the students to do schoolwork. We had to persuade them to put us, and through us, schoolwork, into their quality worlds. We had to treat them well no matter how they treated us. Using choice theory, we were able to build relationships with them, and through these relationships, they began to picture themselves satisfying their needs in school with people. Happiness slowly began to replace pleasure as they began to put the staff and each other into their quality worlds.

As long as the people we want to help have only antisocial pleasure pictures in their quality worlds, all we can do that has any chance of succeeding is to build relationships with them and get into their quality worlds. Punishment, which is used mainly with students, especially with those who come from poor homes and don't like school, does just the opposite. The more we do what most people believe is right—punish—the further we get from what we want. It is a wonder that our schools are doing as well as they are, considering how much we punish and how many students do not have teachers and schoolwork in their quality worlds.

We all need happy, supportive people in our quality worlds; nothing less will do. It is the job of parents, teachers, and employers to be such people. Too many teachers and bosses do not realize how much they are needed just to be warm, friendly, and supportive to those they teach and manage. It doesn't take much; a few minutes of attention a day works wonders. But many who teach and manage don't understand that given care and support, the students and workers who are doing so little now would be willing and eager to work hard.

Without sufficiently supportive people in our quality worlds, we often follow an extreme version of the fourth variation of unhappiness described in chapter 1: We try to force ourselves to do what goes against a basic need or needs. Anorexics are such people. No matter how much they are cared for, they are not satisfied. They starve themselves, ostensibly to be thin but actually to control the people who care about them. Since we all see the world not as it is but the way we want to see it, they may interpret parental care as control. But however they rationalize what they are choosing to do, research has found that they put a picture of themselves in their quality worlds as being thinner than whatever they see in the mirror.

If these young women hold rigidly to this unsatisfiable, changing picture, they will starve themselves to death. In practice, only a very few do, but it's hard to figure out who will and who won't starve herself to death. Why they starve themselves is not an easy question to answer. My guess is that they discover that doing so gives them an unexpected feeling of power over the people they believe are not treating them the way they want to be treated.

When a powerless adolescent suddenly has control over her entire family, it feels so good that she can't start eating. She literally becomes addicted to her internal endorphins and fails to feel the pain of hunger. If she ate, she would lose all this power and the pleasure that goes with it. Later, when I discuss child rearing, I explain how to raise a daughter so she gains reasonable power at an early age and has no need for the abnormal power that an anorexic suddenly gains and has no idea how to handle. The key in rearing all children is to surround them with loving, supportive people in their quality worlds who help them to experience both freedom and power responsibly. Anorexia is a graphic example of the strength of the quality world. The wrong pictures can ruin lives.

To get along better than we do now with another person, we need to try to learn what is in that person's quality world and then try to support it. Doing so will bring us closer to that person than anything else we can do. But it is not easy to find out what is in another person's quality world, and it is not always easy to support what we find out, as the example of anorexia shows so clearly. No parent can or should support that crazy picture. Tell the truth: "I care about you, but I can't support all you want to do." The treatment of anorexia is difficult even if you know what is going on and beyond what I can explain in this book.

Most of us are reluctant to share what is in our quality worlds even with people we are close to because we are afraid they may not support what we want—that they may criticize or ridicule what is so important to us. We know we would choose to feel hurt, angry, or both if they did. For example, a man wants to write a novel but he's afraid to tell his wife. He fears being told, "That's ridiculous. What do you know about writing a novel?" Fearing this put-down, he doesn't tell her. This way he can't get hurt. But since he can't share it with her, he may grow resentful. The thing is, she hasn't actually said anything; it's all in his head. She might be quite supportive if he told her. It's his fear that has led to his discomfort. Still, in too many marriages, fear and resentment are common and start with the early criticism of what may be in the other's quality world. The best thing to do if you know choice theory is to explain the quality world and what you are afraid of to your partner. This is the way to get trust in a marriage when more is needed. If you don't, your resentment may lead you to criticize and blame your partner, which further reduces the trust.

It is common for people, following the third belief of external control psychology—that it is your right to make people do what you want them to do—to put a picture in their quality worlds that goes beyond relating, to actually owning someone. If you own that person, it is right to make him or her do what you want. Any ownership picture is a relationship disaster in the making. It almost always sets us up for disappointment, anger, and conflict. Ownership pictures may lead to murder; prisons have thousands upon thousands of men and some women who killed their spouses who would not be owned. Robert Browning's tragic poem, *My Last Duchess*, portrays so clearly how ownership can turn to disaster when the owner is jealous.

It is especially hard for powerful people to be tolerant of the quality worlds of people who are less powerful. If everyone could learn that what is right for me does not make it right for anyone else, the world would be a much happier place. Choice theory teaches that my quality world is the core of *my* life; it is not the core of anyone else's life. This is a difficult lesson for external control people to learn.

Most of us have two pictures of ourselves in our quality worlds. One is a slightly idealized picture, the other an extremely idealized picture. Because of these two pictures, when you look in the mirror, you first compare what you see with the extremely idealized picture and are not satisfied. You may think about it for a moment; then you quickly realize that matching that picture is impossible, since you may never have looked as good as that generous picture. After a moment of displeasure, you realize it's not worth the effort and stop thinking that way. For most of us, the extremely idealized picture is a fantasy picture. It's there and we enjoy it, but we don't take it seriously. We settle for the slightly idealized picture that we have a reasonable chance of achieving. I picture myself being a better tennis player but nowhere close to a professional.

But just as we can choose to put people into our quality worlds and picture them anyway we want them to be, we can also choose to take them out. Parents and children are generally an exception, which I explain in chapter 9. Even though it is unusual, we can actually remove every single person from our quality worlds except ourselves. No matter how we picture ourselves, we can't take ourselves out. That picture may be totally unrealistic, but as long as it is what we want, we have to keep trying to be like it. We can't escape from this self-imposed task by taking ourselves out of our own quality worlds. To take ourselves out would mean we don't exist. There is, however, one thing we can do if we refuse to change the picture of ourselves being OK all alone. We can kill ourselves, and this may be one motivation for suicide: I'd rather be dead than continue to struggle trying to feel good with the way I choose to be—all alone. This is different from the usual motivation for suicide: I'd rather be dead than struggle for a relationship I can't have.

Because it feels so good to be with them or we believe it will feel so good to be with them, we may get involved destructively with some of the people we choose to put into our quality worlds. It is sometimes dangerous to our health or happiness to put certain people into our quality worlds, and we often know it when we put them in. And to be fair, it may be destructive to them to put us in. We may take drugs, commit crimes, abuse others, cheat, lie, or commit suicide with the someone who is in our quality worlds.

Therefore, whether we like it or not, or anyone else likes it or not, the people we put into our quality worlds are neither good nor bad in the sense that the real world defines good and bad. What the real world thinks may have a lot to do with putting them in or taking them out, but it is what *we think* that counts. They are there because we believe, or at least hope, that it will feel very good to be with them and bad to be without them.

It's the same with things. Almost all the *things* we choose to put into our quality worlds are attached in some way to people because this attachment provides much of the good feeling we all want. There is less satisfaction in owning a fine house, a powerful car, or a great painting if no one enjoys it with us. The things we picture in our quality worlds may not be anything we want to own. They may be pictures of a beautiful sunset, a gorgeous public garden, a full moon, or the sighting of a huge blue whale, but all these pictures are most enjoyable when we share them with people we care about.

What we most *believe in* is our religion, our political convictions, and our way of life. Music, art, sports, almost anything can be part of our way of life. But systems of belief that are strong enough for us to put into our quality worlds mean little to us if we cannot convince another person that what we believe is also good for him or her. We don't have to convince everyone, but it hurts if we can't convince someone who we believe is worth convincing. In fact, if we are able to convince people, this becomes a good reason to put them into our quality worlds. Most of us start trying to convince the people close to us and then, if we are successful, we go on to our acquaintances, but less often to total strangers. If those we know refuse to believe, few of us are ready to go to extremes to convince them.

Of course some are willing to go to extremes. There are terrorists who have systems of belief in their quality worlds that are in violent opposition to the workings of governments and are willing to act on those beliefs. Huge amounts of blood have been spilled in wars in an effort to get others to believe as a few powerful leaders do. Our unwillingness to extricate ourselves from the war in Vietnam is an example of how difficult it is for politicians to change a quality world belief that, right or wrong, the United States should never lose a war. Few of our citizens shared that rigid belief, and the army is now well aware of the risk of going to war when that going-to-war picture is not in the quality worlds of the majority of the people.

With serious threats, you can force most people to choose to say or do anything to stay alive. But this behavior will continue only as long as the force is in effect. What you can't do, no matter how much you threaten or punish, is make anyone change any picture that he or she has put into his or her quality world. The one thing no one can take away from you is the freedom to control your own quality world. This freedom was well illustrated by two recent, closely related newspaper reports.

The first report was that computers in schools are not leading to increased learning, as measured by proficiency tests. The second, a good-news–bad-news story, stated that American fourth graders are now showing significant gains in mathematics and science compared to those in other countries, but American eighth graders are lagging even further behind other eighth graders. What the first story illustrates is that teacher-student interaction is being replaced by computer-student interaction. Computers are good tools, but they are not teachers. Used by a good teacher who understands their limitations and who interacts enough with students so that they put this teacher into their quality worlds, computers can help. Used without teacher interaction, computers mean little, and that, according to my experience, seems to be how many are being used.

The same reasoning applies to the drop-off in learning between the fourth and eighth grades. What is actually being measured in both instances is the number of students who have their teachers in their quality worlds. Go into any first-, second-, third-, or fourth-grade class anywhere in the country and observe what is going on. Then take a look at any sixth-, seventh-, or eighth-grade class in the same school district. You will see a marked difference.

Many more younger students are involved in learning than older students. This is another way of saying that many more younger students than older students have their teachers in their quality worlds. Exactly why this drop-off in learning occurs is explained in detail in chapter 10, but the overall reason is simple. External control psychology is many times more prevalent in the upper grades than in the elementary grades. It is the use of this psychology, not the students or teachers, that is the cause of this discrepancy.

The best way to explain how we learn what pictures to put into our quality worlds is to begin with a newborn baby. All she knows for the first few weeks of life is how she feels. As long as she feels good, she sleeps or, when awake, looks around. It's when she feels bad, for example, when she's hungry, that the survival genes take over. Then she gets purposeful and begins to do what she can to feel better. But besides the few behaviors she is born with, crying and fussing, there's not much she can do.

In no more than a week or two, she learns to put pain, crying, and getting fed together, and from this combination she then directs her crying toward getting fed because getting fed feels very good. She soon learns about sucking and milk and becomes aware that something is feeding her and it feels good. This vital survival knowledge, which feels so good, is the beginning of her quality world. It will grow much larger as she learns more, but even when she becomes an adult, it will never become very large because she will put into it only those people, things, and beliefs that feel much better than anything else she knows at that time in her life.

In a few more weeks, the something feeding her and helping her to feel good becomes someone and then a particular someone, in most cases her mother, the first person most of us admit into this special world. The baby also begins to learn that crying is an all-purpose behavior that leads not only to less pain but often to happiness as her mother and even others go out of their way to care for her when she cries. She doesn't know what happiness is, but she learns that this feeling is associated with close contact with people, which will prepare her for learning what happiness is later. As this happens, she begins to realize the difference between feeling good and bad, a difference that will motivate her for the rest of her life.

By the time the baby is six months old, she is well aware that feeling good is highly related to her quality world picture of her mother, but she also begins to learn that her mother's efforts to comply with her continued demands are not perfect. If the baby has a little intestinal gas, her mother can't do much but pat her back to help her burp. Sometimes her mother succeeds and the baby feels better, but whether she succeeds or not, the baby may begin to appreciate in a dim way that her mother always tries to help her to feel better. But she also learns that there are times when she has to do as well as she can by herself.

Her appreciation that her mother is always trying to help her even though at times she can't is another reason the baby continues to keep her mother strongly in her quality world. But she also learns that helping herself, no matter how good a mother she has, is a good idea. As she learns to help herself, she begins to put a strong picture of herself into her own quality world. She is now planting the first seeds of personal freedom. The more others in our quality worlds let us do things for ourselves, the more we learn to take care of ourselves.

When the baby is around two years old, that strong picture of herself that is starting to form is now given an unexpected jolt. Unknown to the baby, but well known to her genes, she is now being driven by a new discomfort: She wants some power. Who better can she turn to than her parents, to see if they can do something to help her get rid of this new frustration? At some trifle, some small difference between what she wants and what is in her quality world—perhaps she has misplaced a toy—she chooses to scream and keep screaming, no matter what her mother or father does. Some parents call this checking-out-my-power time "the terrible twos" because it becomes obvious when most children are about two years old.

Although she is unaware of what she is doing, the child, driven by power, is now exploring her controlling behaviors that have worked so well to find out if they work well enough to get rid of every discomfort that comes along. That's the ultimate goal of power. No one achieves it, but some babies come pretty close for a while. The baby says to herself, *Why not find out how much I can get others to do for me*. Much of what she is checking out has to do with power, but as time goes on, it may also have to do with freedom and fun. In search of freedom, she may run all over a market and cry her head off when her mother catches her and puts her in the shopping cart. She may find a book in a store and start to look at it—fun and learning—and have a tantrum if her father won't buy it. At times, it's not so much that she wants anything in particular, she just wants to see if her parents will respond quickly and enthusiastically to her demands.

Sometime between two and four years, she discovers there is a limit and restarts the maturing process of modifying the picture of her parents doing everything for her that she had begun to form before the need for power kicked in. She finds that her parents won't do as much as she wants them to, but they are still well worth keeping in her quality world. The preschooler begins to learn that wanting things that depend on others who won't or can't get them for her is just too painful, it isn't worth it. She learns the process of not wanting too much. That adjustment of her quality world based on what is possible is well worth learning. She also begins to take some people, who used to fuss over her but have now stopped, out of her quality world and begins to get more realistic about putting people into her quality world.

Good parents who make clear what they and others will do and what children have to do for themselves can help the children create sensible quality worlds. Divorced parents who compete for a position in the children's quality worlds are not in a good position to teach this lesson, and the children are often more than willing to exploit this situation. How well children learn to deal with reality, and huge numbers learn to do it poorly, has a lot to do with whether they are happy or miserable for the rest of their lives.

But as children grow older and begin school, they get another shock: External control is a two-way street, and most of the traffic is coming the other way. More and more, teachers and parents join together and try to make them do a great many things they don't want to do—like homework, which is seldom in any child's quality world. But homework is strongly in teachers' and parents' quality worlds. If children don't do it, the teachers and parents threaten and punish. Thus, children now get hurt by the same people who used to spend a lot of time and effort making sure they felt good. They have no idea that their parents, now invoking the third belief of external control, know what's right for their children and are acting vigorously on that knowledge.

Still, the home part of these early years between about age four and preadolescence is usually satisfying because few parents are so strongly punitive that their young children even consider taking them out of their quality worlds. If the parents are sensible enough to couple their increasing demands that the children do what they tell them to do with a lot of love and with explanations of why these demands are being made and are strong enough to cope with the children's resistant behaviors by not responding in kind, things usually work out well. The children keep their parents strongly enough in their quality worlds to realize that cooperation is better than trying to force the parents and not succeeding.

By their teenage years, when the sex-power hormones start to flow more freely, the power struggle between parents and children escalates even with children who had been obedient in the past. During these years, many parent-child relationships are damaged severely at a time when teenagers, who are exposed daily to many opportunities to get into trouble, need their parents in their quality worlds more than ever.

Each is trying to make the other do what the other does not want to do, or each is withdrawing from the other because he or she decides that this person is never going to be the person I want him or her to be. And following the external control they are practicing to the hilt, each is convinced that he or she is right. Parents who understand choice theory bend over backward to try to maintain themselves in their teenagers' quality worlds. The advice I can give them that worked well in our house is this: *Pay close attention to what they do but little attention to what they say*. It isn't always easy to do so. But if you know about the quality world and that you are risking your position in your child's quality world by threatening and punishing, you have an incentive to learn to do it.

What makes things so difficult in our society is not our inability to get along well with the people in our quality worlds. If we can't get along with them, we simply stay uninvolved, sometimes going so far as to avoid them. But although staying uninvolved may work for people we know, it will not work for a community. To do as many of us are increasingly doing, hiding behind the external control of security systems, guards, and gated walls, is not the American dream. The biggest problem of our society is our inability even to conceive of getting to know, much less get along with, many people who are repugnant to us. We see them as dangerous or potentially dangerous, and many of them are. They are the last people we would consider putting into our quality worlds.

But neither we nor the people we fear and try to avoid have any idea that we need each other. We and they have the same genes; our need for belonging, if not love, has no conditions. Whatever conditions we impose have to do with the psychology we use; there is no psychology in our genes. As long as external control psychology continues to be the psychology of our society, we have no way of dealing with these people except to punish them and hide from them.

If we would change to choice theory, we would begin to think differently. We might begin to realize that neither hiding from them nor punishing them has any chance of getting us the comfort and security we want. Then we might consider a totally safe and low-cost alternative: reaching out at least as far as teaching choice theory widely in a community. Choice theory could do no harm and would have as good a chance of helping those we fear and shun as it has of helping us. Just one concept, wider knowledge of the part our quality worlds play in our lives, could make a difference. I expand on this concept of community in part 3 of this book.

CHAPTER 4
Total Behavior

ODD, A NICE-LOOKING, well-dressed young man in his early thirties, came to my office for counseling. He immediately told me he was very depressed, by far the most common complaint that brings anyone to a counselor. The therapy or counseling I practice is called reality therapy. It is based on choice theory and focuses on improving present relationships, almost always disregards past relationships, and depends for its success on creating a good relationship between the client and the counselor. As soon as Todd sat down, the following went through my mind.

If he knew choice theory, he would know a lot more about himself than he knows now. But, of course, if he knew choice theory, it is unlikely he'd be in my office because he would not have done what I'm certain he did that brought him to see me today. The need for psychotherapy, or at least for extensive psychotherapy, would be reduced if capable people such as this young man knew and used choice theory in their lives. But he doesn't know it, so my job is to teach it to him as part of the counseling. What I will teach him is that he is not satisfied with a present relationship, the problem that always brings people to counseling. His past could have contributed to the problem, but even though most current psychotherapies initially focus on it, the past is never the problem.

It is possible that the relationship is with a girlfriend, but that's unlikely. In my experience few men go into therapy over a girlfriend. At his age, it could be with his mother or father or with a child, but again it is unlikely. In his case, his wife is doing something he doesn't want her to do. Of course, she may perceive the same of him, but since he is here, he is the person I have to counsel.

When he tells me he is depressed, I'm sure he believes that this misery is happening *to* him. But I believe he is choosing the misery he is feeling. What I will teach him is that he is choosing to depress to deal with something his wife is doing that he doesn't want her to do. I will explain why I change the adjective, *depressed,* to the verb, *to depress.*

Since all we do is behave from birth to death, in choice theory all complaints are changed from adjectives and nouns (the way most of us express them) to verbs. This change is crucial because it teaches that not only are we actively choosing what we are complaining about, but we can also learn to make better choices and get rid of the complaints.

My counseling will offer him two options. If he chooses one or both of them, he will feel better. If he refuses to choose one or both of them, he will not feel better and very likely will feel worse than he does now. He won't like these choices—at least not at first—but if he wants to feel better, they are all he has. First, he can choose to change what he wants his wife to do. Second, he can choose to change the way he is dealing with her. Depending on which option he decides he wants, he may do one, the other, or both. When he does, it is almost certain he will feel much better than he has felt in a long time.

Todd will immediately take exception to my claim that he is

choosing the misery he feels. Whenever we feel bad, it does not seem like a choice; it seems as if it is happening to us. This is the reason I do not tell clients they are choosing what they feel until I have prepared them with enough information about choice theory so they can understand what I am talking about. If I just tell them straight out, they may get up and leave.

But after two or three sessions, this is exactly what Todd began to understand. In his case, it was too late to help his marriage. His wife had left him before he came to see me and did not come back. But these same choices were helpful with the next woman, whom he later married. If he treated her as he had treated his first wife, that relationship would not have had much chance either. The following is the essence of what we discussed in the first few sessions of therapy. A lot of the getting-acquainted talk and banter, during which we learned about each other, is omitted here, but it was important for us to do if we were to develop the warm supportive relationship necessary for successful counseling.

Todd came to trust me, and we quickly got down to what to do about the broken relationship with his wife. It was obvious to me that he wanted a good relationship with her. It was also obvious to me that if he couldn't patch things up, he could probably find another love, but this option was not on his mind when he came in. The following are some short sequences of dialogue, just enough so you can begin to see what reality therapy is. I also pause as I go along to explain what was on my mind at the time, so you can see how I wove choice theory into my counseling. I started this way:

"Todd, what I need is the story. Tell me, what's on your mind?"

"I'm depressed. I feel terrible. I'm so upset I haven't been able to go to work for a week."

"Are you blaming anyone for how you feel?"

At first I look for the relationship that's gone awry. Then I look to see if he does the usual external control thing and blames someone else—in this case his wife—for how he feels. This question will gain his attention and get the therapy started.

"It's my wife. She left me. About a week ago I came home from work. She's usually there, but she wasn't then. I didn't think about it too much, sometimes she has things to do. But an hour went by and she didn't call, and then I noticed it."

"Noticed what?"

"A note from her, held by a magnet to the fridge, two words, *So Long*. And she was gone. I went to the bedroom; her stuff was all cleaned out. All her clothes, everything. I was devastated. I mean, I love her. How could she do that to me?"

"I can't tell you how; only *she* knows that. But I wonder why? That's a big move. She must have been really upset about something. What do you think it was?"

"It's hard to say. It's really hard to say."

When a client says, "It's hard to say," he usually knows what's really going on but doesn't want to talk about it. He may have to admit that he had more to do with what happened than is comfortable. I just break through that reluctance by acting as if it wasn't there.

"Well, say it anyway. This is the place to say hard-to-say things."

"Well, I don't really think I am, but she had been saying I was too domineering—that I called all the shots. But the funny thing was I thought she liked it. She's a lot younger, ten years, twenty-three years old. I know more than she does. I thought she liked it when I kind of always took over."

"Do you want her back?

"My God, of course, I want her back. Can you help me get her back?"

I didn't answer that question. Maybe we need to talk more to try to find out whether her coming back is the best thing for him or even for her. By not answering, I don't say I can or can't. But my next question, asking what he has been doing, implies that maybe he could do something better than he has until now. In my experience, that's how most clients interpret it.

"What have you been doing since she left?"

"Nothing really. I've been so upset. I've just been sitting home.

Some of the guys from the office were worried about me. They came to see me, and one of them gave me your number. I just can't seem to get myself going. I've heard about depression, but I never realized what it was. I'm kind of paralyzed."

I don't respond to that remark because I can't offer him anything that would directly help him feel better. While I listen to him telling me how he feels, I don't talk much about feelings. He's here and he's talking, that's doing something. I focus on what he's been choosing to do. I've got to get him thinking about choice and choosing, and this is a good place to start.

"Since she left, I gather that you've chosen to sit home and not go to work, is that right?"

"Doctor, you don't understand. I haven't chosen to sit home."

"You're right, I don't understand. How can you say you haven't chosen to sit home? Has anyone been making you sit home?"

"But I've been upset, too upset to go to work. I haven't chosen anything. I've been upset since I read that note."

"You chose to come to see me today."

"But I need help; that's why I came here."

"Have you tried to contact her? Have you heard from her?"

"I've been hoping she'd call. I thought about trying to find her, but then I thought we might get into a fight and that would make things worse. For a little while I was real angry, and then, when it sank in that she was gone, I got real sad. Doctor, I love her and I don't know what to do. I don't want to be domineering; it's just the way I am. My dad's like that, but it doesn't seem to bother my mother. Maybe I learned it from him."

"Does it matter whom you learned it from?"

"I thought psychiatrists were interested in stuff like that."

"I'm not interested in your parents. You're grown up. I'm interested in what you're going to choose to do now. I'm interested in what you want. And I'm interested in helping you choose some way to get it if I can. We have to deal with the fact that she left. Do you think she's gone for good?"

"That's just it. I've been racking my brain. I don't know. If she was thinking of coming back, I think she might have left some of her stuff. It's all gone, clean. It all happened so suddenly; I just don't know what to do."

"Suppose you could talk to her right now. What would you tell her?"

"I'd tell her I'm so sorry. I'd tell her I didn't know what I was doing. I took her so much for granted. I was such a blind asshole. I thought she loved the way I stuck my nose into everything. It was my criticism. I'd never admit she could do anything right. Always some little thing was wrong. She called me Mr. Perfect, not in a mean way or anything like that, and I kind of thought it was a compliment. We never fought. We made love. About a week before she left, she said that things weren't working out the way she wanted. She asked if I felt that way. I said that the only thing that bothered me was that she didn't seem real happy. I told her she should try to be happier. She said she had been trying, but it didn't seem she could do it. She asked me if I thought there was anything I could do. I said that I'd always done everything I could do. I didn't see how I could do any more. She said she'd guessed I'd say that. After that she seemed a little happier, and I thought things were better. That was why I was so surprised when she left."

"You still think you couldn't have done anything differently?"

"Oh no, no. Now I see I could have done a lot of things differently. But how do I tell her that? She's gone. I've waited for her to call, but she hasn't."

"Don't you want to tell her that you miss her, that you love her, that you're willing to change?

"Of course, but how? Even if I knew where she was, I'm afraid I'd screw things up worse. I'm not the kind of guy who can admit that it was my fault. The first thing I'd do is blame her. I'm depressed but I'm still a little angry. She shouldn't have left like she did."

"Can I make a suggestion? It's worked for some people I've seen."

"My God, yes, what?"

"Write her a letter. Tell her how much you love her and miss her. And tell her you'll change. I don't want to tell you what to write. It has to be you, not me. It has to come from your heart or don't bother. But you might tell her you're seeing me for help and ask her if she'd come in and see me together with you. This way she wouldn't have to be alone with you, and she might be willing to do this much."

"I could do that. It's a good idea."

"This way there's no pressure; she can read it and think. She won't have you hanging on the phone; that would be too much pressure. Write the letter and bring it in to me. We'll look it over together before you send it. Is that OK?"

"That's good, real good. I like that idea. I'll be glad to bring it in. That's good."

"Tell me, how do you feel now, I mean right now?"

"I feel better, a lot better."

"Why do you feel better?"

"Because I've got something to do. I don't feel as helpless. It may work; it just might."

Todd went home and must have really worked on the letter. It was a masterpiece. If he was still in his wife's quality world, it might work. I thought he had a chance, but her cleaning all her stuff out like that didn't look good. His wife read the letter and called him. She wouldn't talk much, and he didn't pressure her, which was smart. She said she'd come to see me with him, and he made the appointment.

When she came, she didn't say much. He made a long emotional pitch for her to try it again.

She listened carefully but then she shook her head, *no*, and said, "Look, we'd been married four years, I owed you this much. You're not a bad guy; you're just not for me. If you didn't know what I was upset about, that really tells me something about you. I'm only twenty-three; I can't take a chance with you. You sound great now, but it's only because I put pressure on you. It's a game for you, and you hate to lose. It's not a game for me. It's over. I don't want anything that's not my fair share. No alimony, nothing—just my part of what we saved while we were married. I can make it OK by myself."

She thanked me and left.

Todd was quiet for a long time and then said, "I can't live without her."

"That's a pretty dramatic statement. Are you planning on killing yourself?"

If I had any worry that he was going to commit suicide, I wouldn't have said it, but he was not the kind of person who was suicidal. He had too much going for him in other parts of his life. What I said seemed to defuse the tension.

"No, I'm not going to kill myself, but I'm going to feel awful for a long time; I really loved her."

"Take as long as you want. Unhappy people are how I make my living."

"You don't take all this very seriously do you?"

"Not very, because I know the rest of the story, and it's OK."

"What do you mean you know the rest of the story?"

"I mean that in a short time you are going to find someone else. And if you treat her like you promised your wife you were going to treat her a few minutes ago, you'll be very happy. That's how it's going to end."

And that's how it ended. It took a few months for him to get his wife out of his quality world. He was already out of hers. He did find someone and even brought her in to see me. By that time I was so much in his quality world that he wanted me to meet her and approve of her. No one can predict how well a marriage is going to go, so there was no reason for me to do anything but be supportive. He had told the new woman all about me. He had told her the truth about his failed marriage, that he was too domineering. This woman was his age and seemed quite realistic about him.

Since he had told her the truth, I asked her, "What do you think, how has he been with you? Is he taking over your life?"

"No, quite the contrary; he's been great."

"But maybe he was great with her in the beginning. That happens, you know."

He chimed in, "No, it's not going to happen that way."

And it didn't. She was cautious, but in about a year they got married. I saw him a few times during that year. Things were OK. The interesting part is that his first wife called me in about a year to tell me that she was happy, too, that she had met the kind of man she wanted.

Reality therapy now includes explaining choice theory to my clients. While Todd was getting over the loss of his wife and getting started with the new woman, I had a chance to teach him the choice theory that explained what had happened, and he told me that he taught his new girlfriend all I taught him. It seemed to help them both get off to a good start. I especially taught him about his choice to depress. I taught him what to do if a situation arose in which he again was beginning to choose to depress or any other of the common varieties of unhappiness that human beings ordinarily choose.

As I stated, when he came in, I knew he was involved in, or had just lost, a long-term unhappy relationship because that's almost the only reason a client comes to a psychiatrist's office. As I explained, I was almost certain it was with his wife. What is more startling to most people is my claim that he was choosing the misery he was complaining about. This is a radical departure from what most people believe, especially from what every client I have ever seen believed when he or she sought psychological help for the painful symptoms he or she identified as *depression*. When we depress, we believe we are the victims of a feeling over which we have no control. When we depress strongly for a long time, this choice is usually called clinical depression and is considered a mental illness.

A widespread current belief is that mental illness is caused by an imbalance in brain chemicals. To correct this imbalance and to feel better, patients need brain medication, and for depression, most psychiatrists immediately think of a drug like Prozac. I did not think of using any drugs to treat Todd. I did not believe that he was suffering from mental illness. I believed that he chose to depress to deal with the situation and that I would be able to help him make some better choices with no need for medication.

Later, when I was teaching him choice theory, I began by teaching him that all he, or anyone else, can do from birth to death is behave. Examine your own life and try to identify a time when you were not behaving. All your significant conscious behaviors, that is, all behaviors that have anything directly to do with satisfying basic needs, are chosen.

Not only are we always behaving, but we are also always trying to choose to behave in a way that gives us *the most effective control over our lives*. In terms of choice theory, having effective control means being able to behave in a way that reasonably satisfies the pictures in our quality worlds. When he came to see me, Todd had the picture of himself, still with his wife, in his quality world. He knew nothing about choosing his misery or about his quality world; what he knew was that he felt bad and wanted to feel better.

After he wrote the letter instead of sitting around feeling miserable, he felt better because now he was doing something that might help him solve his problem. In other words, he felt better because he believed he was doing something to regain more effective control over his life. Writing a loving letter to a woman who has left you is a much more effective way to behave than just sitting around choosing to be miserable, and he did feel better. Later, when he changed what he wanted from a picture of his wife in his quality world to his new fiancé in that world, he got almost total relief. *Again, these are our choices when we want to stop choosing a painful behavior like depressing: (1) change what we want, (2) change what we are doing, or (3) change both.*

It was clear in the therapy that Todd had the ability to make better choices even when he was strongly choosing to depress. If he was able to make these better choices and to stop depressing, then it is also fair to say he was not suffering from any form of what is commonly called mental illness. There was nothing wrong with his brain that prevented him from being able to make these choices. As I explain later, choosing to depress, no matter how strongly or how long in duration, is not a mental illness. Like all our behavior, it is a choice. It is not as direct a choice as walking and talking, but when you understand the concept of total behavior, you will see that all our feelings, both pleasurable and painful, are indirectly chosen. But an indirect choice is still a choice.

To substantiate this claim, I have to explain that we ordinarily use the word *behavior* much too narrowly. My dictionary defines behavior as the *way* of conducting oneself. I accept that definition, but I want to expand on the word *way*. From the choice theory standpoint, that word is important. There are four inseparable components that, together, make up the "way" we conduct ourselves. The first component is activity; when we think of behavior, most of us think of activities like walking, talking, or eating. The second component is thinking; we are always thinking something. The third component is feeling; whenever we behave, we are always feeling something. The fourth component is our physiology; there is always some physiology associated with all we are doing, such as our heart pumping blood, our lungs breathing, and the neurochemistry associated with the functioning of our brain.

Because all four components are working simultaneously, choice theory expands the single word *behavior* to two words *total behavior*. Total, because it always consists of the four components: acting, thinking, feeling, and the physiology associated with all our actions, thoughts, and feelings. In this book I occasionally use only *behavior,* but I always mean *total behavior.* As you sit reading this chapter, you are choosing to sit, turn pages, and move your eyes and head; essentially, this is your activity. You are also thinking about what you are reading. Otherwise, you couldn't understand what is written. In practice, when you are acting, you are always thinking, and vice versa. Because they go together, we frequently combine them into one word, *doing.* When I say I am doing something, I am almost always describing a particular combination of acting and thinking.

You are also feeling something. You are always aware of pain or pleasure. Probably, you are not feeling much right now, but you at least agree with, disagree with, or are thinking about my claim that you choose the misery you often feel and that thinking is always accompanied by some sort of a feeling. You always feel something, even though a lot of the time you do not pay attention to what you are feeling. Also, your heart is beating, you are breathing, and your brain is working; that is, there is always a physiology associated with your choice to act, think, and feel—your total behavior.

Now that I have introduced *total behavior*, I can explain what I mean when I say that you choose your feelings, both pleasurable and painful. If you pay attention, you can easily become aware that you are feeling something while reading this book. That awareness, however, does not mean that you are choosing what you feel. You may say, I'm aware of my feelings, but they just happen. I'm not aware that I'm choosing them. And I'm certainly not aware that when I'm unhappy, I'm choosing my unhappiness. If I had a choice, as you claim, I certainly wouldn't choose to be miserable.

But if this statement was true, it would make no sense to see a psychotherapist. What good would it do to talk about your life and your problems if you couldn't choose to do anything about how you feel? It's how miserable he felt that led Todd to choose to come to see me. If he had hated his wife and been hoping for her to leave, he'd have felt wonderful and never have come to see me. My explanation of why you believe that you have no control over what you feel is that you have no direct control over what you feel in the way that you have direct control over your acting or thinking.

When Todd told me he felt depressed, it would have made no sense for me to tell him, *Cheer up!* No one can directly choose to feel better. It's not the same as choosing an active behavior like tennis or a thinking behavior like chess. But, if you accept the concept of total behavior, that all four components are inseparable, you find that although you have no direct control over how you feel, you have a lot of indirect control not only over how you feel but even over a great deal of your physiology.

Although all four components are *always* operating when you choose a total behavior, you have direct control only over *your actions and thoughts*. You may argue: *Sometimes I can't seem to control what I am thinking about; I can't get a repetitive thought out of my mind.* I contend that you keep choosing to think that repetitive thought, miserable as it may be, because it gives you better control over some aspect of your life than any other thought you could choose at the time. This idea, that you always try to make the best choice at the time, is essential to understanding total behavior.

The following story illustrates the idea that the best choice is not necessarily a good choice but that it seems good at the time you choose it. A young man was walking through the large civic cactus garden in Phoenix. Suddenly he took off all his clothes, jumped into a huge patch of low cactus, and started to roll around. The bystanders eventually pulled him out, all punctured and bloody, and asked, "Why did you do that?" He said, "It seemed like a good idea at the time." We have all done some cactus rolling in our lives, but not to hurt ourselves. It was always because at the time we jumped in, it seemed like a good idea. Divorce lawyers prosper from people who have rolled in the cactus more than once because each time it seemed the best thing to do.

For example, Todd said that he just couldn't get the painful thought of his wife's leaving out of his mind. There is a good choice theory reason for this repetitive, almost obsessive, choice. As I mentioned, when we are dealing with a perception, in Todd's case, his wife, that is related to a strong picture in our quality world, we try to control the world so this picture is as satisfied in the real world as we can make it. Todd's repetitive thought was his way of trying to do so. His logic was, As long as I keep thinking about her, maybe I'll be able to figure out how to get her back. I don't want even to entertain the idea that she may be gone for good.

But for now, let's focus on the indirect choices of both how we feel and how we indirectly choose our physiology. We have almost total control over our actions and thoughts, and what we feel and our physiology are *inseparable* from these chosen actions and thoughts. If I choose the total behavior of beating my head against the wall, it hurts. *Wouldn't it also be fair to say that I am choosing to suffer the pain associated with this acting and thinking choice?* If I feel miserable, I may choose the total behavior of drinking to try to feel better. From experience with drinking, I have felt better, so why not try it again? *But I have to choose to think and act to get the alcohol into my bloodstream.* The alcohol cannot get in there on its own, and I believe I can't feel good until it gets there.

In the case of Todd, who said he was depressed, while I said he was choosing this misery, I didn't say he was choosing it directly. What he *was* choosing directly were the acting and thinking components of a total behavior that I call depressing or choosing to depress. As long as he was depressing, he continually ran the same unhappy thoughts through his mind. Over and over he thought, I wish she'd never left, I wish she'd come back, I wish I'd treated her differently, what will I do without her?

As he thought these miserable thoughts, his activity slowed, almost as if he were paralyzed. Everything became an effort, and he didn't even feel able to get up and go to work. And as he slowed down, his physiology got more obviously involved. He experienced a constant feeling of exhaustion and indolence—a total lack of energy—as if his get-up-and-go had got up and left. But since this is a total behavior, his feelings and physiology were integrated into this total. Whatever he felt and whatever his physiology, they are inseparably combined with his thinking and physical activity. When we depress, as we all have on many occasions, it feels as if our slowed activity is involuntary. But it is not. If Todd wanted to choose to make more of an effort, he could. He made the effort to come to my office.

Choice theory also teaches that he was choosing to depress for the same reason that all of us choose any total behavior—depressing gave him better control over his life than whatever else he could have thought of in this situation. It was his way of jumping into the cactus. Even though he was not aware of it, he, like all of us, had learned to depress as a child; had depressed on many occasions since then; and, in this situation, chose to depress so strongly that he came to me for help. As painful as depressing is, not to depress in this situation would have been more painful or, in his experience, would have led to more pain.

Shortly, I will explain why depressing is the best choice in this common situation and in almost all the situations in which you choose it. But you will be better able to understand this idea if I first explain why I label the total behavior I have been talking about *depressing or choosing to depress*.

Following choice theory, I label any total behavior by its most obvious component. To attempt to describe it by all four components is cumbersome and misleading. If I see you walking down the street, I would say you are walking. You are also thinking and feeling, and I'm sure your heart is beating, but it is your activity, walking, that is the most obvious. If I saw you pondering a move while playing chess, I would say you were thinking. I would not mention your minimal activity, how you felt or what your physiology was doing. If I saw you upchuck your dinner, I would describe your physiology and call it vomiting; I would not pay much attention to any other component of your behavior. If I brought you to an emergency room and told the doctor you had been vomiting, the doctor would question you about other components, such as what you had chosen to eat and where you ate it, but it is the vomiting, the most obvious component, that would lead to those questions.

When Todd came to see me and said he was depressed, he had correctly focused on the most obvious component of the total behavior he was choosing. He didn't say he was depressing, but he easily learned to do so when I taught him the choice theory that explains why he made this choice. In fact, from now on in this book, whenever I mention a total behavior that is ordinarily considered a mental illness, such as anxiety neurosis or phobia, I will call it by its total-behavior designation. Anxiety neurosis will be called anxietying or choosing to be anxious, and phobia will be called phobicking or choosing to be phobic.

These new names sound cumbersome at first, but when you get used to them, they become perfectly natural. These designations are more accurate than the traditional ones because they are active. Because these are the result of a choice, it becomes obvious that there is hope. If you can make one choice, you can make another—better—choice. Your choice may be painful, but it is not irreversible. Because no one likes pain, it immediately gets both the client and the therapist focused on helping the client make a better choice. To be depressed or neurotic is passive. It happened to us; we are its victim, and we have no control over it. This use of nouns and adjectives makes it logical for us to believe that we can do nothing for ourselves.

Verbs, coupled with some tense of the verb *to choose,* immediately put you in touch with the basic choice theory idea: You are choosing what you are doing, but you are capable of choosing something better. If it is a choice, it follows that you are responsible for making it. With verbs, you are not a victim of a mental illness; you are either the beneficiary of your own good choices or the victim of your own bad choices. You are not ill in the usual sense of having the flu or food poisoning. A choice theory world is a tough, responsible world; you cannot use grammar to escape responsibility for what you are doing.

The common use of nouns and adjectives to describe "depression" and other "mental illnesses" prevents huge numbers of people from ever thinking that they can do something more than suffer. When you learn that you are almost always free to make better choices, the concept that you choose your misery can lead to optimism. This new awareness is a major redefinition of your personal freedom. The idea that a situation is hopeless, that you can do nothing about it, is what makes it so uncomfortable. Without knowing anything about choice theory or mental illness, millions of people, who never see a counselor, make better choices than to depress many times in their lives. So can you.

Try this. Imagine that you were expecting a substantial raise, but all you got was a pittance. You would be *angry* for a while, but because you want to keep your job, you would almost immediately feel "depressed." Now instead of continuing to depress as you usually would, give yourself this little speech: *I am choosing to depress because I didn't get the raise I expected. How is this choice to depress going to help me deal with this situation? If it isn't helping me, can I choose to do something better?*

If you ran that through your mind, you would find it difficult to continue to depress; you would try to find a better total behavior. Although you are blaming this situation on your boss, you could take a look at what more you might have done to get a substantial raise. Or make up your mind that you are not going to complain but are going to look for a new job. Or tell your mate, "I did all I could, so give me a little support and we'll get through this situation. There's no sense my being miserable; none of us needs that. As long as you stand by me and accept that I did my best, I'll be OK." Doing something active like this is so much better than the passive acceptance of misery that so many of us choose now.

If we know about total behavior, we learn not to ask people who are obviously in pain or miserable: "How are you feeling?" This question is most commonly asked when someone is injured or sick and has no immediate chance to feel better. When I was the psychiatrist for the Orthopaedic Hospital in Los Angeles, I tried to convince the orthopedists and others who were dealing with suffering patients who were a long way from getting well not to ask this question. When it is asked, the questioner is looking for the answer "I feel fine" or "I feel better." Both the patient and the doctor know that this is being asked for.

So the patient usually lies and says, "I feel good," and that lie harms the doctor-patient relationship. The question also implies that the doctor's treatment alone can make the patient feel better, when in fact it can't. The better question to ask is this: "What are you planning to do today?" No matter how sick a patient is, he can do something, even in the hospital, besides just lie there. Implying that he can do something positive for himself gives him a sense of control that will help him feel better even in this difficult situation.

If the patient looks at the doctor as if the doctor is crazy, as some of the quadriplegic patients did when I asked them this question, I was always prepared to suggest some activity—perhaps as simple as watching a television program and talking to their roommates about it. If I saw them every week, they began to look forward to that question and had something prepared to tell me. Often they would add that they felt better when they were doing something, which confirms that this change in the usual approach is effective. In a choice theory world, we would get rid of the phony greeting *How are you?* and replace it with *What are you planning to do today?* or *Anything important happening?*—some variation of an active doing question instead of the inactive feeling question that usually traps people into phony answers.

Now that I have described total behavior, let me explain the three logical reasons why so many people choose to depress. These reasons explain the whole gamut of what is commonly called mental illness, such as depressing, anxieting, or phobicking. Even sicknesses like adult rheumatoid arthritis may be explained by these same three reasons. Many doctors believe that there is a psychological component in many diseases and call these diseases psychosomatic. The *psycho* of *psycho*somatic means that the way we are thinking may have a lot to do with what is going on in the *soma*, our bodies. It is safe to say that when we are not in effective control of our lives, as when we are in unsatisfying relationships, our physiology may get painfully involved in that loss of effective control. We may not get sick, but we cannot have a totally normal physiology any more than we can feel good when we are frustrated.

Restrain the Anger

Whenever we are not in effective control of our lives, many of us immediately think about using the total behavior we are born with: *angering*. Angering is built into our genes to help us survive, and since infancy we have used it or thought about using it whenever we are not able to satisfy an important picture in our quality worlds. Based on a lifelong experience with frustration, Todd, like most people, had an immediate impulse to anger when he saw the note from his wife telling him she had left. Angering is the first total behavior most of us think of when someone in our quality worlds does something that is very much out of sync with what we want that person to do.

But by the time we are a few years old, we learn that angering is usually an ineffective choice. It rarely gets us what we want, especially when we use it to try to control adults who are also angering. When we choose to tantrum, and our parents are smart enough not to pay attention, we find out that tantrumming is worthless. It is not getting us what we want, and we end up wasting energy and suffering a lot of pain. If we keep it up too long, we learn that this choice can make things worse—we may get punished or rejected, neither of which we want.

Todd had learned that. In a later session, he told me he knew that if he went after his wife and tried to force her to come back, a thought that had run through his mind for a moment when he read her note, he could make things much worse. Although we are not aware of it, depressing is also one of the most powerful ways that human beings have discovered to restrain angering, and all of us use it a lot. But, as I will soon explain, in its own way, depressing is a very strong controlling behavior.

When you are strongly depressing, what you are most aware of is its miserable feeling, a feeling that takes over your thinking, acting, and even your physiology and tends to slow you down. It takes a lot of energy to block the angering completely, which is why you are so tired. As long as you depress, you have little energy to do anything else. If we were not able to depress quickly and effectively, we could not function in marriage, as a family, or as a society. Depressing prevents huge amounts of marital and family violence. If most of us didn't depress a lot of the time when we were frustrated, our streets and homes would be war zones.

The killing and mayhem that we watch almost daily on television are good examples of what happens when adults choose to rage and strike out. If even a few of them depressed, we and they would be much better off. Most of us know how to depress, and we do it well. Some of us dedicate our lives to this behavior and must be cared for. Those who do so are so immobilized by this choice that they cannot function, but it is still a choice. They can stop choosing it if they can figure out another choice that will give them more effective control over their lives.

Depressing prevented Todd from going after his wife, harming her, and even killing her, a common behavior in this country where weapons are so available. It also might have prevented him from killing himself. Suicide is another total behavior that people choose when they have given up on the idea that they will ever be able to get their lives back into effective control. If a person who is depressing strongly suddenly stops depressing but seems to observers to have no good reason to stop, since his life is no more in effective control than it had been, that person may have decided to kill himself. That decision has given him the way out of his misery; in a sense it has given him the idea, Finally, there is a way to end this suffering forever.

Psychotherapists always look for that *feeling better* sign in people who have been depressing for a long time. When we see it, we suspect they may now be thinking of suicide. The pain of restraining their angering is so great that many people decide it's not worth living anymore and turn the anger against themselves. This was not a problem for Todd, but it might have been if he had not been willing to choose to find another woman to replace the picture of his wife in his quality world. For a man who seemed so social, suicide would have been unusual, but given time, anything is possible.

HELP ME

Depressing is a way we ask for help without begging. It is probably the most powerful help-me information we can give to another person. Because it is so strongly controlling, a lot of people choose it to try to get control over other people despite the pain. What the suffering does is to legitimize our asking for help. If we just asked or pushed for help with no show of pain, others might see us as incompetent or unable to take care of ourselves, and we do not want to be seen that way. For most of us, being seen as incompetent is too painful; too frustrating to our need for power; and too much like begging, which goes against our pride. But in many cases, we are perfectly willing to choose to depress as a way to get help that might not otherwise be offered.

After I had taught Todd some choice theory, he admitted that he had hoped his wife would call him after she left and then he would try to play on her sympathy by telling her he was so depressed that he couldn't even go to work. Since he rarely stayed home from work, that might have impressed her. But she didn't call. He also thought I would be impressed with how badly he was feeling, and if I had been, he would have depressed more to try to get me to solve his problem. But since I know choice theory, it is difficult for my clients or anyone else to control me with any total behavior that has misery as its feeling component. If it is coupled with compassion, not allowing anyone to control us with depressing helps them to see that there are much better choices than to depress.

AVOIDANCE

We often use depressing as an excuse for not doing something we don't want to do or are afraid to do. When someone suggests that we go ahead and do whatever we are trying to avoid, we usually agree and say, "I think you're right, but I'm just too upset right now to do it." For example, your company is downsizing and you lose a good job through no fault of your own. You tell me what happened and how depressed you are. I try not to pay much attention to your depressing. Instead I say, "I know it's hard, but don't sit around; get out your résumé."

But you are depressing for a good reason. You have just been laid off and feel rejected, even though it was not your fault. You are afraid of another rejection, of facing the fact that there may be no good jobs for you at your age and with your experience. As painful as depressing is, it's less painful at this time than looking for a job and getting rejected again and again. Todd had no problem at work, and he had no fear of looking for another woman, but the first two reasons, *restrain the anger* and *help me*, were in full operation when he first came to see me.

After reading this far, especially if you have recently depressed strongly, you may still say, *You may be right, but it still doesn't feel as if I'm choosing all this misery.* To check out my claim that depressing is a choice, force yourself to make a different choice for a short time, for at least an hour. Do something physically hard that, under different circumstances, you can easily do and that you usually enjoy, perhaps a brisk walk or a short hard run. If you can do it with a good friend who is not overly sympathetic, so much the better. While you are walking or running, especially with a friend, you will notice you are not depressing. For a short time, you are not thinking about your unhappy relationship, and you feel much better.

But as soon as you finish, you tend to go back to thinking about the relationship that has gone bad, and the feeling comes back. To depress, you have to keep thinking the unhappy thoughts that keep one or more of the three reasons to depress going. To stop thinking these thoughts, you have to do what I have been suggesting all through this book: change what you want or change your behavior. There is no other way. Todd did attempt to change his behavior toward his wife, but it was too late; she had already taken him out of her quality world. But with my help, he was able to change what he wanted—he took his wife out of his quality world and put another woman in—and he was able to stop depressing for as long as I was in touch with him.

By far the most uncomfortable of all the choice theory ideas to accept is that our chosen actions and thoughts may have a great deal to do with our health, that these actions and thoughts may adversely affect our physiology. For example, are there thinking choices that can lead to what is called psychosomatic disease? I'll touch on this briefly here (a large part of chapter 7 describes how choice theory explains these extremely common and, sometimes, fatal diseases and how we may use this explanation to help ourselves, both in cooperation with a doctor or over and beyond what a doctor can or will do). Let's take a look at the most common disease of men and, increasingly, of women: coronary artery disease or arteriosclerotic heart disease.

You are a forty-seven-year-old movie producer who is frantically trying to get financing for what you are sure will be a blockbuster film. You are doing all you can to get the money, but your option on the property is running out. You feel bad. Eating rich foods and smoking are your attempts to get some pleasurable relief from the pain of getting rejection after rejection from the people who could easily give you the money. Although at first you felt only a heaviness in your chest, this heaviness gradually turned to greater and greater chest pain and shortness of breath.

You go to your doctor and learn that your coronary arteries are badly clogged with plaque. You ask him what can be done, and he tells you that a lot depends on how you choose to live your life. He talks about diet, exercise, smoking, stress, the whole lifestyle now known to be strongly related to heart disease. Your doctor may not understand choice theory, but what he is saying when he mentions stress is that when your life is not in effective control, it is bad for your health. This is the same as saying, bad for your physiology.

But since all your behavior is total behavior, when you lose effective control of your life, you cannot separate your feelings or your physiology from your actions and your thoughts. In this case, from your physician's standpoint, the most obvious result of the altered physiology that is part of all the ineffective behaviors you are choosing to get the movie made is your diseased coronary arteries. Following what I have just explained, heart diseasing could well describe your choice to eat fatty foods, to smoke, and not to exercise.

The doctor has medicine and even surgery that will help, but it is your choice to stop the unhealthful eating, smoking, and sedentary life. I would go further than many doctors and suggest that in addition, you try some counseling to help you learn to take more effective control of your life. Frustration, a much more accurate word for what is going wrong than stress, may be making as large a contribution to your heart diseasing as what you are eating.

As I have stated, when our lives are out of effective control, all four components of the total behaviors we are choosing to try to get them back into more effective control are involved. We may pretend we are happy and nothing is wrong, but we can't pretend to be healthy; we don't have that kind of control over our physiology. When we are choosing to depress, our brain chemistry is not the cause of what we feel. It is the usual or expected brain physiology associated with the acting, thinking, and feeling that together make up the total behavior called depressing. For this reason, I believe that the currently accepted explanation that "depression" is caused by an imbalance in our brain chemistry is wrong.

I can assure you that when Todd found the note on his refrigerator, his brain chemistry instantly changed, as did his feelings, his activity, and what he had been thinking just before he saw that note. He probably wanted to do more, and if he knew choice theory he might have been able to. But, as it was, when he found the note, by choosing to depress, he was able to restrain the urge to get going and do something active to get her back. That activity, if it included confrontation or even violence, would have made his situation much worse.

He chose to depress for the same reason that millions of people all over the world choose to depress: An important relationship was not working the way he wanted it to work. Such people who choose to depress are not mentally ill; their brain chemistry is not abnormal. It is changed from what it is when they are happy, but that change is perfectly normal for the total behavior, depressing, they are choosing. As I stated, we all learned to depress when we were very young, and we have been using it, when needed, all our lives. It is only when the pain of this choice gets severe and long lasting that we begin to recognize that something is seriously wrong.

But few of us are prepared to recognize that something is seriously wrong with our lives. It is more comfortable to blame our discomfort on a mental illness or on abnormal brain chemistry. There is not one person reading this book who is not able to depress strongly when his or her life is out of effective control. To see why our brain chemistry is normal for the depressing we are choosing, consider the following scenario.

I am sitting on my cool front porch on a hot summer day. My neighbor, who is a consistent five-mile-a-day runner, comes up the street and heads for my house. I tell him to sit on the steps, which are in the shade. Without his asking, I get him a tall glass of water, and we chat. I decide to teach him a little choice theory. He knows what I do, so I'm sure he'll humor me.

I ask, "Why are you perspiring so much?" He looks at me as if he doesn't understand, and I say, "I'm serious, tell me." He says, "I was running. No one can run on a day like this and not perspire; running and sweating go together." I say, "I agree that they go together, but why do you say that the running caused the sweating? Why don't you say that sweating caused the running?" He, not knowing about total behavior, looks at me as if I'm crazy and says, "I don't understand what you're driving at."

And he doesn't. We are so used to external control thinking, that when things go together, as do running and sweating, we often say one caused the other. But using the same logic, it makes just as much sense to say that sweating causes running. In actual fact, while they do go together, *neither causes the other*. What causes both the running (the acting component) and the sweating (the normal physiology associated with running) is his choice to run. If he had not chosen to run, he would not be perspiring.

When Todd chose to depress, for one or more of the three reasons I explained, he chose a total behavior for which depressing is the normal feeling component. Whatever brain chemistry is associated with that feeling is also normal. The brain chemistry no more causes his depressing than sweating causes running. It is the *choice* to depress or to run that results in both. That is why I call what I am explaining choice theory. When the neurophysiologists show that the brain activity of a depressing person is different from that of a happy person or from the same person when he or she is happy, they should expect what they find. But in this instance—choosing to depress—not only is the physiology different, but the thinking, acting, and feelings are different, too. In the case of the man who was choosing to run, a much more normal behavior than depressing, only the acting and the physiology are sure to be changed by this choice. What he was thinking and feeling may not have had much connection with his choice to run. But many runners report that they think more clearly and feel happier after they run.

Research that shows that drugs, such as Prozac, reduce the depressing activity in the brain also should be expected. Depressing lowers the brain chemical serotonin; Prozac raises it. A lower level of serotonin is the normal physiology when we choose to depress, and raising the level helps many people who choose to depress feel better. Alcohol, nicotine, and other addicting drugs also help most people feel better because each in its own chemical way injects pleasure directly into the brain. Prozac does the same. And if it gives the user, who has a chronic unsatisfying relationship, a lot of pleasure, it can also be addicting.

Some people who take Prozac say they would not think of living their lives without it. For them, it may be a lot like alcohol. They look forward to their daily Prozac as social drinkers look forward to a few drinks or some wine each day. They are no more addicted to Prozac than social drinkers are addicted to alcohol. But like social drinkers, they would miss it terribly if it was taken away. But some social drinkers move on to become alcoholics. The lonelier they are, the more danger there is of their becoming alcoholics. There may even be more danger of becoming addicted to Prozac because it is prescribed only for people whose lives are known to be out of effective control.

Prozac could not have brought a new relationship into Todd's life. It might have helped him to feel better so that he was more able to look for someone else, but it would no more solve his loneliness than would alcohol or marijuana. We would be much better off getting rid of the psychology that is causing so much misery than looking for chemicals that make us feel better but do nothing to solve our loneliness. If Todd refused to take his wife out of his quality world and all he was offered was Prozac, he might need it for the rest of his life, and even then, it might not be effective. Drugs provide pleasure; they cannot provide happiness. For happiness, you need people.

Drugs like Prozac are often used along with psychotherapy. The rationale is that if people feel better through the chemical boost they get from the drug, they will be able to profit more from the psychotherapy. Most reality therapy counselors who focus quickly on faulty relationships have not found the use of Prozac to be necessary, and in all my years of practice, I have never used brain drugs. Good psychotherapy precludes the need for these drugs. If more people would learn and use choice theory, the use of these drugs could diminish. All the usual psychiatric diagnoses, excluding observable brain damage, are chosen for one or more of the same three reasons that people choose to depress.

Choice theory does not come easily to us in a culture that is external control to the core. But my experience with many people, including my wife and myself, who have learned enough choice theory to use it in their lives, has been positive. The fact that the use of choice theory improves marital, family, school, and work relationships instead of destroying them is what makes the difference. Besides, we all have proof of its effectiveness because it is all we use with our good friends.

CHAPTER 5

Compatibility, Personality, and the Strength of the Needs

B Y THE TIME I was four years old, I realized that my parents were almost totally incompatible. There had been sporadic violence in which my father broke things, and once I saw him hit my mother. Whenever my parents started to argue, I was frightened. By the time I was six, the violence stopped, and they seemed to get along better. Whatever difficulty they had with each other, they were always loving toward me. Much later I realized that my mother had won by the simple tactic of giving my father the message that he would have to kill her if he didn't want to let her rule the marriage. He was a gentle man, and I was aware of how mercilessly she prodded him. As young as I was, I could see that he erupted only when he had been pushed beyond his ability to endure.

If the Olympics had an event in controlling, my mother could have gone for the gold medal. My father was totally choice theory. Never in the more than sixty years that I knew him did I ever see him try to control another person except when he was being goaded by my mother. And even then, his heart was not in it. My parents had been married almost seventy years when my father died; in those days most people stayed married. To illustrate what my father had to contend with, I offer the following example.

When I was twenty-four and married, just before I started medical school, my father called me and said he wanted to come to our apartment to talk with me privately. He had never done so before, and it seemed clear from his tone of voice that it was a personal matter. He was at his wits' end; my mother had done something that was typical for her, but this time she had carried it to such an extreme that he was unable to cope with it by himself. He came to ask me what to do.

For a long time, my mother had been pushing my father to sell his business and retire so they could move to Florida, where they had spent part of each winter for many years. She hated the cold and damp of Cleveland. My father was only fifty-six years old, but he had worked since he was thirteen and could retire. While he was far from sure that he wanted to give up the freedom his business afforded him and the few Cleveland friends my mother allowed him to have, he told me he had sold the business and was ready to sell the house and move to Florida. Now that I was going to medical school and would never go into his business, he felt that there was no reason for him to work anymore. All things considered, he agreed she was right, and he was looking forward to the move.

My mother had seemed pleased with all his preparations and things were going well, but the day he told her that the business was sold and that he was putting their house up for sale, she said to him: "*Why have you done all this? What gave you the idea that I wanted to leave Cleveland and move to Florida? I don't want to leave this house and all my friends.*" She had no friends in Cleveland and acted as if it was all his idea, that he had not consulted her and that she had no intention of leaving. He asked me what he should do. I thought a long time and told him, "Pop, you're only fifty-six. You may live another thirty healthy years (which he did). Divorce her. She's never going to change."

He was not prepared for this advice, but if I had to do it over again, I'd say the same thing. When it registered on her that the business had been sold, that there was no turning back, she did go to Florida. She had what she had been pushing him to do for years. It must have occurred to her that she had nothing more to fight about. He had disarmed her by surrendering unconditionally. But after that initial outburst, she did as she always did. She shut up and acted as if she had never said anything. If he had asked her why she said what she did, she would have denied saying it and responded, "I don't know where you got the idea that I didn't want to go to Florida."

But, of course, he let it drop. My sister moved to Florida a few years later with her family, and the last thirty years of my father's life were much better than any of us, including him, expected. There is a lot more to this story, but I've made my point. My parents were incompatible from day one; it was her way or no way. There is such a thing as personality, and hers was much different from his.

I believe that the way we usually relate to other people, best called our personalities, is, in part, written into our genes. I don't mean that anything specific, such as my mother's fondness for warm weather or that she was an omnivorous reader, was genetic, but her huge need to control everyone she came into contact with was. What gives us our different personalities is that our five basic, or genetic, needs differ in strength. Some of us have a high need for love and belonging. Others have a high need for power or freedom.

The strength of each need is fixed at birth and does not change. Autistic children have a low to almost nonexistent need for love and belonging. This means they have hardly any desire for human interaction and none for the close interaction that most of us want so much. Given enough human contact, some may learn to interact with others a little but never to the extent to which a normal child or adult wants. This lack of the desire to belong, much less love, was illustrated clearly in the movie, *Rain Man*, starring Dustin Hoffman. On the high end of love and belonging would be the kind, unselfish people who care for and give a lot of love to severely handicapped children and adults, those who, compared to what they are given, can give little or nothing back.

The differences in people's personalities, even between brothers' and sisters', is striking. My mother and father were hardly unique; many husbands and wives have very different personalities. Some are outgoing, gregarious, optimistic, liberal, and fun loving. Others are sober, quiet, conservative, pessimistic, controlling, and gloomy. The variations are endless. Our personalities are created out of a genetic need-strength profile that is unique for each of us. Some of these profiles, like those of my parents, are highly incompatible; some, such as mine and my wife's, are highly compatible.

The personalities of some couples are different but complementary; that is, the differences enhance the relationships. But, in my observation, the best marriages are ones in which the husbands and wives have similar personalities. If my father had married a woman who matched his high need for love and low need for power, he would have been a much happier man. My mother, who had an off-the-scale need for power, could love intensely but only if she owned the person; she was not able to separate love from power. This is another illustration of how individual our need strengths are.

What I explain in this chapter is that finding a compatible mate and getting along with a less-than-compatible mate need not be luck. Figuring out your need-strength profile and the profiles of those you want to get along with may not be totally accurate, but it will give you a good working understanding of how you and others deal with people. Not only should you not marry a person with a markedly different personality, but you should not go into any endeavor with anyone whom you may have difficulty getting along with.

Most of the people who are reading this book are already married, and some of you may be wondering, if we are not compatible, is it too late for us? The answer depends on how incompatible you are. In most instances, your need strengths are not so different from your partner's that working things out is impossible. If you are willing to give up trying to control each other and to begin using choice theory in the relationship, you can usually negotiate these differences. But to negotiate accurately, you need to become aware of what these differences are, that is, which need or needs are in conflict.

Once you have this information, you can focus on where you are different and stop criticizing and blaming each other in areas of the marriage where you are actually compatible. If I want more freedom than you are willing to let me have, we can negotiate that difference and not exaggerate it into blaming me for not being loving enough. The love part may be fine. It is foolish to link it to the disagreement over freedom. As long as the differences in the need strengths are not too extreme, they may not do serious harm to a marriage. It is how you deal with those differences that counts. You always have a chance for success with choice theory. But if you use controlling and coercing, the differences will remain, the effort to change the other will magnify them, and you will find yourself arguing over unimportant issues that you wouldn't even think about if you used choice theory.

During our long marriage, my first wife and I had one conflicting need strength that gave us some difficulty. But when we both learned choice theory and started using it in our marriage, we were able to work out where we differed. For me, freedom is a very strong need; for her, it was no more than average. When we discovered this incompatibility and negotiated it, we got along much better. After my wife died, I married an instructor in my organization who also teaches choice theory; however, before Carleen and I were married, we checked the strength of our needs and found we were highly compatible. We also agreed to use choice theory with each other from the start. So far we have had a very happy relationship, and it seems to get better as the years go by.

Since we are dealing with a normal distribution, the odds are against people marrying whose need strengths are so incompatible that the marriage is in immediate danger. But the odds against a perfectly compatible marriage are also small. What a couple, or at least one partner, can learn from the need strengths is to pinpoint any difficulty as soon as it is recognized and then use choice theory to do something about it.

To illustrate what I am talking about, look at how a difference in the need to survive can cause problems in an otherwise good marriage. Even a moderate variation in the strength of this clear-cut need can cause trouble. A common problem is that one partner's lifestyle is more conservative than the other's, usually because of a difference in the strength of the need to survive. For example, one is a saver, the other a spender. That combination does not augur well for the marriage unless the couple recognizes this difference early and sets up a plan to negotiate when trouble arises.

Assume the usual case, that there is enough money but no surplus. When the less conservative one wants to spend, the other says it's not necessary. If each is dedicated to fighting over this disagreement, they will have an argument every time and will soon escalate the argument into the personal, *You don't love me anymore,* which they will then use to blame the other for every difference, large and small, they have. As long as they argue, there can be no resolution. If their need for power is about the same, neither will give in, and in time both will harden their positions. Without knowing what they are doing, they are trying the impossible: to change the other's genes. All they can negotiate is a compromise. Choice theory is the way to compromise; fighting, arguing, and trying to control are the paths to increased conflict.

THE SOLVING CIRCLE

A good way to use choice theory to solve marital problems is to start by agreeing to picture your marriage (or other relationship) inside a large circle I call the solving circle. It helps to draw an imaginary circle on the floor. Then both you and your spouse take chairs and enter the circle. There are three entities in the solving circle: the wife, the husband, and the marriage itself. Recognize that you both have strong positions based on the differences in the strength of your needs, but these positions are not so strong that you are unwilling to enter the solving circle. What you are agreeing to when you enter the circle is that the marriage takes precedence over what each of you wants as individuals. Both of you also know choice theory. You know that if you try to force the other, it is likely that the weaker person will be pushed out or will decide to step out of the circle. Unless both of you are in the circle, you cannot negotiate; all you can do is argue.

The reason you have moved into the circle is that during the time one or both partners are outside the circle, a marriage problem cannot be solved. The marriage has suffered a wound and is bleeding. The wound is not fatal, but it will continue to bleed as long as one or both of you are outside the circle. This is how most marriages end, slowly bleeding to death, one or the other unwilling to step back into the circle. A more severe wound, often fatal, would be if they were so dissatisfied that both stepped out; that wound would indicate that the marriage is hemorrhaging and will soon be dead.

A couple who knows choice theory will not try to make the other do what he or she does not want to do. When they step into the solving circle, they agree not to wound their marriage. No matter how serious the disagreement, they must stay in the circle and negotiate this difference. They would start by one saying and the other agreeing, *We have a disagreement over money. It may be based on the fact that one of us has a much stronger survival need than the other. But that difference does not mean we can't negotiate. We both know that arguing and blaming will do no good. We need to stay in the circle, talk, and find out how much each of us is willing to give to avoid wounding or killing the marriage.*

In the circle, each tells the other what he or she will agree to do that will help the marriage. Within those limits, they must reach a compromise. At times, one may give in completely, but, realistically, a compromise is usually necessary. One may say, *I will agree to your spending this much. It is more than I want to see spent, but it is my attempt to reach a compromise.* The other may say, *I will cut my spending more than I want to, but this is as low as I will go.* If both agree on what is acceptable, the negotiation has succeeded; the marriage has taken precedence over individual wants.

If no compromise can be reached in this first attempt, one or both must be willing to say, *What I want right now is more important to me than this marriage. I am going to step out of the circle now, but I am willing to try again tomorrow.* This is a test. If they give themselves a night or even several nights to think this over, the next time they get into the circle, both should be ready to say, *It is more important that we stay in this circle than that we spend or save any amount of money.* As long as they both know they are willing to do it, disagreements will surface but then fade away. The awareness that this circle is there to use and that both will agree to use it does the job. This simple vehicle can give any marriage a chance. If one or both stays outside the circle, external control takes over and soon dismantles the marriage.

From survival, let's move on to disparities in the strength of the need for love and belonging. It is important to understand that the strength of this need is measured by how much we are willing to give, not by how much we are willing to receive. Most of us would like more love than is usually available. There may be significant differences in the strength of this need, and a difference here can be more serious than a difference in the strength of the need to survive (such as over money). But no matter how much we want, we have to learn that we can't get any more than our partner is able to give. We can't give any more love than the amount that is written in our genes, but in the vast majority of marriages that's enough.

If I am to get all that my wife is capable of giving, my best chance is to try to give her as much as I can. Here, even a little holding back can cause great difficulty. In conflicted marriages, holding back love is a common punishing behavior. A controlling husband sees his wife paying attention to a man at a party and asks her, "Why don't you treat me that way?" She thinks, If you would stop trying to make me over, maybe I would. The other man got the attention because in that social situation, it never occurred to either the man or the woman to be controlling. The husband may not know how much love his wife is capable of giving, but what he wants is well within her ability. He is right to assume she's holding back. What's wrong is that an accusation is unlikely to persuade her to give him more and probably will result in her giving even less. As they are, both are not even close to being in the circle.

Beware of confusing love and sex. A strong sex drive is not indicative of a strong need for love and belonging; hormonal sex is related to the species' need to survive. Early in any marriage, a strong sex drive may have little to do with love and belonging. The test for love and belonging is not early sex but a continuous interest in sex and ongoing attempts to please the other as much as or more than to satisfy oneself. When sex starts to wane early in a marriage, it is not because the couple lacks hormones. It is because one or both partners begin to feel that there isn't enough love attached to the sex. This is rarely genetic; there is usually enough love, but the love has been turned off by too much control.

There can be some genetic variation. If the partner with the strong need for love, often the woman, gives a lot, she may be dissatisfied with what she gets in return. Perhaps the partner with the weaker need is not able to give as much as she wants, or he may be choosing not to give as much as he could. In practice, it doesn't matter. Either way, there is good reason to negotiate, and the solving circle is the best way to do so. Keep in mind that the circle will work only if the couple is committed to choice theory, to understanding the needs, their strength, the quality world, and total behavior.

Step into the circle and tell each other not what you want but what you are willing to give. Remember, we can only control our own behavior, so you should talk solely about what you are willing to do, not what you want the other to do. If a partner is not willing to stay in the circle with the amount of love and friendship the other is willing to give, there is not much hope for the marriage. Because the negotiation in the circle is, in itself, an offering of love, what is offered is usually enough. As soon as the discussion centers on giving instead of taking, the love problem has an excellent chance of being resolved.

Where survival and love are concerned, the closer your need strengths are to your partner's, the better the chance for the marriage. This doesn't necessarily hold for power, the most difficult need to satisfy in or out of marriage. There are so many frustrated people who have no chance to satisfy this need in the coercive workplaces that are the norm in our society that they try to get from their marriages what they can't get anywhere else. If both partners have a strong need for power, this attempt may doom their marriage. Battered wives are often the victims of powerless husbands who are trying get from their wives at home what they can't get elsewhere.

A good workplace, in which you have some power and work for people who don't try to push you around, is very good for your marriage. The only time I saw my mother really happy was when she served for almost six months on the county grand jury. If she had been born fifty years later, she might have been able to use both her brains and her tremendous energy in a job. With her huge need for power, she might never have been able to be happily married, but she might have been a happy single woman. How happy the people who worked under her would have been is a point for conjecture, but she would soon be in charge. My guess is that if they behaved in a way that showed they accepted that she owned them, she would have treated them well. I've seen a lot of employees do so; it's not difficult if you don't have a strong need for power.

Partners who both have a low need for power are almost always compatible. Low power leads to a high desire to negotiate, and low-power couples are usually in the solving circle most of the time. Even if one partner has a much higher need for power than the other, their marriage may be OK because the one with the low need for power won't mind the other calling the shots as long as he or she is loving. I've seen this combination of high-power loving men and low-power loving women work reasonably well, sort of like the last half of my parents' marriage.

But if both partners have a strong need for power, a common occurrence because power attracts power, the urge to push the other out of the circle is almost impossible to resist. *This marriage isn't big enough for both of us* is the battle hymn of these unhappy, often doomed, relationships. The only way for two high-power people to deal with each other if they can't satisfy their need for power outside the marriage is to find a way to work together so that their combined effort gets them both more of what they need. This is what my late wife and I did in our marriage, and it worked well. My present wife has a much lower need for power than did my late wife, and we work well together. We both enjoy power, but it is not as crucial for this marriage as it was for my first marriage. I have seen many successful husband-and-wife teams join together to build what neither could build alone.

Unlike the needs for survival and love, the need for power can rarely be negotiated in the solving circle. High-power people push each other out of the circle before they realize it. By its very nature, power is difficult to negotiate because to negotiate always means that both agree to give up some power. Negotiation cannot take place if neither is willing to give up some power. Since the negotiation is *how much power to give up,* it is essential to try to find out how strong each partner's need for power is before marriage. After marriage it may be too late. I explain this power problem further when I describe the two kinds of people who have need-strength profiles that I believe are incompatible with marriage.

People with a high need for freedom struggle with all long-term close relationships, but they struggle the most in marriage. The very nature of being free is that no one owns them. When someone tries to own them, they don't fight, as people with a high need for power tend to do, they move on. In a world in which almost half the people who marry divorce, a lot are moving on all the time. Marriage has the best chance when both partners have a low need for power and a low need for freedom. If one partner has a high need for freedom and the other has a low need, there is no problem until the partner with the low need tries to limit the other's freedom.

Unlike power, this difference can usually be addressed in the solving circle. In the circle, the partner with the high need for freedom has to tell what concessions he or she is willing to make. Simply by agreeing to accept some restrictions to freedom to please the partner with the low need for freedom, the partner with the high need can ensure that the negotiation will have a happy ending. Just the willingness of the high-freedom partner to call home if he or she is going to be late will make a big difference. If in their frustration they reject each other, they have no chance.

If both partners have a high need for freedom, the marriage may or may not work. It will work if each can accept the freedom the other wants. To do so, both partners must get into the solving circle and tell each other what freedom they are willing to give up. A blank check for freedom can't work in any marriage unless there is a lot of love and belonging to make up for the times the partners are not together, and even then it is very difficult. Marriage is not a situation in which there can be anywhere near total freedom. This is a difficult test of the solving circle, but mutual high-freedom needs will constantly challenge any marriage.

Today, as many couples live together before marriage, this incompatibility may surface before they take the legal step, and that is the time to use the circle—maybe here it should be called the *premarital solving circle*. If a couple finds out after they marry that they both have a high need for freedom, they will divorce or just leave without getting a divorce. Unlike a mutual high need for power, a couple can't unite for increased freedom. Shared freedom for two high-freedom people is an oxymoron. For these reasons, the solving circle makes no sense for high-freedom people. They don't want to be in a circle with anyone; to them any circle may seem like a prison.

Sharing a high need for fun is excellent for every relationship, especially a marriage. If fun is the genetic reward for learning, then partners who learn together have the best chance to stay together. Fun is almost never limited by age, sex, or the lack of money. With a minimal effort, you can laugh and learn anytime, anywhere. But fun is not critical to a relationship. Partners can learn to enjoy themselves independently and not hurt the marriage, and they often do. If both partners have a low need for fun, neither will ever know what he or she is missing, and things may work out fine. I don't think the need for fun, strong, weak, or equal, makes or breaks a marriage if all else is compatible.

Therefore, the best marriages share an average need for survival, a high need for love and belonging, low needs for power and freedom, and a high need for fun. Any deviation from this not-too-frequent pattern will need to be negotiated. The greater the difference, the more negotiation. What this information gives you, whether you are already married or looking, is a clear picture of where there may be trouble. Armed with this information, couples who want a better marriage will use the circle to negotiate. Unsatisfying marriage is, by far, the most frequent cause of human misery. As a friend of mine said years ago when we discussed the value of negotiation in marriage, "Consider the alternative."

If you agree with what I have just explained, you are wondering, How do I assess the strength of my needs and the needs of my partner? I have given a lot of thought to this question, and I don't believe it can be done by any simplistic paper-and-pencil self-test like a questionnaire. The questions have to be asked by each individual on the basis of what the person knows about himself or herself and what he or she can assess in the other. Basically, it is an assessment of quality worlds, yours and your mate's.

By the time you are ready to marry or remarry, you have already had some relationships. Since you were a teenager, you have been looking for Ms. or Mr. Right. It is impossible to have a relationship and not evaluate it against some ideal relationship that has been forming in your quality world for years. But if you are an external control person, the heart of that ideal relationship is what the other can do for you. Having this other-centered relationship as the ideal leaves you unprepared to find what you really need—a relationship that is based on what each partner can do for the other. O. Henry's short story, "The Gift of the Magi," depicts both the sadness and the joy of choice theory love.

To help you create this *right* person in your quality world, you have observed your family and friends, read books, and seen movies and television shows. And during your teenage years, especially if you are a woman, you talked endlessly with your friends about why this boy and that girl were or were not right for each other. On the basis of all this information, you should be able to see where you stand in comparison with others in many of the things you thought or talked about.

Because your basic needs underlie almost all you do and think about, much of your talk has centered on these needs. You may not have come right out and used these words, but you have talked a lot about love, power, and freedom. You have done so because you have seen, and even experienced, that when there are differences in these needs, things are difficult. If you are a woman, you have talked about the fact that all some guys want is sex when you want love, how some of them want to own you (power), and how the guys always want to go off with other guys (freedom). You have done a lot of thinking about relationships in these terms. Driven by a more intense need for power than women, most men rarely talk to each other this way.

If you have found that you are less willing to take risks than most people, you have a high need for survival. If you have about the same willingness as most people you know, you have an average need, and if you are willing to take more risks than most of your friends, you have a low need. The same goes for love and belonging. The key to assessing the strength of your need for love and belonging is how much you are willing to give, not take, compared to your family members and friends. Be careful with this need; look hard before you leap into a loveless marriage. Don't confuse sex with love. Pay attention to belonging. As I said in chapter 2, don't marry someone you would not be friends with if there was no sex between you.

To assess the strength of your need for power, ask yourself if you always want to have your own way, to have the last word, to own people, and to be seen as right in most of what you do or say. If you do, you have a high need for power. If you don't care that much about having your own way, don't want to own anyone, and won't often fight for the last word, you have a low need for power. If you care somewhat, you probably have an average need for power.

If you can't stand the idea of following rules, conforming, or even staying in one place or with one group of people very long, you have a high need for freedom. If you are a little this way, you have an average need. If it doesn't bother you to conform, you have a low need for freedom. And the same goes for fun. If you enjoy learning and laugh a lot when you do, you have a high need for fun; if you enjoy teaching a class that tends to laugh at what you do and with each other, you have an even higher need. A little less enjoyment of learning and laughing make you a person with an average need for fun. But if you really don't want to make much effort to learn and you depend on others for enjoyment, you have a low need for fun. If you hardly ever laugh when others are laughing and are not much interested in finding out more than you know now, you have a very low need for fun.

Another way to assess your needs is to take a look at your quality world. If you and your partner or prospective partner trust each other enough to share your quality worlds, there is a good chance you love each other. As you assess your own quality worlds (separately or together), look for the following: If your quality world is filled with people you get along well with, you have a high need for love and belonging and are a happy person because you have been able to satisfy this need. If your quality world has just a few people, but you are very close to them, you may have a high desire for love but a lower desire for belonging.

If you have a lot of people in your quality world but are not close to any of them, you may have a high desire for belonging but a lesser desire for love. And if you have only a few people in your quality world and are not close to any of them, you have a low need for both love and belonging. This does not mean that you have no need, but it may mean that you have a lower need than does your mate. If your desire is more in the area of belonging and less in the area of personal closeness, this could be a problem.

As I have already explained, use this information to negotiate and use the solving circle as a vehicle for negotiation. As long as you can stay in the circle and accept that you can control only your own behavior, you can negotiate almost anything. If you are able to see the rationale of choice theory, you understand that there is no sense blaming the other partner because that is the way he or she is. It's like blaming the other partner for not being tall enough or being allergic to seafood. Working together to become aware of your need strengths can give you information you can both use. If you are willing to use it for the sake of the relationship, you will get closer to each other just by starting this assessment. Most people are not *that* incompatible. The solution is as much in what you are willing to try to do as it is in actually doing that much. A small compromise sends the message, *I care more about our relationship than I do about what I want personally.* This is a powerful message.

I have described some simple and obvious parameters of need strengths. In any individual instance, you may vary from what I have described and be high or low for another reason. I can't go through all the possible variations. That is a task for you. Take your time, discuss it with people who know you, try to be openminded, and you should be able to do it well. Remember your feelings and how good you feel when your needs are satisfied. The better you feel, the stronger the need. It doesn't take much to satisfy a weak need. Base your assessment on total behaviors that felt good, and your profile will be reasonably accurate.

If you are beginning a relationship and it seems as if it could get serious, you may think of making a compatibility assessment before the other person's picture is so strongly in your quality world that you have little chance to see him or her as he or she actually is. Even if the person is already too much in your quality world for accuracy, doing so is still better than doing nothing. Try to assess him or her in the same way you have assessed yourself. If you see a problem, talk about it while you are very attracted to each other. Your assessments may be biased by your love, but your love will make you more willing to compromise at this stage than at any other time and well before you have used so many controlling behaviors on each other that negotiation is impossible.

Try to make sure that you do not let good sex or the desire for good sex become too much a factor in making this initial assessment. If, however, sex is not good or the desire for sex is not strong, you can be assured that this situation is unlikely to change for the better. Sex in the beginning of a relationship, before you have learned things you don't like about each other, while you are firmly in the circle, is about as good as it is going to get. In a good relationship, it may lessen in frequency but will stay satisfying. If sex starts out good and gets bad, it is not sex but the relationship that has gone downhill.

If your relationship is not going as well as you would like, but you think that assessing the strength of the needs is too difficult, inaccurate, or not worth the effort, you are throwing away an important opportunity to know yourself. After you are married and the dissatisfaction with your partner begins, there are not many opportunities to help the marriage that both partners are willing to try. This is a golden opportunity—use it. If you depend on the widespread lover's delusion, With my love he or she will change, you have little chance to help yourself. This delusion is external control to the maximum. If things are not good in the beginning, they are very likely to change—but not for the better.

Here is what I promised earlier, the two personalities that are totally incompatible for marriage with anyone. Marrying a person with either personality will result in nothing but misery. There are no silver linings in these two clouds. If you are not yet married but suspect that the person you are involved with has either type of personality, run as soon and as fast as you can. Start packing your bags as soon as you read this section. Don't wait to finish this book.

If you are married when you discover that your partner has one of these personalities, realize that no matter how bad the relationship is now, it is guaranteed to get worse. Begin now to think of what you can do to extricate yourself. With this kind of a person, man or woman, whatever you are feeling now, you are well off compared to how you are going to feel later. But I don't have to tell you that your relationship is bad; you already know it. What I explain here is *why* it's bad.

The Sociopath

The *sociopath* seems to care only about power and personal freedom and has no real consideration for the needs of anyone else. Most sociopaths are men because genetically men have a lower need for love and belonging and a higher need for power than do women.

The survival need of a sociopath is below average, but he has enough of a need to survive that he can concentrate on what he is doing for short periods. What is characteristic about him is that his need for love and belonging is almost nonexistent, while his need for freedom is high. He is always on the move trying to satisfy his need for power and doing so at the expense of anyone he can cheat, swindle, or steal from. His need for fun may vary, but if he has a high need for it, he will enjoy learning all the ways he can exploit you and everyone else he meets. He also enjoys putting you down, no matter how competent you are. The only person he sees as competent is himself. In the beginning, sociopaths may be exciting because they are so active and full of charm that they get things going. But because of their low need for survival, most have little follow-through. Life may be miserable around them, but it isn't dull.

A sociopath is good at fooling people because he believes he is much better than almost everyone else. He may be funny and even seem kind. When you notice he has some flaws, he may cheerfully admit them and compliment you on how perceptive you are. He'll tell you how much he appreciates your love, that with it he'll change. He's been looking all his life for a woman like you, and that's true. But you have not been looking for a man like him. For this unscrupulous predator, life is a hunt and you are the game. He'll use any weapon to get you; there are no rules in the games he plays.

This man is genetically incapable of feeling love or belonging for anyone. He may be charming and sexy, but only to exploit, never because he really cares. Once he has gotten all he wants from a woman, he will run away if she attempts to cling to him because of his need for freedom. If she is too clinging, he may beat her in the hopes that she will do everything for him and expect nothing from him except more beatings. He may even beat her for not guessing what he wants—he won't tell her—but after he beats her he will say, "You should have known."

If you have *any* suspicion that you are involved with a sociopath, look for his friends. You will find that he doesn't have any; they are always far away or about to visit, but they never show up. One thing about him that you can absolutely count on is that you can never count on him. Never! If he does what you ask, it was a mistake or it's part of a scheme to exploit you further. If early in the relationship he takes you out to an expensive place and tells you he's forgotten his credit card and asks to borrow yours, never see him again and make sure you get the card back. If he says he misplaced it, cancel it immediately. He has no credit cards, but he is already thinking about going on a spree with yours.

THE WORKLESS

The workless person is the most puzzling of all the people we encounter. He easily relates to others and, at first, you may easily relate to him. But if you get close, if you marry him, you will become increasingly frustrated. There may be women among the workless, but they are less visible because it is still more accepted in our society for a woman not to work and to be supported.

Unlike a sociopath, who quickly shows his true colors, the workless person goes about what he does slowly. You may get deeply involved before you realize who you are involved with. Also he doesn't prey on you directly; you are hurt more by what he doesn't do than by what he does. But, in the end, because of your longer involvement with him that may take up years of your life, he may hurt you more than the year or less of *adventure* that you will have, if you survive, with most sociopaths. I call this person *workless* because he doesn't work. Although he doesn't usually drink or use drugs excessively, he is like an alcoholic in that he needs enablers—wives, family members, and friends—to survive. And like an alcoholic, he usually finds them.

The workless person seems able to work and may hold a job for a while, especially when he is young, but never for more than a few years. Mostly he gets fired, but sometimes he quits. By the time he is in his forties, it is unlikely that he will ever work again. He depends on others to take care of him.

I believe that the workless person has a very low need for survival, significantly lower than the sociopath, and a very high need for power, much like the sociopath. But he has none of the *ganas*, the desire to work hard to survive that I talked about in chapter 2, so he rarely if ever is able to satisfy his need for power.

The low need for survival has left him with insufficient drive to do anything for himself, much less for others, even for an employer who will pay him. The high need for power has inflated his opinion of himself to the unrealistic idea that almost anything he is asked to do is beneath him. But it is the relationship between these two needs, a lot of power but no drive to achieve it, that is the critical part of his need profile. He talks and dreams big, but he performs small.

The workless person's need for freedom may be average or slightly above average. He does move around a lot but I don't think it's so much for freedom as just for something to do. He likes to drift around, meet strangers, and talk about himself. The latter is characteristic. He talks to you, never *with* you, about himself or people he knows. He is not interested in what you have to say. He has no real interest in anyone but himself. He also seems to have no insight into the fact that he is the way he is, especially, that he doesn't work.

The workless person does have the ability to receive love, an ability that is foreign to the sociopath. He likes to be loved and, even more, to be befriended. Unlike the sociopath, he has no problem making and keeping relationships, as long as nothing difficult, such as holding a job, is required of him. When he is asked to do the things that are normally done in a close relationship like a marriage, he won't do his part. If you marry such a man, you are marrying a child who will never grow up. He is so pleased and appreciative when you give him love and friendship that this show of appreciation will fool you and his parents into thinking that he can give some back, but he can't; he has none to give.

He does, however, have a very high need for fun in a childish sense. He tends to like school and makes up a significant proportion of the group called perennial students. Sometimes he finishes what he is studying, but mostly he doesn't. It is typical for him to get right to the end and then drop out. What he fears is finishing and having to go to work using what he has learned. If he goes to work, he does nothing. He acts as if he doesn't know what to do or what is expected of him.

The workless person has little contact with the reality of the world; his reality is almost all of his own making. He seems normal, and as long as nothing is expected of him, he can act as if he's normal, but he's not. If you marry such a man, you may have a good companion as long as you support him, do almost all the work, and don't ask anything of him. When you ask him to take a little bit of responsibility, he won't do it and can get quite mean and abusive if you persist. When he does something, which at times he may, it is more for himself than for anyone else.

Generally, if the workless get into top jobs through family influence, they do nothing, just sit there, paralyzed, while things fall apart around them or bark a lot of senseless orders that no one pays much attention to. The workless man tends to live in the past with the fantasy that before now, I was very competent and things were fine. He is perfectly willing to talk about his nonexistent *accomplishments* and may talk about school, where he may have done fairly well.

If the workless person worked a few days, he talks about it as if he'd worked for months. The past, as he remembers it, is always good. He also treats the future like a world of opportunity that is waiting for him. What he doesn't want to do—and doesn't do—is live in the present, work, take responsibility, get things done. For him, life is always back then or soon to be; it's never now.

The workless often marry and have children so, if this condition is in their genes, it can be passed on. They say they love children, but they do not love children enough to do much, if anything, for their own. When their children are young, they enjoy playing childish games with them. When their children are teenagers, these children may see their fathers more accurately than anyone else. At this point, many of the children lose interest in their workless fathers, and their fathers seem to lose interest in them. The fact that the children of the workless lose interest in them is a positive for the children; otherwise, they would be disappointed.

Almost all of us have known some workless men, and we want to help them. They are frequently sent to psychiatrists—I've seen a lot of them—but few are amenable to psychotherapy because the goal of therapy is to help people to develop better relationships, which they can use to live more effective lives. When the workless start therapy, they often fool their counselors because they are often charming, relate easily, and give the appearance that with a little help, they can straighten themselves out. But this is the point: They just *seem* to want help.

The workless love therapy. Instead of acting as clients and trying to get some help, they quickly become cocounselors, always talking, suggesting, and helping out. In a sense, what they try to do is to go into business with their counselors. If their counselors realize this is going on and become confrontational, the workless get angry, blame the counselors, and break off the relationships. In therapy, they act the same way as they do everywhere else. As long as nothing is asked of them, they are fine. But they are fine only for themselves, not for anyone else.

In their efforts to deal with the hand their genes have dealt them, they may choose the up-and-down behavior that goes by the common diagnosis of bipolar disease or manic-depressive disorder. But whether they are up, down, or in between, the workless are never competent. This is what makes them different from other bipolar people who are quite competent when they are not choosing to go too far up or down. Unlike bipolars who are sometimes helped by lithium carbonate, I don't think lithium or any medication will help the workless. (That doesn't mean it shouldn't be tried.)

The workless choose bipolar behaviors because this up-and-down activity reflects their struggle with reality. Driven by their huge need for power, when they are on the high or the upper part of the bipolar cycle, they put pictures of themselves as very powerful, almost omnipotent persons in their quality worlds and go around acting as if they were such persons. They have no desire to see themselves as they really are. As high as they are, with all the energy the high releases, they cannot do anything of value. They are like cars burning a lot of fuel to keep the motors racing, but they seem unable to stay in gear. For them, the only gear is neutral.

Eventually, reality—other people's, not their own—begins to impinge on their activities. They run out of money and a place to live. Wives, families, and friends stop helping them; they run out of gas and the engine turns off. Now they start to depress seriously. What they are depressing about is the fact that they live in a cruel world where no one seems willing to recognize their talents enough to stay with them. They never think of how little they give and delude themselves into not seeing that they are mainly takers.

They depress not because of all the lives they have damaged;

they never see it that way. Their depressing is a kind of resting and forgetting phase. After a while, they start up their motors again, and the process repeats—up and down but always standing still. When they are low, they may be suicidal, but not as suicidal as competent people who are better able to recognize reality.

If they run out of money and need care, their families or who-ever else cares for them should offer them a structured home set-ting in which they have to prepare their food if they want to eat. It should also be an environment in which they can just sit if they don't work. They should not be locked in; they should be free to come and go but given only enough money for the food they have to buy and prepare. There should be no passive entertainment, such as radio or television, except in a special room that they can gain access to only by working. Active entertainment like basket-ball should be available if they can find someone to play with. Ac-tivity is good for them; they are generally inactive. The staff should not talk with them unless they do something tangible for the house that is, in the staff members' judgment, worth talking about.

I have described sociopaths and the workless as if they were pure cases. Sociopaths are close to pure cases; they don't vary much, except that some are killers and others are not. What makes one a killer and the other not I don't know. I suspect that the killer has the worst possible or nonexistent relationships, but this is a guess. If I was involved with one of them, I would always suspect the worst.

The workless come in many shades of gray. Some of the high-grade workless can hold special jobs in which nothing much is asked of them and they don't even have to be present all the time. Some work for themselves doing odd jobs but never steadily and never if there is any hard work to do. If they have jobs when they go into their high phase, they will walk off them because they view themselves as overqualified for whatever they are supposed to do.

But I can't think of any workless man of any shade of gray

whom you would want to marry. But if you are married to one of the high-grade workless and he treats you well, you may be able to stay with him. That is the real difference between the high-grade and the usual workless. The high-grade workless man treats the wife who takes care of him well. It's like being married to an adult child. He won't change, but he may not get worse. If I were married to one, I would make it clear that this trip through life with me will last only as long as he treats me well.

I have described these types of people partly so you may realize that the strengths of the needs lead to some unusual people, people you need to beware of. But only a few people have need profiles that push them to become sociopaths, although the workless are much more common. The vast majority of us have genes whose strengths lie well within three deviations from the norm, a wide range but still considered statistically normal.

Most of us can create quality worlds that work in the real world and are strong enough to create an effective life with good relationships. We are, of course, limited by things, such as our age, sex, size, looks, health, and talent. But even within those real-world limits, we have more choices than most of us even conceive of using. We are much more limited by external control psychology than by our genes.

CHAPTER 6
Conflict and Reality Therapy

WHEN THERE ARE two opposing pictures in your quality world at the same time, you have a conflict. The more you move in the direction of one, the more you frustrate the other. There is no escape as long as you want both pictures. For example, I want to be thin, but I don't want to diet or exercise. I have one ticket for the game of the year, and the girl I have been begging to go out with me for weeks tells me that's the night she's free. My office meeting is going overtime; if I leave now, the boss will be furious, but if I don't, I won't make it to my daughter's school play in which she has the lead. It's been a struggle, but I've been dry for a year; a good friend who has invited me for dinner shows me a fine bottle of wine and says, "This is a great wine; try a small glass, I just want you to taste it, that's all."

The list is endless, and the severity of the conflict is proportional to the strength of the conflicting pictures. When both pictures are strong, the conflict is very painful. The severest conflicts, which have been grist for plays and novels since the Greek tragedies, are between love and loyalty. Should Anna Karenina stay with Vronsky or return to her husband and son?

What makes conflict so severe is that there is no immediate solution. But there may be something you can do even though it does not solve the conflict. My great teacher, Dr. Harrington, said, "If it's at all possible, when you don't know what to do, do nothing in either direction." At least, you won't make things worse. In the end, time will move the conflict in one direction or the other, and the decision will become less painful. But there are many times you can't wait; if you don't decide, one of the pictures may be lost forever.

Another solution is good counseling. The counselor can't tell you what to do, but he or she can frame the options. In doing so the counselor may be able to help you see that what seem to be equal choices are not in fact equal at all. And while you are talking to the counselor, time is passing. The talking helps you to stand pat for a while. But many times you decide what to do. You settle for one side and give the other up. Now you are miserable because the other side is still in your quality world. The suffering won't end until you remove one or both sides from your quality world. The most common thing to do when you are in conflict is to depress strongly, and this may provide you with both the incentive to see a counselor and to stand pat. Seeing how down you are, the people around you may encourage you to seek help, giving you the support you need to go.

What the counselor may do, which I have done successfully in helping people in conflict, is to lead the conflicted person in the direction of a third option, one that is not in conflict and may lead to satisfying the same need or needs that were frustrated by the conflict. In this chapter, I show you how I used the reality therapy I introduced in chapter 4 with a forty-five-year-old woman who was suffering from her unsuccessful effort to resolve a severe conflict. I take you, word by word, through the first counseling session and, as I go along, explain what I did as I did it. By doing so, I give you direct access to the counseling process. By now you know enough choice theory to understand what I was trying to do.

Choice theory provides a framework for reality therapy, the counseling method I developed in the early 1960s. But it is only a framework; it does not tell me what to say. Each client is different, and I have to figure out how to tailor what I say so that it best serves the client. As I have already explained, through the use of choice theory, which explains how we function, I know a lot about any client I see. As with Todd, even before I saw the client discussed here, I knew that she had a severe relationship problem. I also knew that she was choosing to depress and that to help her, I would have to persuade her to make a better choice. As you will see, she needed to focus on getting something she wanted that was not in conflict. As long as she was in the conflict, nothing she chose to do would resolve it.

Most people who need help are similar to this client. They can't afford months and months of counseling. Because so many people would benefit from counseling if they could afford it, it is important that the time for counseling be reduced. With the addition of choice theory to the reality therapy I have taught and practiced for years, a lot can be accomplished in ten sessions or less.

Most of what takes so much time in traditional psychotherapy is eliminated in the way I counsel. Specifically, what can be eliminated are the following:

1. There is no need to probe at length for the problem. It is always an unsatisfying present relationship. Usually, the problem is obvious, but even so, sometimes the client denies that it is the case. If I accept that denial, I may spend a lot of time probing for something else or someone in the client's past. I should be able to handle that denial and get to the current relationship in the first session.

2. Since the problem is always in the present, there is no need to make a long intensive investigation into the client's past. For example, if a client never learned to trust people because he was

abused as a child, it would be impossible for him to have a satisfying present relationship. However, if too much time is spent on the past, he may be misdirected and believe that he cannot solve his present relationship problem unless he understands what went wrong in the past. A long examination of the past may even lead him to believe that so much happened there that he will never be able to be effective in the present. It is much more important for me to tell him the truth: The past is over; he cannot change what he or anyone else did. All he can do now is, with my help, build a more effective present.

3. In traditional counseling, a lot of time is spent both inquiring into and listening to clients complain about their symptoms, the actions of other people, the world they live in, and on and on—the list is endless. The more they are encouraged or allowed to do so, the more important the complaints become and the harder it is to get to the real problem, *what the client is choosing to do now.* Choice theory does not deny that clients have legitimate complaints, but it teaches that the only persons we can control are ourselves. We can't control anyone else, including our counselors, with these complaints. Reality therapy emphasizes what clients can do to help themselves and to improve the present relationship that is the problem. Doing so not only saves a lot of time but focuses the counseling and makes it more effective.

But finding the present relationship, avoiding the past and excessive complaints about the present, and sticking to what clients can do not only shortens therapy, it also helps clients understand that they are free to lead more effective lives. They are not free to have all the freedom they may want in a present relationship, but free to forget the past and stop blaming others, which is taking up a lot of time that would be much better spent making more helpful choices now in their lives. To do so, I begin to teach the clients choice theory, which they can then use to make better choices and learn to handle many problems that might have lengthened the therapy. It's kind of a therapeutic stitch in time that saves nine.

To set the stage, imagine that in 1965 I had an office in a suburb of Des Moines, where a woman named Francesca* came for counseling. I began with a little speech to help her settle down. I could see she was nervousing, and I think what I said helped.

"I have your name and address, and that's all I need to get started. On the phone, you told me you've never been to a counselor and you were a little nervous. The best way to deal with that is for you to start right in and tell me the story. Don't worry that I'll judge you. I won't. Everyone who comes has a story. Please tell me yours."

Quite often (especially in the fifties and sixties), people feel ashamed about coming to a counselor, as if they should be able to take care of this themselves without help. They worry about being judged inadequate, so I tried to dispel that concern.

Francesca then started to tell her story:

"About six weeks ago, I died. You are looking at a dead woman. I thought about killing myself, but then I realized I didn't need to, I'm already dead."

For me this is a new opener. This woman is seriously depressing and is trying to impress me with how down she is. She succeeded; I am impressed. Usually, I try to inject a little humor when people start out so far down, but I don't think I'll try that now. She may take it the wrong way. But part of her choice to depress is a test. She's trying to see how I deal with it. Will I get nervous and show upset or will I be strong enough to deal with her misery? Right from the start I have to communicate that I appreciate that she is suffering, but I'm quite adequate to help her deal with her pain.

"Francesca, you drove fifty miles for a good reason. I'd like very much to hear your story."

"I don't know where to begin."

"Begin anywhere, it doesn't make any difference."

---

*As you may have guessed, I took the liberty of using the main female character, Francesca, from James Waller's *The Bridges of Madison County* (Secaucus, N.J.: Warner Books, 1992).

"I'm married and I have two teenage children, a girl and a boy. We live on a farm in Madison County. Up to six weeks ago I was OK, not happy but OK. I'm Italian, I guess you can hear my accent. I married Richard while he was in Italy with the army just after the second World War. I came here as soon as he could make arrangements. He's a good man, a very good father. We've lived on that farm all our married life. The farm does OK. We aren't close, but we get along. But then, God it sounds so banal, about six weeks ago I met Robert. He was in the neighborhood and drove up to the house for directions. He was looking for a bridge. He said he was a photographer and had an assignment to take pictures of some of the old covered bridges around where we live. I was there alone, Richard and the kids had gone to Illinois for the fair. They're 4H; they go to all the fairs with their animals. . . . Look at me, I'm a farmwife. I was in an old cotton housedress. I'm forty-five years old, look at my hands, look at my face. I looked a sight."

"I think you looked OK to Robert."

Francesca burst into tears and sobbed uncontrollably. Of course, she looked OK to Robert. She was a good-looking woman. Even if she wasn't dressed up, a photographer would see that in a minute. I could see that she had made an effort to look good for me. Whatever she may want to do with her life, her looks would be an advantage. I waited while she cried for a few minutes, and then I interrupted. She was suffering, but it would do no good for her to cry too long. Her tears would take up too much of her time. If crying would do any good, she wouldn't be here. What I'll do with her is what I usually do, try to go on with the counseling while she is crying. She came for help, and I owe it to her to get started. Once she starts talking, she'll be OK.

"Tell me more of the story; you can cry while you talk, you came here for help."

"I'm ashamed."

"Tell me about it."

"It's a short story. I fell in love with him. We had four days, and then he left. And now I'm dead."

"You sent him away?"

"I couldn't go with him. I thought about it. I wanted to, but I couldn't just up and leave my husband. My kids. How could I? I don't see how anyone could do that."

Now we see the oldest conflict in the world, the conflict between loyalty and love. She is being torn apart by it. There is nothing I can do immediately to help her resolve it. Only time will resolve it. But I can help her take a good look at it and maybe help her choose to do something need satisfying while she waits that has nothing to do with the conflict.

"It was hard, but you made a choice to stay. And you made a choice to come here. I'll bet this wasn't an easy choice either."

In recognizing that she made a difficult choice to come here, I'm appreciating the fact that she is an independent person who is used to trying to solve her own problems, not to reaching out for help, but that her decision to come here may have been a good choice.

"You're right. I hung up that phone after I dialed you a half a dozen times before I let it ring. Some woman at the church had mentioned you about a year ago. For some reason your name stuck in my mind. But now that I'm here, I keep thinking, what for? What can you do? What's the sense of going through it all again? It happened, it's over, he's gone. I'm not here to ask you how to get him back."

The reason my name stuck in her mind is that she was unhappy long before Robert came into her life. I won't mention this to her now, but I'll keep it in mind. And as she began to talk, she stopped crying. That's good. She asked an important question, "What can you do?" I have to answer it.

"I'm here to try to help you deal with what brought you here. I have helped a lot of unhappy people and I should be able to help you. All you have to do is to talk with me, think about what we both say, and be honest. It may be difficult for you. If I get off base, tell me. This much I know. He's been gone for six weeks. You haven't been able to talk to anyone about what happened. You're in pain. You need to talk. As long as you keep talking, listening, and thinking, I can help you."

That was the truth. Robert is not in the past; he is very much in the present. If she talks, listens, and thinks, I will help her. I think it's important to tell this to clients as soon as possible.

"But I feel so hopeless. I feel dead."

"Think about this: Suppose I could wave my magic wand and whatever you had with Robert would never have occurred. You'd be the same woman in the same marriage on the same farm as you were before he came to your door. Would you like me to wave the wand and make it all disappear?"

As bad as she feels, I have to establish that there was some good in what happened. If she's "dead," at least she didn't die in vain. If she can tell me that she doesn't regret what happened and I don't put her down or criticize her for what she did, she will see that I am on her side. The only use I have for what I hope will soon be in the past is if there is something good in it.

"No, no, I'd never give up those four days. They were the best four days of my life. Please, don't even suggest taking them away."

"I was hoping you'd say they were good. These things happen, but there is usually some good in them. If there weren't, you wouldn't be so upset. Sometimes the woman who's left behind is so upset that she doesn't think what happened had any good in it. And sometimes there isn't, and she hates herself. I think the way you feel about what happened is better. You say you're dead, but when you think about him, you seem alive."

"If I didn't think about him, I'd really die. I think about him all the time. I keep seeing him, feeling him. That's why it hurts so much. That's why talking about him hurts so much. That's why I was so nervous about coming here. I knew I'd have to talk about him. But I also knew I desperately wanted to talk about him."

Here, you can clearly see the thinking component of the total behavior of depressing. How could she have normal brain chemicals thinking and feeling as she does?

"Francesca, we weren't created to suffer alone. Talking about him with me will help."

She seems a little more relaxed after I say this. She's found out she can talk to me about him and feel safe, that I don't judge. Maybe I can lighten things up a little; it's worth a try. The heavier the going gets, the harder it will be for me to help her. If it can get a little lighter, she will be able to think more clearly. If it stays real heavy, she'll just be aware of her misery.

"It's like something from a storybook, isn't it? Like he turned you from a frog into a princess, and now you think you're going to have to go back to being a frog."

"But that's it exactly. I hated being a frog. I was a frog for so long I'd even stopped thinking I could ever be a princess. Robert came in for a drink of water and talked to me. When he did that, suddenly I was a princess. There's not much talk around our house. We're all frogs. We go *brrrp brrrp*. In my house it's *brrrp* the farm, *brrrp* the kids, *brrrp* the parents, the blue ribbons, the high school, the price of corn, the worn-out tractor. All day *brrrp brrrp*. Robert talked to me, he was interested in me, he made love to me over and over. I've never felt that kind of love; I didn't know it existed. And he had a life; he traveled with his camera. I went with him to the bridges. He asked me my opinion as he took the pictures. I loved being something more than a pair of working hands. I can't tell you how good it felt to be alive for four days. When he left, it hurt so much. I could go on and on, but what good would it do? He's gone and I'm dead."

I understand her pain. But if the session focuses mostly on pain, I may do her more harm than good. And she is talking. The *brrrp brrrp* showed a little spark of creativity, which is always encouraging. But I have to figure out a way to get her to where she can see some hope. I have to practice what I preach—try to show her she has some satisfying choices even in this painful situation. She can't change what she or Robert did, but she can control what she chooses to do now. I have to try to find something she wants now, something that she has control over, something that depends only on her and that no one can take away. This is the way to live through a conflict. Don't focus on the conflict. Focus on something possible that isn't part of the conflict. That will give her time and maybe some hope. It's about the only way a conflict can be successfully resolved. Things change, and in time most conflicts get diluted and forgotten. But right now I've got to get her to see that there's more to life than the conflict.

"Francesca, think for a moment, why did you choose to come to see me? You knew I couldn't undo what happened."

There was a long pause, but I had introduced the word *choose* in a positive sense. I intimated that she made a good choice when she finally let my phone ring. Now my job is to steer the conversation around so she sees that something good actually happens in this hour. I don't know what it can be, but I'll keep thinking and something will come to me. Or maybe to her.

"I came to see you because I had to tell someone. You know that, you just said I had to talk. There is no one in Madison County who could even begin to understand why I would do such a thing. I'm not sure you understand how bottled up I was. That house was on fire for four days. Then my husband came home, and it was cold as ice again. I've tried to put up a front, but I haven't been able to do it. I've been a zombie. He knows something's wrong; the children sense it. I can't go on like this. I didn't come here looking for a miracle. I'm not asking you for a happy ending. The way I feel right now I'll be satisfied if you'll get me back to being a frog."

"I agree you had to talk, but there is more to talk about than what happened with Robert. Suppose you had come a year ago, what would you have talked about then?"

"I didn't come a year ago. Frogs don't go to therapists."

Frogs don't go to therapists. Good. Another spark. I think we can get off the misery track.

"You're wrong about that. A lot of frogs come to see me, but I can't help them. I don't think a counselor can do much for a frog. But what you just said, if you came to see me, it means you still want to be a princess. There's a place in the world for princesses, even miserable princesses. I've helped more than a few of them."

"There's no place in the world for me. The world left with Robert; the world is gone."

"The world is gone? I'm not so sure of that. If you go home and your daughter has been hit by a car and is in the hospital asking for you or your son is there telling you his girlfriend is pregnant, are you going to sigh and tell them the world is gone? Francesca, the world is very much here. What may be gone is your marriage. You had a visit from a messenger. Was that the message?"

"What are you telling me, that I should leave my husband?

"I'm telling you that we have to take a look at your marriage. You looked at it hard for four days with Robert; you took a good look at it as soon as he walked in the door. You came here to talk about your marriage and we had better get started."

If I can persuade her to take a look at her marriage, I think we can make progress. She can't do anything about Robert, but she can do something about her marriage. If she is to stay married to Richard, that marriage has to change. She knows it. Change doesn't have to be the end of the marriage. That will be up to her and up to him, too, if she can send him the message that the marriage, as it is, isn't working.

"The children need their father."

Good. She's accepted my invitation to talk about her relationship with her husband. That's something over which she has some control. There is little sense wasting time talking about things over which she has no control. I've got to deal with her as if I may never see her again. Time is precious; we've got to make some progress.

"All kids need their mothers and their fathers. But they don't need them together if they are miserable with each other. You thought about that. It crossed your mind that they may all be better off if you dropped out of their lives, if you went off with Robert."

"I did, but I knew it was a fantasy. I told you I could never go off with him. I couldn't leave my husband, my kids; I couldn't. I told you."

"I didn't say you could. All I'm saying is you thought about it. Your mind opened for a moment to that possibility. But Robert's gone. Have all the possibilities in your life gone with him? You've had six weeks and you know how you feel. Do you really believe you can just go back to the way you were?"

"What else can I do? What reason do I have to leave? It wasn't his fault that Robert came in the door."

"Let's not talk about the reason to leave. Let's talk about the reason to stay. What do you have with Richard?"

"I have a family. I have my children."

"And right now, the way you are, what do they have with you?"

"Not very much, a zombie, a dead woman."

"Excuse me, for a moment I forgot you were dead. I was beginning to hope you were thinking about looking for a new life. Francesca, this is what I do. When people come here and tell me that their old life isn't working, I help them to figure out a new one. If your old life was working, you wouldn't have gone to bed with Robert. He wasn't some traveling seducer. He did what he did because he could see your life wasn't working. You had it written all over your face. He couldn't miss it when he walked in the door. But it wasn't only Robert you fell in love with; it was also the idea of a new life. Robert is gone. Are you prepared to give up the idea of a new life, too?"

"You're being cruel."

"Why do you say that?"

"Dangling a new life in front of me. The way I feel right now I'm better prepared to be dead than to even think about a new life. You're talking as if I can just shuck all this pain like you shuck an ear of corn. I can barely get through the day; I can't even think of what to make for dinner. A new life is as remote to me right now as the far side of the moon."

You can see the power of depressing. It's so immobilizing. What she is struggling with as I talk about a new life is the third reason to depress. It's easier to continue to depress than even to think of a different life, much less a new life. She's preparing herself to spend the rest of her life depressing, and if I don't help her, she may. Part of the reason she came here is to reassure herself that counseling can't help her. I'm now saying it can, and she calls it cruel. That's the way depressing works; the misery destroys hope. To say nothing, when I know she may choose to depress for the rest of her life, would be more cruel. If I can do something about it, I'm going to. By calling me cruel, she's trying to scare me off, but I don't scare off easily. She's finding out how persistent I am, and I think she likes it.

"If you're dead, you don't have to get through the day. Dead is the perfect excuse for doing nothing. Robert brought you back to life. If he was here, he'd tell you, *I'm gone, Francesca, but please stay alive.* I know he would."

"But look what happened, look at me. I looked in the mirror this morning and I saw my dead face. If this is what being alive for a few days ends up doing, I don't want any more of it. I know what you're getting at. It's not so bad; take another chance. What else can you say? I don't blame you, you have to say something. You offer a new life, but to me it's just words. Go ahead, tell me what you mean. What would a new life for me be like?"

I've taken her to the point where she's asked the real question. She's beginning to doubt the depressing she's choosing. She wants specifics, something tangible. She's calling my hand. Is it all talk or can I offer her something? And she wants to be offered something. She's interested, she's depressing much less right now.

"OK, I can tell you this. It would be a life in which you were in control of some of it. For you, that would be a new life. When you married Richard and came here from Italy, you gave up what little control you had. He's been in control. From his standpoint, he's done all the *right* things, but have they been right for you? He just took it for granted that you wanted what he wanted, and it's not really his fault. When did you ever tell him anything different? You made the same mistake with Robert: He came here, he loved you and you loved him, and he left. I doubt if anyone had ever loved him like you did. But he was in control. He knew as soon as you went to bed with him that you were giving him your heart, and he took it. And he left with it. After you made love, did he ever say, 'My God, Francesca, you really love me; tell me what do you want. I don't know if I can give you what you want, but please tell me; maybe I can do something.'"

"No one has ever asked me what I want. No one, ever. My God, why are you telling me this? I feel awful. How can you do this to me. How?"

She burst into tears again. She cried much harder than before. I didn't say anything. But I was ready to tell her something as soon as she stopped. After about five minutes, she slowed down and then stopped.

"Now you're making sense. You're crying for something you can do something about. You can't do anything about Robert or Richard—what they did or what you did with them. But you can do something about your life right now."

"What can I do? What do you mean? I don't understand."

"I mean like coming here to see me. You did it; you didn't ask anyone else, you didn't depend on anyone else. And you haven't hurt anyone else. No one in the whole world is going to get hurt because of what we talk about. This is all for you."

"But what if I decide I want a divorce? Won't Richard get hurt?"

Now we are at a critical point. Right now, a million men and women are at this same point—if I leave, won't I hurt my husband or my wife? Of course, Francesca's husband will be hurt. But there is another question that must be answered: Doesn't Francesca also have some responsibility about how she feels and what she does in this situation? Is Richard all right and Francesca all wrong? The answer is that neither is all right and neither is all wrong. That will always be the answer to that question until we evolve into a race of perfect people. Francesca's problem is not whether she will hurt Richard or Richard has hurt her. The answer to that question, if it is to be answered, is what Francesca can do now that may help *her* and may also have the potential of helping the marriage. She chose to stay behind; she was too loyal to leave. But does loyalty also mean accepting a life she can no longer live—the life that led her to Robert? She changed her life when she fell in love with Robert. Now, if she chooses to, she can figure out how to have a better life with Richard. It can't be the same as it was. And in figuring out how to have a better life with Richard, she has to have some help from him. Not just his help for a better life for her, but his help for a better marriage, which would mean a better life for him, too. This is the direction in which I want to try to take the counseling—the direction that all marital counseling should take. I may not succeed, but it is clear that without some good counseling, she may never get any further than depressing by herself.

"We're not talking about doing anything right now that will hurt anyone. We're trying to figure out how you can help yourself. If you can do that, maybe you can help Richard, too."

"What do you mean help myself? You're talking about me leaving the farm. I do a lot on that farm. He'd lose all I do for him. He'd be devastated."

"He'd lose what he gets from you. He'd lose the work you've given him for over twenty years. And you're right, he'd be upset. But I'm not talking about the work, I'm talking about him losing you. If you are as miserable as you are now and don't say anything, that's not being fair to you or fair to him. Tell him the truth. Tell him you are unhappy. Not unhappy with him, that would be cruel. Unhappy with the life you lead on that farm. Would you be willing to tell him that?"

"He wouldn't understand. He'd say, 'What are you talking about? You've never complained before. I don't understand.'"

"So tell him. He's not here, so tell me. What would you say to him about your life on that farm? It's safe; you can say anything you want to me."

"I'd tell him I can't stand the loneliness, the drudgery, the same thing day after day. The constant worry about the weather, the bugs, the bank. I want to talk to people who don't farm and who don't care about farming. I want soft hands again and pretty clothes once in a while. I don't want to watch every goddamned cent I spend. Look at this pink dress. I bought it for Robert, but I bought it for myself, too."

Francesca sat forward in her chair and looked at me. She was tuned in; things were much different from when she walked in. She had just described a new life. I've got to say something that will get her to think about a little action and something that might get her mind off Robert.

"Do you want to go back to Italy?"

She must still have relatives in Italy. She must keep in contact with someone. That's what family is for when you need someone, when you need comfort. That question can't hurt her, and it hasn't. It hit her hard, but she liked it. She's taking a long time. She's thinking, but this is good thinking; it's forward thinking away from Robert.

"I've stopped thinking about that. I brought it up a few times, but he always says we can't afford it. The farm seems to eat up everything. I've stopped asking."

"But you haven't stopped thinking about it, about taking your kids and going for a visit."

Now I can see that something new has opened up. I'll follow up on it, maybe use it as a way to get her off the farm. We both know she has to get off the farm.

"He'd still say we can't afford it."

"Tell him you'll earn half the money and that the kids can do what you do; they are both big and strong."

"But how would I earn the money?"

"I don't know, get a job; there are plenty of jobs in Des Moines. It's not that far. You'd probably enjoy the ride. Go to an employment agency, tell them you're used to hard work. I think it'll take you no time to get a job. Sales, maybe, but a job where you'll meet people and wear pretty clothes. You're here, go out today and look around. And don't get stuck. If the job you are offered isn't right, look for another one. Don't settle for what you don't want. I'd like you to see me again next week. Will you come?"

"I'll come. I'd like to think about this. I feel better."

"Next week at the same time is good for me. Call me during the week and tell me what's going on. Call me a little after noon. I usually pick up the phone then. I don't want you ever to think you can't talk to me. Bug me a little; you need the practice. You won't call too much; I'm not worried about that."

I dealt with her conflict by diverting her to an area over which she had some control: Get out and start a new life. I'll bet as many farmwives work off their farms as on them. Even if she has to pitch in and still do some work on the farm, she will have regained control of a big part of her life. Once she settles into a life separate from the conflict that brought her in, she will be able to put that experience into perspective and talk about it without tears. What came to my mind, but I didn't mention it because she's not ready for it, is that she could hook up with a travel agency and lead tours to Italy. Farmers travel plenty in the winter and, in that setting, she may even like being with them. She'd be the leader; she'd be in control. If she went for a visit and liked it, I might mention it then. I have no qualms about suggesting things to clients if they seem to make sense. They are always free to accept or reject my suggestions.

Let me review this session with Francesca. First, I stayed strictly with the present problem. I did not take her back through her unhappy life with Richard or the lost fantasy of a life with Robert. There was no point in going through her childhood, why she left Italy or her relationship with her mother and father. But there is a point in seeing her family now when she may need them. My counseling technique works in the present. I don't believe it does any good to revisit the past in the hope of finding something there that corresponds to the present problem. I disagree with the usual psychiatric thinking that you can learn from past misery. When you focus on the past, all you are doing is revisiting the misery. One trip through the misery is more than enough for most people. The more you stay in the past, the more you avoid facing the present unhappy relationships that are always the problem. But if I do go into the past, I look for a time when she was in effective control of her life. We can learn from past successes, not from past misery.

Second, Richard is worth talking about; he's still there. Robert is not worth talking about; he's gone. If he resurfaces or if she decides to go after him, then he will be worth talking about. There is no sense talking about people who are not involved in her life and in what she chooses to do with it. It has not yet crossed her mind that Richard could be different from the way he's been for years, so I've worked with her on the ways she can be different. Richard has surely noticed her choice to be a zombie and he may be concerned, or at least curious.

If she can follow through and tell him she's tired of being stuck on that "sacred" farm, that may get his attention, especially if she seems happier. I can't predict what Richard is going to do, but if he becomes supportive, she may be able to work things out with him. Especially if she can get some kind of a life off the farm. Old dogs can learn new tricks, but someone has to teach them, and if she's happy, she is in a better position to do it than if she's sad. I didn't see any rush for divorce, but from what I did, you can see that I think there is some rush to get her new life started.

In the next session she told me she had been a schoolteacher and wondered if she should go back to teaching. We talked about it and why she quit. The problem with discussing teaching is that it's a part of a past that she didn't like so much. We decided that since she has a college education and good references from the school district, she could get a good job easily. If she wanted, she could always go back to teaching school.

Even before Robert, she was suffering from trying to force herself to accept the life she has with Richard. She can't do it without depressing. I would never imply or promise that others like Richard in a client's life will change without the client changing what she is doing. I tried to establish in the first session that the only person we can change is ourselves. And people *can* change. Most people who are able to come to a counselor's office on their own are competent people. They are looking for happiness, not just pleasure. It is the counselor's job to treat them as if they can do something more with their lives than what they have been doing.

Clients come to counseling believing they are helpless, and it is not the counselor's job to perpetuate that belief. Their pain and misery are the ways they have learned to deal with their helplessness and to tell others about how upset they are. No one, not even counselors, should allow clients to control them with their choice to suffer. As much as this goes against our common sense, misery is their choice; our job is to teach them better choices. By the time Francesca left my office, she was thinking about a much better choice than to sit home depressing. All her strength was being consumed by the depressing. She doesn't need drugs; she should not be taught that she is mentally ill and dependent on a counselor. She needs to learn what she can do to help herself and begin to do it. Ten sessions spread out over the next six months should get her well on her way. We'll decide how often she should see me, and we'll spread the sessions out so I can help her deal with problems that may arise at work or with men she may meet.

After a few more sessions, I will start to teach her some choice theory—that no one can make her miserable; only she can do that to herself. When she changes, Richard may start to depress to try to get her to stay on the farm again, and she can explain the choice theory that she has learned in therapy to him. She can treat him well but tell him that she is not responsible for his or for anyone else's misery. She can ask him to see me or come in with him. There is a good chance that choice theory will make sense to him, and then they can both use it.

Since all people who come for counseling have at least one unsatisfying relationship, it is incumbent upon counselors to form good relationships with all clients, to let the clients know that they care for them and that if the clients are willing to talk, listen, and think about all that goes on, the counselors will be able to help them. All clients are lonely when they come in and have to have a friend and ally in their counselors. As the counseling proceeds, the counselors teach them, as I began to teach Francesca, that they are responsible for their own lives and that others may change, but they can't depend on it.

It is also crucial to teach clients that life is not fair, that in the real world some people give more to relationships than do others. If counseling is successful, the client will have worked to improve old relationships or create better new ones. To be happy, we all need a few good, close relationships. Our genes demand that we work on them all our lives.

Creativity

I WAS DRESSED IN A white space suit, helmet on, all ready to go into space on the soon-to-be-launched shuttle. But I was in Cincinnati and had to get to Wright Patterson Air Force Base in Dayton where liftoff was in a few hours. I didn't think it was at all strange that the shuttles were now lifting off from Dayton, but I did think it was peculiar that NASA had not arranged my transportation from Cincinnati to get there. NASA had, however, let me know that the best way to go was by public transportation, and I was on a city bus. People stared at me in my space suit but no one commented. I kept changing buses, but none seemed to be going to Dayton. I grew more and more frantic, I was sure I was going to miss the liftoff. I kept asking people for help, but they just shrugged and didn't seem the least bit interested in my problem.

That was a dream. I had it several years ago while living in Cincinnati. It was so vivid and so frustrating I have never forgotten it. We all have dreams, and many of them have this theme of trying desperately to do something that never seems to work out. While the dreams are going on, they seem so real, even though what is actually happening may have little to do with reality. Dreams, like all behaviors, are total behaviors. They should be called *dreaming* and, since they all take place in our heads, they are the thinking component of that total behavior. During the dream, I was mostly acting, but I was also thinking about getting to Dayton, I felt the pain of my frustration, and my physiology was certainly normal for what I was doing.

I mention that dream not because it was of any significance in my life but because it is a vivid example of how creative all of us are. Dreams have no boundaries, little logic, and no necessary grounding in anything that could be called reality. Literally, anything can happen, but while it is happening, it all seems to make sense. In that dream, I was sure I would be on my way to outer space if only I could get to Dayton on time. Although researchers believe that dreams help us get the maximum rest from sleep, it is the inherent creativity they represent that is what this chapter is all about.

A life without creativity would be hardly worth living. But unless we are given creativity-destroying drugs, often used to treat psychosis, or have Parkinson's disease, where we lose our ability to move creatively, this can never happen because in our brains we have a *creative system* that adds creativity to all our total behaviors. The creative system may operate when we are sleeping as in dreaming but what it does while we are awake is far more important. It can add creativity to one or more of the four components of any total behavior.

We see it clearly in the *actions* of great athletes, dancers, surgeons, and others who perform neuromuscular feats that are creative beyond compare. Michael Jordan comes to mind as one of the most creative athletes who has ever lived. It is their creative *thinking* that sets great writers, artists, musicians, and scientists apart from the rest of us. Einstein, Shakespeare, Mozart, and van Gogh are examples of a group that could fill the pages of a whole book. It is the ability of great performers to create and express *feelings* that hold audiences spellbound. There are also instances of new and creative *physiology* when people who are given up for dead create a way to recover from a severe illness in ways that cannot be explained by medicine.

While these are examples of the phenomenal ways the creative system works, in this chapter I will explain that there is also the possibility this same system can cause us great harm as it goes about its business by creating painful and self-destructive total behaviors. This destructive creativity is most often seen when we want good relationships and are not able to get them.

For example, when we are lonely, as Francesca was when Robert left, there is nothing effective we can do to close the wound. But because there is nothing effective we can do does not mean we do nothing. This is exactly the situation for which our creative system evolved. It never shuts down or gives up. It keeps trying on its own to help us deal with our lonelinesss or anythng else we want either by adding creativity to a behavior we already have or, at times, creating a whole new behavior that might be more effective in the given situation.

In many instances, it offers *new actions and thoughts,* which we can reject if we believe that what is offered will make things worse. It is difficult to reject what it offers, and often we could use counseling to help us, but we usually have enough voluntary control over our actions and thoughts to do this, especially if we are able to understand this is a choice. What I am talking about here is when we are offered violent or suicidal thoughts and actions that for us are very new. Also when we are offered psychotic or crazy thoughts or what is commonly called schizophrenia or bi-polar disease. Or when we obsess and compulse as we frequently do when we are lonely. And when we are exposed to a traumatic situation as in posttraumatic stress disorder and handle it painfully but creatively. In almost all instances, by improving our relationships, we may be able to reject these thoughts and actions. Many people do. Later in the chapter I will discuss all of this in more detail.

When we are lonely or frustrated our creative system may also offer us new feelings. Depressing is the most common but there are also anxieting, headaching, backaching, and other painful feelings. While we cannot reject the feeling—we have no direct control over how we feel—we can try, with counseling or without it, to improve the relationships we have or find more satisfying new ones. This is what my client in chapter 4 was able to do and what Francesca began to think about in the previous chapter.

When our creative system offers us new but destructive physiology, we cannot reject this offering. Unless we know that improving our relationships may actually slow or stop the destructive process, we may suffer great harm. The most common examples of this destructive physiology are the autoimmune diseases such as rheumatiod arthritis. Even though this process is so destructive and so puzzling I still believe there is a choice we can make which could help. I use the general heading of psychosomatic disease to describe this process.

Psychosomatic Disease: The Darker Side of Creativity

There is no way to predict when these diseases will occur or how much out of control our lives need be for them to occur. We can find out that we have rheumatoid arthritis, for example, only when it appears. But if what I explain here is correct, there is something helpful that we can do on our own or with good counseling at the *first indication* that we are becoming destructively creative. I want to emphasize that nothing I suggest has any chance of doing harm, and I advise anyone with these diseases to seek accepted medical care and to follow their doctors' advice.

Most doctors believe that adult rheumatoid arthritis is caused by the victims' immune systems attacking their own joints as if these joints were foreign bodies. Another way of putting it is that their own creative systems are trying to protect these people from a perceived harm. If we could figure out a way to stop this misguided creativity, millions of people who suffer from this disease and a host of other relentless diseases, called autoimmune diseases, could be helped. They might even be cured if the attacks were caught early enough.

Norman Cousins succeeded in aborting such an attack. As he described in detail in *An Anatomy of an Illness*,* when he began to suffer pain and stiffness in his back, he was diagnosed as suffering from an acute ankylosing spondylitis, or rheumatoid arthritis of the spine. If it continued, the doctors told him, he would be severely disabled by a badly bent and painful spine. The pain and inflammation might eventually stop, a common occurrence in the life history of many of these diseases, but the deformity would be permanent.

His doctors told him there was nothing that could be done for him medically and no pressing reason for him to stay in the hospital even during the acute phase of the disease. Therefore, he left the hospital and chose a regime that seemed to lead to what was medically confirmed as a complete cure. What he did had nothing directly to do with his immune system, but it had a lot to do with taking more effective control of his life.

Cousins's explanation of the circumstances in which he got sick, clearly showed that he had lost control of a significant event in his life. Cousins was an important man who was used to people both listening to and appreciating what he had to say. Yet some foreign officials, vital to one of his many help-the-world projects, ignored him. His picture of himself in his quality world as a well-known, powerful man was severely frustrated, and his life quickly went out of effective control. As it always does when we are frustrated, his creative system got involved. This involvement was not in the thinking or acting component of his total behavior, however; it was with his immune system, a vital part of our physiology. The immune system began to attack and damage his spine as if it were a foreign body.

_____

*Norman Cousins, *An Anatomy of an Illness as Perceived by the Patient: Reflections on Healing and Regeneration* (New York: W. W. Norton, 1979).

My explanation of what was going on in the physiological component is that his immune system, whose major purpose is to protect us from outside invaders, such as bacteria, viruses, and poisons, misread his loss of control and wrongly concluded that he was being attacked by a bacterium or virus. When we become sick with a severe infection caused by an invading bacteria or virus, it is accurate to think we have been attacked. I have often heard people say, *I am fighting a bad cold* or *wrestling with the flu.* But people also say, *I am fighting to save my marriage, my job, my reputation, my beliefs, my way of life.*

Because this is such a common way to think, it is not far-fetched to infer that what was going through Cousins's mind was, I've got to overcome this indifference to my ideas; I see it as an attack on the important work I am trying to do. Because the immune system reads only the physiology of thought, it can't know anything about the psychology of that thought or any thought. It may mistake the physiology of the being-attacked thought for the similar physiology of an actual bacterial attack. It certainly seems possible that the immune system is alerted by that thought and begins to hunt for a microorganism that is not there.

Finding no microorganism, but not wanting to shirk its duty, the immune system somehow targets an organ or body part and attacks it as if it was infected with a microorganism. To confirm what I am trying to explain, experiments have shown that a person who is allergic to strawberries may break out in hives when he or she goes into a room papered with strawberry-patterned wallpaper. The hives are caused by an overactive immune system. The pathology in rheumatoid arthritis is almost the same as if the joints were infected by bacteria. Medically, this mystery is called a sterile infection.

For unknown reasons, adult joints seem to be the prime target of the autoimmune system, and rheumatoid arthritis, no matter what joints it attacks, may be the most common autoimmune disease. Other target organs and their corresponding autoimmune diseases are the skin, scleroderma; the kidneys, glomerulonephritis; the blood vessels, periarteritis and lupus; the lungs, adult asthma; the sheath that covers or insulates the nerves, multiple sclerosis and other common diseases that are too numerous to mention here.

But a feature story in the *Los Angeles Times* of April 4, 1997, reported that medical researchers seem to have discovered a new widespread autoimmune disease in which the immune system attacks the lining of coronary arteries.* The article began: "A subtle but unexpected attack on the coronary arteries by the body's own immune system may be the cause of as many as half of all heart attacks and coronary artery disease. It also may explain why aspirin is so good at preventing heart attacks." At the end of the newspaper article, Dr. Valent Fuster, of Mount Sinai Medical Center in New York City, offered this opinion: "Such inflammation may be a response to the accumulation of even small amounts of cholesterol in the walls of blood vessels." The conclusion I drew from this research and Dr. Fuster's comment is that the immune system may be misreading this cholesterol in the lining of the coronary arteries, a common, almost normal, accompaniment of aging in men, *as a foreign body.*

This is strong evidence of what a few doctors, including me, have been speculating for years. In a chapter on creativity in an earlier book, *Take Effective Control of Your Life,*† I wrote the following:

As the cardiovascular system is tensed for years on end, the blood rushing through the arteries begins to erode the artery walls and produce rough spots. The excess clotting elements already circulating are trapped by these rough spots and begin to form small clots at these sites. The immune system, "seeing" a clot that normally would not be there, somehow (no one yet

---

*Paul Ridker, "Inflammation, Aspirin, and the Risk of Cardiovascular Disease in Apparently Normal Men," *New England Journal of Medicine* (April 3, 1997).
†William Glasser, *Take Effective Control of Your Life* (New York: HarperCollins, 1982), p. 112.

knows why) becomes crazily creative and attacks the clot as if it were a foreign body. This quickly causes the clot to become inflamed and the inflammation enlarges the clot just like a scab on a skin wound is always larger than the initial blood clot. As time passes, the clot continues to enlarge through the repetition of this process until the clot obstructs the flow of blood through the artery.

What Fuster described as "small amounts of cholesterol" could be part of "the rough spots" I mentioned in the preceding paragraph. The rest of what I describe is the well-known process of inflammation, including the proliferation of clotting elements in the blood. People with heart disease are routinely given anticlotting drugs, such as coumadin, to reduce the circulation of clotting elements in the blood. In recent years, aspirin, an anti-inflammatory drug, has often been added to this regimen. As you can see, I have been thinking for a long time about what part this self-destructive— I call it crazy—creativity may play in coronary artery disease.

When your doctor tells you that you have an autoimmune disease, he or she is trying to tell you it is caused by your immune system attacking the part of the body involved. Cousins couldn't do anything directly about what his immune system was doing; at that time, he may not have even known this was what was going on. What he did know was that he was miserable and that he thought he could do something about it.

He decided to leave the hospital and make himself comfortable in New York's Plaza Hotel. He hired some cheerful, attentive nurses; ate great food; and asked his friend Allan Funt to visit and bring videotapes of some of his funny *Candid Camera* sequences, often too risqué to show on television. Cousins watched these videotapes and laughed and laughed. The combination of good food, attentive nurses, good friends, and a lot of laughter gave him the sense that the world need not end because a few foreigners he hardly knew refused to listen to him. He stopped fretting about what had happened and regained effective control of his life, and his creative system stopped pushing his immune system. He quickly became normal; the disease never recurred.

Cousins wrote about taking massive doses of vitamin C and continued to see his doctor. But he took the vitamin C on the advice of Linus Pauling, a renowned physicist, not his doctor. There is no indication that this is an effective treatment for rheumatoid arthritis. But Cousins believed in the vitamin C and made the point that he did more than laugh his way to good health.

Anyone who suffers from rheumatoid arthritis or any other destructive, or potentially destructive, creativity, could attempt to take more effective control over his or her life. But even though what Cousins did seemed to have worked for him—of course, his regimen has never been proved—it is not the only way. I also suggest that when you become aware that your immune system has harmed some aspect of what should be your normal physiology, concentrate on trying to improve the frustrating relationship that may be the cause of what is happening.

Although it seems simple, most people with a psychosomatic disease don't even think of doing what Cousins did or of entering counseling with a counselor who knows choice theory, which may be easier and equally effective. People who are sick often make the logical mistake of concentrating their efforts on the symptoms of the disease, which they can do nothing about. Instead, I suggest that they give equal time to the relationships in their lives that may not be in effective control.

It is difficult to live in such a way that all our relationships are in effective control, and usually it doesn't make that much difference as long as some relationships are satisfying. But when you get sick, it is a good idea to review all of them. Some may be more rankling than you are willing to admit. You can review these relationships by yourself; with the help of a friend or family member you trust; with your doctor if he or she can give you the time; or, best of all, with the aid of a good counselor.

To illustrate what a counselor can do, I would like to share with you the most dramatic incident I have ever been involved in as a psychiatrist. It occurred in 1956 while I was working as a resident on the psychosomatic ward of the Wadsworth Veterans Administration Hospital in West Los Angeles. A forty-year-old man who had been suffering from intractable asthma for the past ten years had been given every known medication with essentially no relief. His lungs were scarred and clogged as if his immune system had been attacking his bronchioles. He could hardly breathe; it was difficult for him to talk, and he had been put on a positive pressure respirator once or twice a week to keep him alive during the attacks he frequently suffered. The medical resident who called me in told me his condition was hopeless, but if I wanted to try to help him, I could see him.

The man's human relations were nonexistent. He was in the dry-cleaning business with his brother, but he could do so little that they were not on good terms. This hospital admission had lasted six weeks, and the medical staff doubted they could ever get him in good-enough shape to leave the hospital. The man could barely talk, but I was patient and told him that even though it was hard, I was determined to counsel with him.

I saw him for several weeks almost every day, and we gradually got acquainted. He kept telling me it was worthless; he needed good medical care, not a psychiatrist. But I persisted. Several times he had a mild attack of not being able to breathe during the sessions and begged me with gestures to let him go back to the ward, but I told him that even if he couldn't talk, this was our time together and I didn't want him to go back until it was up.

He seemed to be doing a little better, and I was encouraged. But then he got an attack so severe that I had to call the respirator crew, who put him on a respirator and wheeled him back to his bed. I got the idea that he was choosing the attack to get away from me and from having to talk about his present life. I decided that when he had the next attack, I would keep counseling even while he was on the respirator, and he could respond with his hands or nod to my comments. The next attack was the worst yet. The respirator crew pumped and pumped but couldn't seem to get enough air into him, and he turned blue. The respirator crew; the medical resident; and, of course, the patient thought I was crazy. I paid no attention; I continued to counsel and could see his expression get more and more desperate.

This went on for about twenty minutes, when suddenly he ripped the respirator from his mouth and nose and screamed at me, "For Christ's sake, I'm dying. Won't you leave me the fuck alone?"

I said, "No, I won't leave you alone. You need counseling and I'm not going to give up. You seem OK now; let's go on."

And he was OK. His face, which had been blue-black from anoxia, had a little color, and he seemed to be breathing easier after the outburst than I had ever seen him breathe. We continued, and his breathing took a sharp turn for the better.

The man stayed in the hospital for another two weeks getting his strength back but then was discharged. His lungs were badly scarred and he had to walk slowly, but he was able to breathe well enough to take care of himself. He came back to see me as an outpatient three or four times and said he thought he could handle things on his own.

The key in this therapy was his trying to push me away and my not letting him do it. When I persisted, it was as if something had happened that he had never dreamed would. As much as he tried, he could not get me to reject him. It was enough to help him get back into some kind of control. His lungs were damaged, but he could breathe and take care of himself. There is tremendous power in good counseling. The medical resident who witnessed that dramatic episode was astonished and, truthfully, so was I. What I learned was never to give up, and I don't.

I will now go into greater detail so you can see exactly how choice theory applies to what I am trying to explain. Again, I want to state that it is important to know that even if what I suggest does not help, it can do no harm. It is also free or moderate in cost, depending on whether you can apply it yourself or seek several months of counseling, which should be enough, especially if the counseling involves learning choice theory, which explains what the problem may be and what the client can do to cope with it better in the future.

When we face a large frustration in a relationship, as did Norman Cousins, my veteran with asthma, and Francesca, we don't know what to do to reduce the frustration. We search our memories for an old behavior that has given us some relief in the past. In almost all instances, we immediately find depressing, a familiar behavior we learned as a child. I am sure Cousins and the asthmatic were depressing strongly, as was Francesca, when their lives spun out of control. But depressing is not an effective behavior; it hurts and immobilizes. Still, it gives us more relief than anything else we know, for three reasons.

First, depressing, and all other symptomatic behaviors, including arthritis, restrain a lot of anger, which, if unleashed, would make things worse. Second, these behaviors include a powerful call for help, and in many instances good counseling is effective. If we have an autoimmune disease we will also look for a doctor who may counsel or recommend counseling, which could be helpful. Third, these behaviors keep us from trying to do something we fear we may fail at. It's easier to depress or to be sick than to look for a new relationship or a new job, especially if we've had some experience with rejection, which most of us have.

Although depressing gives us some control, it does so at a very high price: misery. Even as we depress, our misery and our continued frustration force us to keep looking for better behaviors. Even when we seem resigned to what has happened, we are not. It is not in our genes to accept a major frustration, such as an unsatisfying relationship, without getting our creative systems involved. Our creative system may not come up with anything effective; rather, it may come up with something that is mentally or physically more harmful than depressing. But whatever it does, its purpose is to try to find a new total behavior that will lead to some resolution of the problem.

However, it is not uncommon for people who cannot find a way to regain more effective control over their lives or who, for a variety of good reasons, refuse to give up on an unsatisfying relationship to choose to depress for the rest of their lives. That they may have additional symptoms is common, but often a new symptom like arthritising may give them enough control over their lives so they no longer choose to depress.

Arthritis did so for two women I counseled in my practice. It gave them something tangible to struggle with that they could try to do something about. Not much, but something. They were not willing to struggle with their unsatisfying marriages. They were not going to leave, and they didn't want to change the way they dealt with their husbands.

But besides physiological behaviors, it is far more common for us to be offered usually one, but sometimes a whole group of, psychological acting, thinking, and feeling behaviors by our creative systems. Together with depressing, psychiatrists call these total behaviors mental illness. Most of these total behaviors fall under the heading of neurosis; psychosis; or physical pain, such as headaching and backaching, for which there is no evidence of a physical cause.

If they are psychological, we may never, even with counseling, discover the reason we choose them, but it almost always has to do with a relationship problem. The problem does not have to be love; it may be that we want more care or less demanded of us, but whatever it is, an important relationship is not working for us. If you look for the unsatisfying relationship, you are on the right track. This is the usual method in our madness.

But because these behaviors, called mental illness, are offered does not mean we have to accept them. In psychosis, our creative system offers hallucinations and delusions, even physical creativity as in catatonia, and offers them so strongly it is hard for us not to accept them. If our lives are far out of effective control, it may be almost impossible for us to reject them. We need to restrain the anger. We often want help, and we can use the symptoms to avoid having to take care of ourselves or to look for and hold on to a new and necessary relationship. Good counseling can often persuade us to stop accepting the offered psychological creativity. But even with no help, not everyone who chooses to accept craziness stays crazy.

Hundreds of thousands of people who function very well today have had episodes of craziness in their lives. Millions more who have chosen to depress, phobic, obsess, compulse, anxietize, panic, and ache and pain with no physical basis for that pain no longer do so. Some start to refuse these creative offerings on their own, and many go to counselors. With counseling, they are able to gain enough effective control over their lives that they no longer choose these behaviors. Finally, the creative system may offer the idea of suicide: Get rid of the problem and, with it, the pain once and for all. People who commit suicide make their last creative move. But many of them, if offered counseling, would welcome it and avoid the final step.

The following case that I dealt with in the first month of my psychiatric residency illustrates my contention that craziness is offered and accepted and that the offer can be refused if the person believes it is not working in a particular situation. In 1954, I was a ward doctor in the Brentwood Veterans Hospital in West Los Angeles. The patients had all been diagnosed with schizophrenia, and one man was almost frightening in his delusional behavior. Each morning when I made the rounds, he would curse me and spit on the floor when I approached. He was very threatening and kept yelling at me to get the imaginary monkey off his back who was tearing the flesh off his bones. He acted as if the monkey was there and cried out in pain and cursed me for being such an inadequate doctor that I could do nothing about this small animal who was making his life a living hell.

I had no experience with this kind of problem, and I was a little frightened of him. He was a World War II veteran, and the symptoms started soon after he was discharged from the military. I dreaded going up to him, and I could never get any conversation going no matter how hard I tried. This went on for three months, when one day, instead of being threatening, he asked me politely (not even mentioning the monkey) if I could see him in my office after rounds. I was uneasy, but the attendant said it would be OK; he would stand by. I was baffled by this total change, but curious. After rounds I beckoned for him to come to my office, which was right off the ward, forty feet from where he usually sat.

He told me in a perfectly normal way that he thought he was sick and asked me to examine him physically. He said he was feverish and was having trouble breathing. When I felt his head, it was hot. I then tried to listen to his lungs, and it was like listening to a brick wall; he had lobar pneumococcal pneumonia. I told him that he had to go to the medical ward; we could not treat him in the psychiatric unit. Because of antibiotics, this disease was becoming rare and I had never before seen a case.

I walked him over to the medical ward in a nearby building, and during the walk there was no sign of any psychosis. He kept thanking me for being so nice to him. I introduced him to the internists, who confirmed my diagnosis and were glad to take care of him. This was a disease that some of them had never seen either. During the two weeks he was in the medical ward, I visited him every day as I had promised, and he never showed any signs of craziness. The hard part was to convince the medical residents that he was crazy, actually the craziest patient I had ever seen and that he did need to be on the psychiatric ward. I never convinced them, and I took a lot of ribbing for keeping a sane man in the hospital.

If I knew then what I know now, I think I could have helped this patient when I saw that he had the capability of choosing to stop being crazy. But I didn't know what to do, nor did anyone else. Gradually, the monkey reappeared, and all his symptoms returned, but he was always polite to me when I made my rounds. He kept telling me how well he had been treated on the medical ward. He still told me about the monkey, but he never accused me of being incompetent or blamed me for not relieving his suffering. I tried to work with him, but I didn't know what to do. I think that he had put me into his quality world, and today I could use that fact to try to work more intensively with him.

I believe he was talking and acting right out of his creative system, as do most severely psychotic people, but he was able to choose to turn off his creative system for the few weeks he spent on the medical ward. My guess is that staying alive took precedence over whatever problem he was choosing to psychose about. After he was cured of the pneumonia, he chose to go back to the craziness, rather than try to deal with the problem. But with me, he was able to choose some sanity; he was never as crazy as he had been in the past. This was in the days before psychiatric drugs, some of which might have helped him. In the course of my residency, I learned how to deal with people like him, and a year later, during my last four months on service, using the beginnings of reality therapy, I was able to discharge thirty-two of the thirty-six patients I was assigned. Many had been crazy for years, and all but four chose to be sane enough to leave.

One of my techniques was to spend time with my patients, get close to them, and then ask them, "Please pretend to be sane with me. I have no interest in your craziness." I reasoned that even the craziest people do a lot of sane things every day. They eat, sleep, smoke, watch television, go to the bathroom, clean up around the ward, and go to various therapies like arts and crafts where many do fine work. When I asked them to be sane with me, someone they liked, I wasn't asking for much more sanity than what they were demonstrating in much of what they did in the hospital. In my experience, it is not difficult to help people stop listening to their creative systems in the safe confines of a good hospital. What is hard is to guide them in the direction of the better relationships they need to stop being crazy when they leave. The main purpose of a hospital is to take care of their physical needs, provide them with the good relationships they need, and prepare them to stay close and try to get along with people when they leave.

Let me now return to Francesca and use her huge frustration to explain some of the other ways our creative systems can get destructively involved with our lives and what we can do about it. I use Francesca because there is hardly a married woman who hasn't occasionally thought, My life would be a lot better with someone else. It is the acting on that simple thought that is so tragically portrayed in thousands of books, plays, and movies.

In Francesca's case, her husband, Richard, as a lover and her life on the farm had not been in her quality world for years. But she was able to accept the status quo because she had no pressing picture in her quality world of a better life than what she had. What sustained her was a picture of her children doing well and needing her and a picture of herself as a loyal, if not loving, wife.

She handled her dissatisfaction with Richard and farm life by mild, long-term depressing. Her choice to depress satisfied the first of the three reasons we depress—it restrained her anger—and that was enough for her. Angry outbursts would have made the situation worse. The other two reasons did not apply. She didn't want help, and she wasn't thinking of doing anything else but keeping the life she had. The level of depressing she chose was high enough to give her enough control of her life so that her creative system did not get involved physiologically. She was healthy; she was not crazy; and before Robert came, she had chosen to do nothing that anyone would have labeled a mental illness or even abnormal.

The four days with Robert upset the fragile equilibrium that Francesca had maintained for years. Afterward, to keep the anger in check and to maintain the status quo, she had to depress much more intensely. She felt terrible. She could do little or nothing around the farm, and she was worried that she would not be able to keep the bargain with Richard that she had kept for years. Now she had the picture of a satisfying life with Robert in her quality world, a picture so discordant with the take-care-of-my-children and loyal-wife pictures that had sustained her for years.

Francesca was in a conflict, by far the most serious frustration we can suffer because there is no good solution. Either way, Richard or Robert, there is misery. She was trying to depress so strongly that she would not even think of making the choice. She recognized that life with Robert was an impossible picture. She said she couldn't leave her family under these circumstances, and she didn't.

All her energy was going into the effort to depress, and she was immobilized. She wanted some help with how she felt and with her difficulty in doing even the routine chores around the farm. In the first session, she said that she would be satisfied if I could help her get back to the mild depressing—her life as a frog—that she'd been choosing for years. The problem is that our quality worlds do not recognize the impossibility of any picture we put into it. If a picture is in our quality worlds, we want to achieve it in the real world and do so as soon as possible. The only way we can stop wanting that picture is to take it out of our quality worlds.

When she came to see me, she had not even thought about finding a picture to replace Robert, and she didn't even want to. It was he, no one or nothing else. But because she knew that what she wanted was impossible for her, she was dealing creatively with that impossibility. Her creative system had told her, *Francesca, forget about living without Robert. Without him all you can do is go through the motions. For all practical purposes, you are dead.* That may not have sounded creative, but it's not something most of us are even willing to think much less to say. If dead is that you can no longer do anything or feel anything, this was what she was trying to achieve when I saw her.

In counseling, I tried to help her toward another picture, not a sexual or love picture, but a picture that might give her some of what she wanted—a social, if not a sexual, life off the farm in which she would have some power and people would listen to her and respect her for what she was saying and doing. I believe that if she could have had such a life and enjoyed it, she might eventually give up the picture of Robert or live better with it. Time would tell if that would ever happen. All I saw her was for a few sessions.

In Waller's book, Francesca doesn't seek counseling. She dealt with her life by choosing to depress, which restrained her anger enough so she could be a reasonably good mother and wife. Writing in her journal helped her to accept the life she had. She was able to come up with the creative fantasy: My children will read this journal after I die, understand me better, respect me for what I did by staying home, and appreciate how hard it was to give up Robert. It also helped that Robert did not forget her. He had his belongings shipped to her when he died, including the note she wrote and pinned to the bridge that brought them together. All this, especially all the misery, is very romantic, which was Waller's intention. I liked the book. I felt deeply for this woman and for the love she had and then gave up.

What also helped Francesca to gain enough control over her

life was to seek out a relationship with a neighbor, Mrs. Delaney, who had gone through a similar situation but had not been able to keep it secret and had been ostracized by the narrow-minded community in which they lived. The two women became close and stayed close until Francesca died.

What actually happened or didn't happen to the fictional Francesca is not important. I want to discuss what might have happened to her or to anyone who suffers a long-term high level of frustration and how our creative systems can get involved with our behavior in ways that are destructive to our lives. Let's start briefly with the autoimmune diseases I have discussed.

If Francesca's immune system had gone crazy several months after she sent Robert away, she might have noticed that her fingers had become very painful, swollen, red, and hard to move. Even Richard might have noticed and said, *You ought to see a doctor.* Her family doctor would have immediately recognized that she was in the early stages of rheumatoid arthritis. He would have taken tests and X-rays, noted that her sedimentation rate was up, and confirmed the diagnosis.

He might have referred her to a specialist in Des Moines. After a few more tests, the specialist would have started her on an anti-inflammatory medication, but that treatment is palliative; it does not cure. The specialist might have even asked her if there was anything in her life she was upset about, but it is unlikely that she would have told him about Robert. Why risk his disapproval? Besides, Robert was gone; what good would it do?

Whenever we are frustrated, it is impossible for our physiology to remain aloof, for us to say to the acting, thinking, and feeling components of our behavior, *You guys, get creative and deal with it; leave me out of it.* So in this example, her physiology got involved. My experience counseling people who suffer from rheumatoid arthritis is that they have very frustrating personal relationships, often blatantly unsatisfying marriages that they are trying to preserve at all costs. They cannot risk angering or even depressing because doing so might impair their ability to keep up their side of the relationship and maybe lose it.

It is not easy to deal with these frustrations, and I am not implying that I could have helped Francesca if she had come to me with rheumatoid arthritis. If she didn't tell me about Robert, I would have probed for the breakdown in a relationship that I believe is behind most chronic frustrations and tried to help her deal with it. If she could have resolved the frustration favorably, as she began to do in counseling, there is a good chance her arthritis would not have gotten worse and might have improved or even gone away. If you can apply choice theory to your life to improve or eliminate your own unhappy relationship, you have a chance to help yourself.

Francesca was not likely to become psychotic because she was both capable of good relationships and of taking care of herself and her family. The kind of people who become psychotic often lack *ganas*. Their profile is similar to that of the workless. They want good relationships but are not capable of giving the amount of care to others that it takes to get them. That has been my overwhelming experience with people who have dealt with an unsatisfying life by choosing psychosis.

Some people who become psychotic want to be taken care of; they don't have the confidence that they can take care of themselves. They can often be helped as much by a good live-in situation in which they are slowly introduced to the demands of the real world as by good counseling. Most of them need a place where they feel secure and have people to talk with; it does not have to be a hospital.

It is interesting that psychotropic drugs that control hallucinations and delusions all tend to paralyze the creative system so severely that even the muscles get involved. This is seen in the Parkinson-like gait and other symptoms that usually accompany the use of these drugs. Under the influence of large doses of these drugs, many people lose their ability to move smoothly, their faces lose expressiveness, and their voices may become altered and lack timbre. Although these drugs may reduce the crazy creativity by paralyzing the creative system, they do not really solve the problem. I am not saying don't use the drugs, but understand that there is almost always a frustrated relationship involved. If it is dealt with in counseling, my experience is that with some clients, those who have some strengths or who are taken care of can stop choosing psychosis and live much better, though somewhat sheltered, lives.

Bipolar or manic depressive psychosis, discussed earlier in connection with the workless, is another variation of crazy creativity. It is not restricted to the workless, however; some successful people choose this up-and-down behavior when their relationships are extremely unsatisfying. Furthermore, it is usually more up or more down, not the complete swings from way up to way down that is commonly thought. With manic depressive psychosis, what is often in operation is the third reason: The sufferer is trying to avoid facing the reality that a long-term relationship is not working out.

Francesca did not do much about her problem except to depress, but at least she faced it. Bipolar people can't even seem to do that. When they are in their manic state, they are living right out of their creative systems. Their brains are going as fast as they sometimes do in long, complicated dreams during five-minute naps. I'm always amazed at how much can happen in dreams in such a short time.

When bipolar people are in the normal part of the swing, they can often be helped by good counseling. Sometimes they are so successful in their lives that when they are not in the up or down position, it is impossible for anyone, including counselors, to believe that they are having problems in their relationships. And maybe they are not. But my guess is that most of them are and that anyone who counsels them should check out their relationships first.

There is also a whole group of creative total behaviors that are commonly called neuroses. People who choose these behaviors don't deny reality, as in psychosis, they just have trouble dealing with it. Phobicking, anxietizing, panicking, obsessing, compulsing, or posttraumatic stressing are common examples of these creative choices. For example, Francesca could have told me nothing about Robert, or mentioned him but not shown much concern over the loss of their brief relationship. Her complaint might have been that she was afraid to leave the house by herself. If her husband couldn't take her somewhere, she couldn't leave the house. He would be in the waiting room to drive her home. Once in a while she could go out with her son or daughter or with a neighbor, but she would really be comfortable only with him.

My guess is that the real fear from which the phobicking would protect her would be that if she left the house alone, she might go looking for Robert. Her choice to phobic would prevent her from doing that. As long as she wanted Robert but felt loyal to Richard, she would continue to phobic. This creative choice would help her to think, It's not Robert that I want at all. My problem is that I'm afraid to leave the house. Here you see all three reasons we choose what is usually called mental illness operating creatively. First, as long as she phobicked, she could replace angering with fearing, which is more acceptable. Second, she would have an excuse to go for help. Third, since she would feel safe only at home, going to Robert would be out of the question.

As the years went by and the memory of Robert faded, she would need the phobicking less, and as the frustration disappeared, the symptom would disappear with it. Counseling would be very helpful, and I would counsel her much as I did. But to help her, the same as I would if she were arthritising, I would have to probe for Robert and the unsatisfying relationship with Richard. Richard, however, would be close to the surface and not hard to find. With my help to get out of the house and into a less lonely life, she could accept that Robert was gone and, with that acceptance, no longer have any reason to phobic.

Francesca could also have chosen panicking, a similar but disabling symptom. As long as she was in fear of a panic attack, she wouldn't stray far from home or from people she trusted. She might even panic at home if she thought of Robert, but home would be a safe place to have such attacks. For example, if Francesca was a panicker and lived in constant fear of an attack, when she came to see me, I would have known that a painful relationship was involved. As I probed for the relationship, she would protest but not too much. Part of her would be pleased. She would want desperately to talk about Robert, and if she trusted me, my office would be a safe place to do it. When she told me about Robert, she would say, "It's over." But I would know that it was not over; the panicking would be proof that it wasn't.

Still, Francesca would insist, "It's over"; I don't want to think about him anymore. In a sense she would be right about that, too. She wouldn't think about Robert very much. Rather, she would think and worry about when the next attack would occur, and that thought would keep her and a lot of other people busy worrying about her. All these dramatic symptoms are marvelous ways for lonely people to get attention and ask for help without begging.

An attack might have occurred in my office when I started to probe, and I would have welcomed it. I would have told her, "That's marvelous; now we can really deal with it." It saves a lot of time when clients discover that, with my help, panicking can be handled. My job would be to get Francesca to think about Robert, not to be more miserable but to learn what she could do to find a life without him. I would have gone into great detail about what was happening when she had the last panic attack. She could have chosen to panic when she saw a couple about her age walking down the street holding hands, which could have revved up the whole affair with Robert. I might have told her to think about Robert and, if she could, choose to panic right then with me. She might not have been able to do so, but this statement would have made it more difficult for her to panic from then on because she would have gotten some understanding that a choice was involved.

This technique of thinking about what you are trying not to

think about is called paradoxical counseling, and it can be very effective. To do it properly takes some experience, and it is not something anyone without experience should try to do on his or her own. Choice theory is about making better choices, but we have to understand the reason for the bad choices before we can make good ones. As much as Francesca was infatuated with Robert, I believe there are few one-person people, certainly not a person one has known for only four days. In my counseling, I offered her a way to find belonging, if not love, by going to work.

Francesca could have chosen obsessing, saying over and over that she was sick and going to die or that her husband was sick and going to die. She could have also started compulsively washing her hands over and over and developed an overwhelming fear of dirt and germs. Either obsessing or compulsing could have kept Robert from surfacing in her mind. People who choose compulsive hand washing frequently feel guilty, and Francesca certainly could have felt enough guilt to have chosen it. The counseling would be the same as with phobicking.

Posttraumatic stress disorder, or PTSD, is another frequent diagnosis in the external control world where it is common for people to think: *I am the victim of something external over which I have no control.* After a painful, unexpected injury, accident, or exposure to a frightening situation, the people involved are so traumatized they cannot cope and need counseling to deal with what happened. The symptoms may be physical, such as a pain in the head, neck, or back; a disability, such as being unable to walk; or psychological, such as fear and anxiety that are so severe that the person can't work. A huge disaster, such as an earthquake, is a classic cause of this condition. I worry that the assumption that the people involved can't cope without expert help is frequently made too quickly.

By now, this assumption is so widespread that a whole posttrauma care system has come into existence. This system consists of doctors, lawyers, and therapists who have a financial incentive to convince the world that those who have been traumatized need help for what happened and compensation for their suffering. All this may be well intended, and the victims did indeed suffer, but it may also convince some of them to choose to perpetuate their suffering.

What is wrong with this assumption and the subsequent diagnosis of PTSD is that thousands of people who are exposed to huge amounts of trauma gather themselves together and deal with it. They do so because they have good relationships and a belief they are doing something worthwhile with their lives that they want to get back to doing. People who suffer so much disability after a trauma that they can't go on with their lives do not usually have strong relationships and may not be doing anything they consider worthwhile with their lives.

For these people—uninjured physically—the choice to disable themselves after a trauma is widely supported by the common sense that we are all controlled from the outside and provides a good excuse for people who are not coping to escape from their own inadequacy. The possibility of insurance settlements helps them believe they have been disabled. I am concerned that money to compensate them is being diverted from people who have suffered more tangible injuries. I do not have the answer to this dilemma, but I think it would occur less in a choice theory society. The more we teach people that they can deal with what happens to them, the better off we all will be.

It is important to me that I not be seen as lacking compassion. I never tell people that they are choosing any painful or self-destructive symptoms. I help them to make better choices and better relationships and teach them some choice theory. In almost all instances, they are very pleased with the therapy and are willing to give up the symptoms or beliefs when they find better ways to take control of their lives. It is no kindness to treat unhappy people as helpless, hopeless, or inadequate, no matter what has happened to them. Kindness is having faith in the truth and that people can handle it and use it for their benefit. True compassion is helping people help themselves.

It has been my experience that helping people to look at a psychological problem as a choice is a liberating awareness. The mystery, the fear that something beyond their control has suddenly come over them, is removed. They can now learn that other choices are possible, and acting on those new, more effective choices sets them free to explore lives filled with creativity that does not harm them.

PART II

The Practice

CHAPTER 8
Love and Marriage

WE OFTEN FALL in love when we least expect to. Neither Robert nor Francesca was expecting to fall in love, but they were lonely, and their loneliness left them vulnerable. In that situation, all we have to do is come into contact with a person who is close to our picture of someone we could love, a picture we all carry in our quality worlds. If that person reciprocates, suddenly we are in love. Even if this picture is a fantasy and there can be no reciprocation, we enjoy the fantasy. I, for example, was deeply in love with both Ingrid Bergman and Audrey Hepburn for much of my early life.

Fantasy loves are rarely a problem; it is our tangible loves that often don't work out. In the beginning it felt so good; we had found a person whom we seemed to be able to get very close to, and it was exciting. The closeness was partly sexual, but it went beyond sex. We had found a person who not only accepted us the way we were but accepted what we were trying to be. Whatever it was, if we wanted it, he or she wanted us to have it.

It felt good to be with someone who, unlike most of the other people in our lives, did not judge us or want to change us. The world took on a rosy hue. With this person we could relax, and we laughed together at everything. It was fun to learn about someone who seemed to care for us without reservation. The more we learned about him or her, the better it felt. We had found someone with whom we could share our quality worlds with no fear of rejection, ridicule, criticism, blame, or complaint.

It is this willingness, even eagerness, to share your hopes and fears that defines love. As long as you can do so, you have a very good chance of staying in love. *If you can't do this freely in the beginning, no matter how much it feels as if you are in love, your love is weak.* A weak love may be based more on hormones than freely sharing, and it will not last. Of course, most people who fall in love know nothing about their quality worlds; nevertheless, the experience is the same whether they know about it or not. But if you and the person you fall in love with know choice theory and know about your quality worlds, you can use this knowledge to stay in love with each other. From the beginning, you can make a pact to share a great deal of what is in your quality worlds and never criticize or complain about what has been shared.

Because it is impossible not to fantasize about others, you are not obligated to share your fantasies. To share them might be asking too much of your partner. But if you find that you can't share what's real, your love is beginning to fade. Francesca may have had fantasies of a man like Robert, but until he came along there was still a chance for Richard. After she admitted Robert to her quality world, there was no more chance for Richard. But there need not be anyone else for you to fall out of love. When there are differences, as there have to be the longer you know each other, you must work them out to stay in love. When you can't, you are no longer in love.

Without choice theory, when there is a disagreement early in a relationship, instead of understanding that it is based on a real difference in your quality worlds, you may revert to external control psychology and try to make your partner change. These early attempts to force the other to change are well expressed in the popular saying, *The honeymoon is over*. But that saying is indicative of the fact that in an external control society, few people expect that marriage is going to stay close to what it was in the beginning. The best that most people expect is that it won't get much worse.

Choice theory is useful, even vital, well before marriage. To illustrate this belief, let me begin with a conversation I had with Tina a few months ago. Before this time, we had talked a little about choice theory, but it was mostly talk. It had not occurred to Tina to put it to work in her relationship with Kevin. Tina wanted Kevin to propose, but he was unwilling to commit. In a world in which both sex and love are widely available without marriage, what she was experiencing is common.

Tina knew enough of what we talked about to have some awareness that the external control psychology she was using was not working. But knowing it wasn't working doesn't mean that it was easy for her to switch to choice theory. To make this change, she would have to admit that the only person's behavior she could control is her own, that she had no control over what Kevin chose to do. We must be willing to make this difficult admission if we are to use choice theory in our lives.

Tina is twenty-eight and competent in almost all aspects of her life. She is a high school drama teacher who does community theater in the evenings when she is not rehearsing a school production. Kevin, aged thirty, is an up-and-coming assistant principal of a nearby middle school, with an interest in physical fitness. He and Tina have been going together for two years. They seem compatible, have a common interest in education, and think they love each other. She doesn't mind waiting, but she wants a family and needs some reassurance that marriage is a possibility. She wanted my advice on how to get from where they are to marriage. She didn't expect me to tell her exactly what to do, but she was becoming more and more frustrated.

"You know the story, I've talked to you about Kevin. We've

spent over a year and a half with each other and enjoy each other's company both socially and sexually. After the last time you and I talked, I even went through our need strengths with him, and we are very compatible. We have traveled together, but we don't live together because I don't want to play at being married. After I give up my apartment, I don't want to chance being told that what we have isn't going to work. So how do we get beyond this point? I'm starting to wonder if we should even try. This constant worry about where we're going is having a bad effect on how I feel about myself. It's gotten to the point where I'm not even sure I love him anymore."

"Tina, if you didn't love him, I don't think we'd be having this talk. All I can tell you is what I've told you before: The only person you can control is yourself. OK, OK, I know I've said that a lot, but you can't make him love you or marry you. You can't make him do anything. If you try, it will make things worse."

"So I should just wait. Let him string me along. Doesn't what I want count?"

"Absolutely it counts. But as unhappy as you are now is nothing compared to how miserable you'll be if you push him into a marriage and it doesn't work out."

"I know that. That's why I don't even want to risk moving in with him. So *you* tell *me,* where am I?"

I paused here to think. That was a difficult question. I'm not sure even Kevin knows where they are. There is no sense trying to answer it. Instead I decided to focus on what she can control. That's the only sensible place for me to be.

"Let's let that question go for a while. I wonder if you could tell me what marriage means to you. What's your idea of marriage?"

"It's us living together; committed to each other; enjoying each other; and having a family, a home, a life together."

"I don't think anyone would disagree with that perfectly reasonable picture of marriage. Now this may seem to be a silly question, but it isn't. How is that picture different from being single, I mean being single right now, with what you have with Kevin?"

"How is it different? It's way different. I don't have him. I want him and I don't have him. He's kind, he's loving, he tells me he loves me, we have good sex together. But there's this thing. The way he behaves. It's like most of the time when we reach out to each other only the tips of our fingers touch. I'm never sure of him. I want to be married. I think I'd feel sure of him if we got married."

"Is he sure of you?"

"I think he's more sure of me than I am of him. He knows I want to marry him; he knows I don't have anyone else. It's different for a man; he can wait, he can wait for ten years, more maybe, but I can't. You're a reality therapist; his reality is different from mine. He can wait and still have a family. I know a man sixty who is starting a family with a young woman."

"You're right, reality is not the same for any of us. His and yours are different. But you have to go with yours; you have no control over his. And your reality is that right now you're very unsure of him. If that doesn't change, the future won't make much difference."

"But that's what I've been telling you. What are you trying to tell me?"

"I'm trying to tell you that you shouldn't even think about marrying him until you are convinced he wants you for a wife, so you can say, 'He and I feel very sure of each other.' You can't predict the future, but if you can get that far, you have a chance for a future with him."

"But that's what I've just told you. I don't see how this is helping me."

"No, it's not exactly what you've told me. You've told me that if he'd marry you, which right now he won't, you'd be more sure of him. Like marriage sort of guarantees the future. But nothing guarantees the future. Certainly marriage doesn't. You know a lot of divorced people; they had no guaranteed future. But Tina, listen, the way you are with Kevin, you don't even have a good present; you're not enjoying him very much right now. I think that's your problem—the present, not the future."

"But I'm doing all I can. I love him, I go places with him, I told you I don't want to move in with him. What more can I do?"

"I think you can stop talking about the future, stop implying there's even going to be a future. All this talk about the future is killing what you have now. Focus on getting along with him much better than you ever have, maybe better than it was in the beginning. You have no control over the future. He knows you want to marry him; you don't have to keep reminding him."

"OK, I stop mentioning marriage and our future and we get along great. How long am I supposed to play this role?"

"What role? Is it a role?"

"Of course, it's a role. I want to get married or get a commitment from him. I don't want to be loving, forget-about-the-future friends. That's not enough for me."

"I know it's not enough, but right now it's where you are. And there is nothing you can do to change it. You can't make him do anything. Even if you could, I don't think you'd want to force him into marriage if he doesn't want it. If you want a future with him, all you can do now is improve what you have. Get rid of all this future tension. To hang on trying to make him do what he doesn't want to do makes no sense. Like I said, you can't predict the future even if you get married. All you have any control over is what you do right now. Life is like auditioning for a part in a play. All you can control is what you do. That's all you can do with Kevin. If you want the part, do the best you can. You keep trying to force him to think about the future, and you're both uncomfortable. A good present has a chance to lead to a good future. A lousy present has a very good chance to lead to a lousy future or no future."

"But I feel so frustrated. I know what you're saying makes sense, but I want him to make a commitment now."

"Tina, you don't know what I'm saying makes sense. You're stuck in external control psychology, in wanting him to change. If you knew what I'm saying makes sense, you wouldn't be frustrated. Choice theory people don't get so frustrated. They focus on doing what's best now and know that the only people they can control are themselves. You keep thinking, *What can I do that will change him?* You've given yourself an impossible task. That's why you're frustrated."

"Are you telling me that even though I'm in love with Kevin and he acts like he loves me, I can't do anything about what he does? He can just go his merry way and I have to put up with it?"

"No, not at all. You can do a lot of things. You can choose to depress, anger, rant, rave, threaten, see other guys, drop him, get sick, do the Ophelia thing and go crazy. I explained all this to you months ago when we were talking about how people mess up their lives. And if you choose any of these things, you'll mess up yours. Do you want to do that? Or do you want to take a good look at where he and you as a couple stand in your quality world right now? You know about the quality world; here's a good chance to use what you know. What is your picture of you and Kevin?"

"I told you. I see us happily married. I see a home, a little family, the things I've wanted all my life."

"That's a wonderful picture, but it's a future picture. I'd like you to take another look. Where are you and Kevin right now, today, in your quality world? Try to forget marriage for a moment and tell me what's your present picture, the picture that tells you right now you love him."

"I see us loving each other, having a good time, getting along well. Laughing, talking, sharing what we feel with each other. All the things we used to do."

"Used to do?"

"No, not used to do, I don't know why I said that. We still do; that hasn't changed."

"Good, those are great pictures. When are you going to see him again?"

"We're planning to spend this weekend together."

"Are you looking forward to it? Honestly?"

"To be honest, yes and no. We get along great, but then there's always some tension. He says something or I say something."

"About the future?"

"Sort of. I guess it's what he doesn't say. And then I say something, you know. And then I get a little dissatisfied and I sulk a little and then he withdraws a little. It doesn't ruin the weekend, but I'd rather it didn't happen."

"It doesn't have to happen. You don't have to say what you say."

"Of course, it doesn't have to happen. But how can I help it? I keep thinking, *Here we are, but where are we?* I get all bottled up and it happens. My God, I'm a human being, do you want me to stop feeling?"

"I don't want you to do anything. I want you to be aware of what you're choosing to do."

"I knew it; I knew you'd harp on that *choosing* crap. What about him?"

"You know you can control only what you do. You said you love him."

"I do love him, but we're not going anywhere."

"OK, say you're an actress in a play. You love a guy who says he loves you but he can't marry you. A while ago he promised to marry someone else, but he doesn't love her. And there are complications; the family business is tied up with her father's business. If he backs out now, her father will ruin his family's business. And ruin not only his future, but also his father's, his brother's, and a lot of other people's. Her father is a ruthless man. Your lover can see you secretly, but in six months he has to marry the one he doesn't love. He says, 'Let's keep seeing each other, I can't live without you. If things don't change, we'll kill ourselves.' The play has you killing yourselves with pills, but in the end as her father gets the news, the audience sees the stricken look on his face as the curtain falls. It's so tragic; the audience is in tears. They applaud. What do you think of that part?"

"I love it. I'd love to play it."

"You don't mind giving up the future for love in a play, so why do you mind it so much in real life?"

"Because it's stupid. I don't want to be dead, I wouldn't even want him to be dead. If he loved me, he'd kiss her good-bye and take a chance. He doesn't owe his family his happiness, his future."

"So what would you do in real life if Kevin told you, 'I don't know if I'm ever going to be ready to marry you?'"

"I'd be miserable, I'd cry, I'd be devastated."

"But?"

"But I certainly wouldn't kill myself if that's what you're worried about."

"Is there anything to stop you from dropping him now, this weekend? To have a beautiful, totally loving weekend and then say good-bye when he drops you off at your apartment."

"If I had a beautiful loving weekend, why would I say good-bye?"

"Because you're scared that's all there's ever going to be. That's what you've been telling me since we started to talk."

"But I don't know, it might still work out."

"That's right, that's exactly right. You can't predict the future. But if you had a beautiful, loving weekend or you had a tense weekend, which weekend would give you the best chance for a future together?"

"But what if after a great six months, I come to the conclusion there isn't going to be any future?"

"Then tell him. Tell him the truth. Tell him, 'Things have been great, but now I want more.' It will be the truth. But here's the hard part. Make sure you are ready to drop him if he can't give you some kind of a commitment. He has no right to try to control your life any more than you have to try to control his. Six months you can deal with, especially if you know that's your limit. Let it go longer, and you'll make yourself into a basket case."

"It's up to me, isn't it?"

"It always is. That's choice theory—it's up to you. He knows how you feel; you've made that clear to him. If he loves you enough and you stop bugging him and try to get closer than you ever have, it may work out. The more you pout, the more you try to force him, the more he'll wonder, I'm not sure I want to marry a woman who tries to control me. Show him you are in control of yourself. He knows what you want. If he can't deal with it, he's not for you. If he's so weak you can force him into marriage, it's not going to work anyway. It might last long enough for you to have a child or two to raise on your own."

"I know you're right. But I don't think I can do it."

"What can you do that's better? This is one of those times in your life when, as much as you want something, maybe you're not going to get it. But at least you'll know that you did the best thing. You didn't nag him or try to force him. You gave him time. I can't see that there is anything more you can do. Do you want to keep hanging on and nagging or waiting until he asks, knowing he may never ask? It's tough. Choice theory is tough. But you have a much better chance with it than just nagging and waiting. You'll hate yourself if you wait too long and nothing happens. If anything is going to happen, doing what I suggest has the best chance. There has to be a cap on this thing. And you have to put it on."

Our conversation helped Tina to see that she had some control, and she made a plan. There is a lot of security in a plan; there's a sense of control, it's what *you* can do, not what he can do. She stopped sending the promise-to-marry-me message. They got along great for the next three months. She concentrated on having a good time with him, did not try to force him into anything; she let the future go, and the tension stopped. He had a chance to see what life with her could be all about. After about three months, they had the following conversation.

"You haven't said a word about marriage. Have you changed your mind about it?"

"I've decided not to talk about marriage anymore. Is that all right with you?"

"Aren't you interested in marriage anymore?"

"Kevin, I don't plan to talk about it. I certainly don't ever plan to ask you to marry me if that's what you're waiting for."

"What if I don't ask you?"

"Then I guess we'll never get married."

"It's great the way you've been, but I can't believe you're just going to keep being this way."

"I'm not going to keep being any way. I'm enjoying the way we are now. I'll tell you when I don't want to see you anymore."

"When will that be?"

"I don't know, but as soon as I know I'll tell you."

This is how Tina began to learn to use choice theory in her life. Kevin wondered why she had stopped nagging, and she taught him some choice theory. He was very interested, especially in the idea that she had no intention of ever trying to force him to do anything he didn't want to do. There was to be as little nagging, criticizing, blaming, or complaining as she could manage. It was hard, and she would have relapses, as do all recovering external control psychology people. She said that she could not control his behavior, only her own, but if they were to have a future, she wanted it to be a choice theory future. She reminded him how much happier they were since she gave up external control. Obviously, this is the time to give up external control psychology, not after an unhappy marriage and, perhaps, a divorce. Kevin and Tina got married and, with the help of choice theory, their relationship continues strong.

What they are doing now, which is the core of a choice theory marriage, is thinking before they do anything that may lead the other to choose to move away. There are only two ways people move away from each other: They resist or withdraw, fight or flee. To prevent fight or flight, which is the beginning of the end of any relationship, whenever they have a problem, they ask themselves, *If I say or do this right now, will it bring us closer together or will we end up further apart?* And they do not engage in nagging, criticizing, complaining, or put-downs to try to control the other person. Even those who have used external control psychology all their lives are well aware that these all-too-common behaviors harm any relationship. If we want to stay close, we do not have the luxury of using them.

What Tina and Kevin have done is form a solving circle. Inside that circle, described in chapter 5, they no longer try to change the other; everything they choose to do is based on how it will affect their marriage. They talk everything over, and if something has any chance of harming their marriage, they don't do it. As a married couple, they now know that it is no longer how what one spouse says affects the other, it is how it will or could affect the marriage.

This doesn't mean Tina and Kevin have no disagreements. It means that they have a tool to deal with disagreements before they escalate into separating them from each other. They understand that when they make a choice in favor of the marriage, it may not necessarily be the choice either of them would make for himself or herself if they were not married. But they are married, it is a reality, and it is not the same as being single. But they also work hard to understand each other's need for a life outside the marriage. There are obvious sexual and social restrictions on that life, but within those restrictions they do not have to be Siamese twins. Each will bend over backward not to restrict the other from having a life separate from the marriage to the point of encouraging each other to do so.

For example, Kevin is an avid runner; every day, rain or shine, he needs to run. Tina is interested in the theater; she needs time to do her community theater work. They have agreed to give each other that time, and it works fine. He runs, she acts, and neither has to fear that the other disapproves. Since success in life is dependent on good relationships, they have learned to apply choice theory to their lives outside the marriage, and it has been effective there, too. Kevin is much more successful as the school disciplinarian using choice theory, and Tina is more successful using it with the students in her drama classes. With choice theory and the solving circle, they feel free to talk to each other about anything anytime because they have agreed that the marriage takes precedence over what each wants individually.

I am sure that many of you may have a few *Yes buts* to add to the rosy picture I have painted of this marriage. You may think it is too ideal, that with no conflict they will soon get bored and fall out of love. If much of the joy of an external control marriage is making up after a fight, a choice theory marriage lacks that plea-sure. Choice theory does not guarantee a wonderful marriage; it guarantees a way to deal with the problems that will come up in the best marriages. If a good marriage goes sour, it is much more often because one or both partners have reverted to external control psy-chology than because getting along well together is so boring.

We should never forget creativity. It is the best antidote to boredom that humans have yet discovered. Most of us fear being creative because we are afraid that something new will be criti-cized, a common practice in an external control relationship in which one or the other partner is always looking to find fault. Couples who have moved to choice theory have no such fears. Be-cause of the freedom in the relationship, they are always willing to try to enlist their creative systems anytime things begin to get stale or predictable. They are not afraid to talk about doing new things both together and separately. The circle provides a safe place to be creative.

To keep long-term sex satisfying, the couple must have the freedom to communicate without fear. If they can't talk, how can they solve the usual sexual problem of a lasting marriage, which is always some variation of *Let's do something a little different the next time we make love*? Even in a good marriage, sex, like any other repetitive behavior, easily gets stale. If the couple does it when they are tired, without consideration of what the other wants, and without agreeing on the preliminaries or if they believe that married sex can't be exciting, sex starts to fade away. Our genes have provided us with one of the most enjoyable of all op-portunities, but many couples are unable or unwilling—it's really the same thing—to take advantage of this opportunity.

They are unwilling partly because, in the beginning when sex is new, we don't have to worry about being creative. But as time goes on, to keep it exciting, we all have to infuse it with a little creativity. If not, one or both partners may grow disinterested and start to take sex *with each other* out of their quality worlds. As they do so, they often start fantasizing about someone else when, with a little creativity, each could still satisfy the other. The idea of sexual excitement with a new partner is the reason for all the sexual banter that frequently goes on between men and women. They want to reexperience the fantasies they had when they were starting out, and a lot of the flirty banter is creative.

Remember, creativity that helps you get closer to another person feels good no matter what it is attached to. In a good marriage you can attach it to sex with your mate and heighten the hormonal pleasure. Creative couples who follow choice theory are not afraid to do or say something different; do it in a different place; and be willing to use some kind of sexual aids, such as games, videotapes, and toys, to keep each other interested in sex. But a further problem may be that sex is simply not enough on their minds or is on the mind of one but not the other. They may not realize that in this hectic world, it is necessary for both to make an effort to have sex with each other on their minds to get the most out of it. Thinking a lot about sex need not be restricted to the unmarried or to someone besides your spouse.

What compounds this problem is that in many marriages, one or both feel that sexual aids should not be necessary—*If he or she really loved me, we wouldn't need these aids.* They fail to understand that it is not the aids themselves, whatever they are, that are important. It is that when you use them, or even consider using them, they get sex on the minds of both participants. Once sex is on your minds, the aids become less important. Just thinking about them accomplishes a lot of what needs to be done.

Good sex is like planning to go to a great restaurant. To begin, it helps to make a reservation and to keep it. If you have to wait a week to get one, the interest may increase. When you finally sit down to eat, good food is on your mind, and you are in the mood to enjoy it fully. Do the same for sex. Enjoy it spontaneously, of course, but don't be hesitant to make a reservation. Reserve the time and the place. Don't be any more in a hurry than to finish a good meal and you will find that you can keep sex with each other active in your quality worlds for much longer than many of you think is possible now.

Long-term marriages that have used external control psychology for years and are not very satisfying to either partner can also be helped if one or both partners are willing to take a look at their need strengths. In any long-term marriage, there is usually enough compatibility. Rarely do the differences in need strengths make the marriage impossible, but checking them out shows clearly where there may be difficulty.

When a difficulty is found, if both partners are willing to stop using external control psychology—willing to get in the circle and talk about what each is willing to give, not take—they may be able to stop the drift apart that has been eroding their marriage. When sex starts to go, it should be a wake-up call that you need to talk and plan. Just getting in the circle feels so good that it can lead to what has been put off for too long. Once you get started, you are setting the stage for more. But you have to start. It may be that your external control marriage is beyond repair, but there is no predicting. No matter how rancorous the couple has been, the solving circle may work. As I have said many times in this book, there is no downside to choice theory, really nothing to lose.

In marriage, as in all human relationship problems, someone has to take the initiative and stop using external control. This was Tina's problem and, to her, it seemed to be unfair. *He's making me unhappy, why should I change if he won't?* was her refrain for months before we had that talk. But trying to implement choice theory can be a trap if the willing partner tries to *make* the other move to his or her choice theory way of thinking. Even with the best intentions, this is external control to the hilt. Besides, whenever we try to do anything to force anyone, we run headlong into *The harder you try to make me, the more I will resist.* Control begets control. To resist pressure is the norm in an external control world, especially for the underdogs.

ABUSIVE MARRIAGES

In an abusive marriage, the husband is following the most destructive external control practice: He believes he owns his wife.

And to a great extent, the legal system of the external control society we live in supports that belief. Men can beat, abuse, rape, or exploit their wives and get away with it because the men who run our present society are, for the most part, afraid they will lose power if wives are legitimately protected by the law. If a man beats or abuses anyone except his wife or a long-term partner, the law steps in immediately and protects whoever suffered the abuse. This acceptance of spousal brutality needs to be changed, and teaching all people, including abusive men, choice theory may be a way to do it.

Wives are not chattel. No one has the right to beat anyone, and people who are beaten need legal protection. In some, but not enough, jurisdictions, this protection is being enforced. The abused woman's testimony is no longer needed; the bruises are allowed to speak for themselves. It does little good if all we do is punish the men. That again is using control to deal with control, and too many men use the excuse *She got me punished* to be even more abusive. What is needed is a court-ordered diversion program that offers husbands and wives the chance to choose to learn choice theory and reality therapy together in a group setting with others who have the same domestic violence problem.

This diversion from traditional court-ordered punishment or even worse, court neglect, is being successfully pioneered in the *First Step Program* in Fostoria, Ohio.* There, a community application of choice theory and reality therapy is made available to all who want it, regardless of whether they can pay. The program's research[†] shows that only 17 percent of the wives who participated with their husbands in the Passages Part of the First Step

---

The First Step Program is directed by Terri L. Mercer, who can be reached at Box 1103, Fostoria, OH 44830; phone (419) 435-7300. Its logo is: A program for victims of domestic violence.

[†]In a detailed report that quotes many statistics, the statement that only 17 percent of the wives reported further violence after they and their husbands participated in the program seemed very significant. The report was sent to me by Terri Mercer, director of *First Step*, in a letter dated March 25, 1997.

Program reported threats of or actual violence since they finished the program, and half the men reported increased self-control.

STRUCTURED REALITY THERAPY MARRIAGE COUNSELING

Destroying marriages is the crowning achievement of external control psychology. Once this psychology has taken over a marriage, the best hope to overcome it is the kind of counseling that offers the couple a chance to move their marriage from where it is into the solving circle. Once the marriage is safely inside this protective circle, it is immune to the cancer of external control. But to be effective, the marriage counseling must be tailored specifically to the needs of the relationship, rather than to the individual needs of each partner.

In most instances, the partners in a failing marriage are not themselves failures. We all have friends and relatives who have divorced but who, individually, are competent. A large number of these people are even competent enough to succeed in a subsequent marriage. When they do, it is because, unknowingly, most of them have learned enough choice theory to avoid the mistakes of their previous marriage. But this is a haphazard process, and many continue the same control and ownership and fail again. If these competent people had been offered the structured marriage counseling I will now explain while they were still married, I believe many of these marriages could have been saved.

In this choice theory-based marriage counseling, the counselor takes an active role and asks specific questions or makes requests that each partner, in turn, responds to, or the counseling will fail.

1. Are you here because you really want help? Or are you here because you have already made up your mind to divorce but want to be able to say you tried to get help?

2. Very briefly, what do you believe is wrong with the marriage?

3.   Whose behavior can you control?

4.   Tell me one good thing about the marriage as it exists right now.

5.   Think of and then tell me something that you are willing to do this coming week that you believe will help your marriage. Whatever it is, it must be something you can do yourself. It must not depend, in any way, on what your partner should or should not do.

6.   During this coming week, are you willing to try to think of an additional thing besides what you thought of here? And then do it following the same I-can-control-only-what-I-do conditions as in the previous question?

In answer to question 1, if both partners are able to say they really want help, then the counseling has a chance. If they are not able to convince the counselor that they want help, the counseling has no chance. Counselors should not try to help couples when both are not committed to seeking help. Individual partners seeking help for themselves is not marriage counseling.

The purpose of question 2, in which one or both partners invariably blame the other, is to be able to point out later in the counseling that this is external control and it is always destructive to the marriage. If only one partner blames the other—a situation I've never seen—the counseling will be even easier than if both blame the other. In this situation, the counselor must monitor each partner's responses to prevent this Pandora's box from opening into a rancorous outpouring of accusing, blaming, criticizing, and threatening because that is what most people who come for marriage counseling expect to do and want to do. Following external control psychology, they both think they are right and both are looking for the counselor to support their positions. Their answers should be restricted to a few short sentences. If their answers are left to run unchecked, they will destroy the counseling effort.

The purpose of question 3 (Whose behavior can you control?) is to lay the groundwork for the essential requests, 5 and 6 (to do something positive at home). This is not a hard question. After the outbursts that are the answers to question 2 (What's wrong with the marriage?) it should be obvious that each partner can control only his or her own behavior.

Request 4 (Tell me one good thing about the marriage) is difficult. Both partners are so into external control psychology that this request comes as a complete surprise. The counselor should be patient here and keep fending off their initial statements, *which will be what the other needs to do if the marriage is to become better*. In the end, most couples will come up with quite a few things that are still good about the marriage. If they couldn't do so, they would not have come for counseling. As they talk about some good things, much of the anger and blaming will drain out of the session, and it should be smoother sailing from then on. They will be surprised by what they say, but these are all positive surprises.

Request 5 is just an extension of request 4, but it gives the partners something new to think about and build on and thus is very important. Again, the counselor should be patient, and they will come up with something positive and be pleased that they have. They will now leave the counseling session with something specific to focus on instead of the bad marriage. It gives them a little hope and, because it is so different from external control psychology, it is very powerful.

Request 6, asking the partners to come up with an additional helpful task during the week, gives them another positive focus to look forward to. If they do it, fine. If they just do request 5, the marriage is still well on its way to getting a lot of help. Both 5 and 6 give them a lot to talk about when they come in for the next session a week later.

If, toward the end of the first session, the partners are much more amicable and their interest in what has been going on has replaced the anger that they came in with, this is the time for the counselor to explain the solving circle and to point out that they are now in it. And to point out further that whenever they talk about their marriage, they should make sure they are in the circle or else what they talk about has a chance of becoming external control and destructive.

Now I would like to demonstrate how this structured marriage counseling is actually done. Ed and Karen came to me for marriage counseling. Karen called, told me that she was very dissatisfied with their marriage and that Ed had agreed to come. Before I saw them, I knew that their quality world pictures of each other as husband and wife were very shaky, but as long as they still had each other in their quality worlds at all, there was a good chance that this structured approach could help them. If one or both had taken the other out, there probably would be nothing anyone could do to save the marriage. I assumed that they are both practicing external control psychology and that each believed that to help the marriage, the other had to change.

Ed and Karen are in their early forties, it is their first marriage, both work, and they have two children ten and twelve. As long as they are reasonable in handling their money, there are no major financial problems. They came in to my office and sat down opposite me, but before they said anything, I started with question 1. I include it in a prepared introduction that I use with all couples in this situation.

"I assume you are both here to try to help your marriage. By this I mean that neither of you has made up your mind that the marriage is beyond repair or that what you really want is a divorce. Is that a fair assumption?"

They both agreed that this statement was true, so I went ahead with my next prepared question. I use this question to make sure that the partners hear themselves blaming the other for what is wrong with the marriage. I do my best to restrict the answer to a few sentences; I don't want a diatribe. I just want short examples from their own mouths so that later they can clearly see how they have changed, or how they haven't changed if the counseling is unsuccessful.

"I need each of you to give me a short answer to this question.

Please don't go on at length, or I will have to interrupt you and I hate to be seen as impolite. Just a sentence or two will be enough. *I want each of you to tell me what you believe is wrong with the marriage.* To avoid arguing over who goes first, I will ask one of you to respond and then the other. Karen, you called, so please go first."

"It's him, he's what's wrong. It's like being married to Ebenezer Scrooge. He watches every cent I spend. I work, but it's all his money. You can't believe what I have to put up with. He makes me—"

I tried to interrupt but, before I could, Ed jumped in, "Me. I'm what's wrong? If you didn't spend every goddamned cent we have. Doctor, we're up to the max on all our cards. We're paying a fortune in interest we can't deduct."

"See, Doctor, see what I have to put up with all day long."

"Look, please, we have to stick to the rules. Just answer the question, no arguing or pointing fingers. Ed, what do you think is wrong."

"I'll tell you. Doctor. I hate to say this, but I don't think she loves me anymore. All she does is complain. Calls me a tightwad. It's got to the point where I don't know what to do that will satisfy her—"

Again before I could say anything, Karen jumped in, "Oh, he's right about that; he doesn't know what to do that will satisfy me. Him talking about love, that's the joke of the century. He treats our dog better than he treats me. That dog—"

This time I was able to get in a word before she could go further, "If you just keep fighting and sniping at each other, I can't help you. Please don't do here what you have been doing at home. It hasn't helped there, and it won't help here. You've answered my questions very well; I get the picture. This is a critical time in your marriage. Please try to follow my directions and let me try to help you."

You can see that external control psychology was in full flower. As I expected, they didn't listen to my request for a brief answer and jumped in, blaming each other and trying to get me to take their side. But I was not worried. I could get this situation under control if I didn't make the mistake of appearing interested in their sniping. Also, while it may seem as if they were doing badly, actually I've heard a lot worse in the first few minutes. I thought that they did care for each other and that I could help. The next question was not difficult, and it got them started in the right direction, beginning to accept that they could control only their own behavior.

"Tell me, whose behavior can you control?"

I used this question to attempt to get them out of their habit of focusing on the other person instead of on themselves. It took a while, and then Karen spoke. They were already into it, so I no longer had to worry about whose turn it was. To be fair, I directed question 4 to Ed, but I also wanted to hear what Karen had to say.

"I guess it's pretty clear I can't control his behavior. But God knows he's tried to control mine."

I said, "Has he succeeded?"

"He's succeeded in making me miserable and wrecking our marriage."

Ed spoke up, "C'mon Karen. If I could control your goddamned spending, we wouldn't be here."

I started to end it by saying, "OK, I think it's pretty clear that you've tried but you haven't been able to control the other. It may be redundant, but please tell me, who is the only person you can control."

Ed confirmed what I said, and Karen seemed satisfied. He said, "I think what you're driving at is we can only control ourselves. I know about that; I tell the salesmen who work for me that all the time."

This seemed to settle them down. They were quiet and were waiting for request 4, which is crucial in directed counseling. If they could deal well with this totally unexpected request, it might change the whole mood and help them settle down further.

"OK, Ed, it's your turn. This is the most important question I am going to ask. Take your time and think about it. I want each of you to tell me something good about your marriage right now. There has to be something good, or there is little hope. If there weren't, you wouldn't be here; you'd have gone to see a lawyer."

As I expected, request 4 floored each of them temporarily. They looked at each other and then at me. This is the request that had the potential to get them away from all the blaming and complaining. If I allowed them to stick with the negative, I'd help kill what little they still had that was positive. In my experience, once couples start thinking positively, they find there is more good than they realize. Even though I asked Ed, Karen jumped right in.

"This isn't at all what I expected. I came here to tell you what's really wrong with our marriage. I didn't expect you to shut me up. What kind of counseling is this anyway?"

"It's the way I counsel. Give it a chance. Don't waste your time and money asking me to take sides. I'm not interested in whose fault it is. You'd never agree on that in a million years. Please Ed, take your time but answer the question. What's good about your marriage right now?"

"That's a hard one. I can't think of anything that's good."

"Go ahead, try, there must be something good."

There is always a little impasse here. He knew more than one good thing but thought that to admit it wouldn't be cool. I decided to be patient and supportive. He would come up with something. She was thinking, too. I could see that she was very interested in what he might say.

"OK, I'll say this for her. She's loyal. When I hear her sister tell her I'm a jerk she doesn't agree. I like that a lot. I just wish she'd do more than tell it to her sister, tell it to me once in a while."

Karen liked this, but still she burst in, "Of course, I support you to my sister. Compared to the goofball she's married to, you are pretty good. But you're going to have to be a lot better if you want me to tell you that."

"Please Karen, Ed did his part. Now it's your turn. Tell me what's good about the marriage right now. It's important that you say something; take your time."

She had something in mind, but I could see that she hated to say it. It was as if by saying it, she'd be more vulnerable, as if it was almost wrong to say there was something good about the marriage. But she wanted to. I could see her softening. This question was getting to her.

"Look, it's like I'm married to two men. Most of the time he's Mr. Hyde. Criticizing all I do. Complaining—"

I interrupted, "We know about Mr. Hyde. Tell me about Dr. Jekyll?"

"It's when we go on vacation. He takes three weeks, we plan it together, and he's great. It's usually two weeks with the kids and then one week by ourselves. But that's what pisses me off. Why is that all there is that's good? I'm not willing to settle for a three-weeks-a-year marriage. It's been eight months since that week in Hawaii."

Ed broke in, "For Chrissake, Karen. Hawaii was good because you couldn't find anything to buy except that fucking muumuu you never wear. If you'd stop your compulsive shopping, we'd get along great."

"If you'd pay attention to me the way you do on vacation, I wouldn't shop so much."

So far so good. It sounded bad, but they could both see that there was some substance in the marriage. This last exchange was positive even if they were still into blaming. I followed up with a little confirmation of the fact there was some good in the marriage.

"See Karen, there are some good things. Believe me, I counsel people who don't have one good day a year in their marriages, let alone three weeks. It's not enough, but it shows that you and Ed can get along. All we have to do is figure out how to get more. No, no, please don't say anything right now. Let's go on to another question. It's another hard one, but if you can concentrate, I think you can come up with something."

I was being very supportive, and their thinking was starting to turn around. They could see what I was doing. It was obvious, but it was grabbing them and it seemed to be what they wanted. I decided to be very patient with the next question. I projected a kind supportiveness, sending them the message that answering this request might take a while, but they could do it.

"I'd like you to take your time and be very serious. Please no snide remarks. Think of something that you are willing to do this week that you believe will help the marriage. This is for each of you to do on your own. Not for the other guy to do."

There was a long pause during which each looked sheepishly at the other. I could see a little affection in their eyes, a very positive sign.

Ed said, "I can go a whole week and not mention money once. I may as well, I can't stop her from spending it anyway."

A good comment spoiled a little by the last dig he threw at her. But it didn't seem to bother her. I guessed that she was past the point where digs even registered.

She responded, "I'd like that Ed, I really would. But who're you kidding? You'll be all over the bills as soon as they come in."

"Why don't you stop putting me down and wait and see. What I want to hear is what you're going to do."

There was a very long pause. I could see that Karen was struggling with something that she wanted to say but she had a hard time getting it out.

Finally, in a kind of coy way, she said, "I could be a little more affectionate."

As soon as she said these unspoken-since-who-knows-when words, I could see that Ed was pleased. I think she was expecting some sort of wisecrack like, "It's about time," but Ed just continued to look pleased. I didn't ask how long it had been since they had sex, much less made love, but my guess was that it might have been in Hawaii eight months before. I now wanted to bring up the last request. If they would agree to do it, it would give me a way to segue into mentioning the solving circle.

"I wonder, now that you are thinking this way, if during the week, one or both of you could figure out another thing you might do to improve the marriage—kind of a homework assignment—and then next week when you come in, tell me about it. During the week, each of you do something more than what you just said would help the marriage. If you are able to do so, next week is the last time I'll want to see you for a month unless you want to see me. But look, we've got a few more minutes. Do you have any questions or comments?"

If a marriage needs extended counseling, I don't think it can be saved. Marital problems are not individual problems. Most of the couples I've counseled are like Ed and Karen, individually competent. What they can't figure out is how to get along with each other. But here, in this brief time, Ed and Karen actually entered the solving circle, and I wanted to explain it to them before they left. I thought they would be able to use this information, and by the following week, we would know.

Ed had a comment, "I feel better. I came prepared to fight, but I guess I really don't want to fight anymore. What do you think, Karen?"

"It's weird. It's not at all what I expected. I'm not sure what happened, but I feel better, too."

What happened was that these two supposedly confirmed external control psychology partners had encountered choice theory, but I didn't explain it to them then. I could begin that next week. But as long as they were in this receptive mood and essentially in the solving circle, this was a good opportunity to explain the solving circle to them. If they could use it in the coming week, they would definitely make progress.

"Karen, I'd like to delay answering your question until next week. But here's part of what happened. Look, I have a big piece of imaginary chalk in my hand and watch what I do with it. I am drawing a circle on the floor around you and Ed. There you are, in the solving circle. Tell me, what do you think the solving circle is? It has to do with what you are both feeling and that you don't feel like fighting right now."

Karen said, "That's what's so weird; it's like Ed said, I don't feel like fighting anymore. And that's all I've felt like for so long. But what does this imaginary chalk line have to do with it?"

Ed ventured a guess, "We're not fighting. I don't even feel like fighting—"

Karen finished the sentence, "We're solving something, is that it?"

"That's part of it. But it's more. In the circle, the marriage takes precedence over what each of you wants. Right now you're in it. Were you in it when you came here?"

Karen said, "It's like that guy wrote about Venus and Mars. I don't even think we were on the same planet when we came in here."

Ed nodded in agreement.

I said, "That's right. Not only don't you fight as long as you're in the circle, it's safe to talk about what you want from the marriage without worrying that you're going to be put down. But, of course, in the circle, it's up to you to add to the marriage, not wait for the other person. All you do in this circle is what we've started to do here. There are no shoulds and musts in the solving circle. No you-do-its. Only I'll-do-its. If you get into the circle whenever you talk about anything to do with your marriage, you'll be fine. Here, I'll give both of you a piece of this imaginary chalk; use it. And one last question, whose behavior can you control?"

Ed and Karen came back in a week and had a lot to say. Things were better. I had no illusion that money was their only problem. I'm not sure there is an only problem. In a failing relationship, everything's the problem. The beauty of the solving circle is not that it's good for this or that problem, but that it's a powerful tool that any couple can use at any time. But when a problem comes up, don't take for granted you're in the circle because you have been getting along. Get out the chalk and actually go through the motions of drawing it every time you want to use it. Don't say anything until you have drawn the circle and are inside. This is a purposeful and focused activity.

When Karen and Ed came in, they told me they thought the solving circle was a gimmick, anything that simple could not possibly work. But when they tried it and it worked, they found themselves using it more and more and were surprised at how effective it was. They asked me to tell them what was going on. This request gave me the opening that I wanted to begin to explain choice theory to them. I gave them a copy of my 1995 relationship book, *Staying Together*.* It explains how any couple can apply choice theory to a relationship.

---

*William Glasser, *Staying Together* (New York: HarperCollins, 1995).

CHAPTER 9
Trust and Your Family

I F, BEFORE I WAS BORN, I knew all I have learned and experienced since childhood and was given the chance to pick my parents, I would not hesitate to pick my father. No son ever had a better father, and I owe much of what has been a good life to how he chose to relate to me for the more than fifty years I knew him. Although he has been gone for many years, his picture is still strongly in my quality world, and I feel certain mine was in his as long as he lived. As I look back over our long relationship, I see that what I had with my father was trust. It never crossed my mind that he ever meant anything different from what he said. From my father I got the gift of personal freedom, love without control. I was a very lucky child.

Although she had some outstanding qualities, I would not pick my mother. It wasn't that she didn't treat me well as a child or even as a young man, but I would not want to relive the way she treated me and my family later on. I don't mean that what she did after I was an adult harmed me or that her good treatment of me as a child did not contribute to my success. But knowing what I have known for many years, I believe I would have been better off with someone else. From the time I was very young, my mother was unpredictable. I never felt free really to trust her. In that respect, she was far different from my father.

Unlike all others who are in our quality worlds, we do not consciously choose to put our parents in. By the time we become aware of them, we have made that choice; they are there. Many animals bond with their young for survival for a short time when the young are growing up. We don't bond genetically, but what we do when we put our parents into our quality worlds and they put us into theirs may be stronger than that short-term bonding. For most of us, it lasts a lifetime.

It is almost impossible for children to take parents who raise them out of their quality worlds because in most instances there is no one to replace them. For the same reason, it is difficult to take many other family members, even stepparents or adoptive parents, out of our quality worlds if they have been there from close to the beginning. Even if they treat us terribly from the moment we are aware of them, most of us struggle to keep these people in our quality worlds far longer than anyone we meet later in life. And it is the same for our children. No matter how our children choose to behave, we find it next to impossible to take them out of our quality worlds. In this respect, the child-parent relationship is unique.

Abused or severely neglected children know nothing about their quality worlds, especially how strong these worlds are and that their parents or parent substitutes are so firmly in them. Because they don't realize the strength of their quality worlds, I think they sometimes wonder why they can't seem to give up on their abusive or neglectful parents. Frequently, they accept the mistreatment in a desperate attempt to please the people they need so much. The pain of the abuse is far more bearable than the idea of separating from what children believe are irreplaceable persons, which, of course, means taking these persons out of their quality worlds.

This was the problem of the hero of the movie *Shine*, young David Helfgott: Neither he nor his father could remove the other from his quality world. The movie painfully depicts how his father loved him, but Helfgott could not help but perceive that this love was conditional. To get it, he had to submit to his father's domination. When he first asked his father to let him leave home to pursue his gift as a pianist, his father cruelly rejected this request, all the while protesting how much he loved him.

Even when Helfgott finally summoned up the strength to escape his father's domination and leave, the separation was only physical. He still was not able to take his father out of his quality world. He suffered unbearable pain over the conflict between his need for his father and his need for the freedom to pursue the piano.

Finally, to escape from this painful conflict, to find the personal freedom he needed so badly, he chose to turn his life over to his creative system, not an unusual choice for a talented person such as Helfgott who is already well in touch with this system.

I believe that Helfgott's choice to give up playing the piano by choosing to become psychotic was his final resistance to his father's insistence that he could not have his love unless he was willing to be the musician his father wanted him to be. But after ten years—time does heal some wounds—he felt free enough to return to the piano. Shortly afterward, he was fortunate enough to meet his wife and, with her love, he has come back as far as he has.

Because of well-intended but brain-damaging electric convulsive treatments Helfgott was given during his psychosis, he may never regain the creative artistry he once had. But we should not underestimate the ability of our creative systems to work around brain damage. He still jabbers, he still needs that protection his creative system gave him, but he is no longer psychotic. He is criticized unfairly for not being as normal as some righteous critics think he ought to be to perform. But he has triumphed over a lot of adversity, and the audiences enjoy seeing how far he has come back.

Now that he is happily married, he may finally be close to taking his father out of his quality world, as was depicted in one of the last scenes in the movie. While visiting his father's grave, his wife asks him what he feels. Helfgott answers, "I feel nothing." Even that answer does not mean he has taken his father out of his quality world. It may mean that with the love of his wife, he is finally able to deal with the father who may always be there and retain his sanity. The healing potential of finally satisfying his need for love, without believing he has to satisfy anyone else's conditions to get that love, is equally clear.

Many abused or neglected children are in similar situations. They are stuck with the pictures of their abusive or neglectful parents in their quality worlds. Because of the abuse or the neglect, when they are young, they are too weak and frightened to do much but suffer. As they grow older and separate from the weak relationship they had with a parent, many of them are too distrustful of people to consider trying to find happiness in human relationships. They now have no one, not even their parents, in their quality worlds. But they want to feel good—*we all want to feel good*—so many of them pursue what is available to them, the pleasures associated with violence and drugs. Study after study has shown that prisons are filled with people who were abused or neglected as children.

For many of these children, the only people besides their mothers and gang members whom they could relate to are their teachers. But the external control system that dominates our schools deprives many of these needy young people of this opportunity. It is also sad that many teachers who try to care for these children are criticized and ridiculed by the external control system that dominates our schools. The educational message of our existing schools, *Learn what we tell you whether it is useful or not or we'll punish you,* compounds this problem, a problem that only the schools have any chance to solve. I explain this situation in more detail in the next chapter.

Huge numbers of people are not willing to settle for lives with no happiness. They are not willing to give up on people or turn their lives over to the search for pleasure without happiness.

Many of these unhappy people want very much to find others to love, but because of the reality of their life situations—they are poor, old, uneducated, unattractive, workless, homeless, sick, or criminal, the list is long—they are unable to.

There may be an answer to the poignant question posed by the Beatles: *All the lonely people, where do they all come from?* They come from a world in which they are separated from their husbands, wives, children, teachers, and employers by this destructive psychology.

I will now explain how we may prevent many of these relationship problems by applying choice theory to families and, especially, to rearing children. As I stated earlier, by far our best chance for good relationships for our whole lives is with our families. If we could get rid of the urge to control, our families would be much stronger than they are now.

CHOICE THEORY, FAMILIES, AND REARING CHILDREN

Child abuse, rejection, and neglect, widespread as they are, are far from the main reason families are unhappy. The vast majority of family unhappiness is the result of well-intentioned parents trying to make children do what they don't want to do. And in search of freedom, children, often adult children, resist their parents' efforts. Much later, the same conflict is commonly revisited when adult children try to make elderly parents do what they don't want to do, such as give up driving, move in with a child, or move to a place where they can have the care they need.

What makes these struggles so much more miserable than marital or nonfamily conflicts is that parents and children are stuck in each other's quality worlds forever. I have no good answer for what to do with elderly parents; there may be no answer to this problem. But the better the elderly and their children get along together while the parents are still able to take care of themselves, the later this problem may occur.

I can hear parents of school-age children saying, *Are we sup-posed to abdicate our responsibility as parents? Let our children do anything they want to do?* Of course not. When we deal with children, we have to learn our limitations and do as much as we can do within these limitations. To try to do more results in ac-complishing less. What bothers people, especially parents, is that choice theory, which states that we can control only our own be-havior, imposes such strict limitations on what we can do when we want children, or anyone else, to behave differently. This limi-tation does not change when we deal with children who are using drugs, failing in school, or being sexually promiscuous any more than it changes when our mothers or fathers become alcoholics, start running around, or keep losing jobs.

This limitation needs to be repeated because it is so hard for people, especially parents, to accept how limited they are in what they can do when they are dissatisfied with how their children are behaving. *They are limited to controlling their own behavior. All they can give to other people, including their children, parents, and mates, is information.* This information may be threats, bribes, beatings, and incarceration, but it is still information. Short of extreme measures, such as incarcerating an uncontrol-lable child, there is nothing that external control psychology can offer to this problem. Since this psychology is all we have, it is no wonder that many of these problems seem insoluble.

Few of us are prepared to accept that it is our attempts to con-trol that destroys the only thing we have with our children that gives us some control over them, our relationship. The choice the-ory child-rearing axiom is this: *Don't choose to do anything with a child whom you want to grow up to be happy, successful, and close to you, that you believe will increase the distance between you.* It is all but impossible for controlling people to accept that axiom when it means don't criticize, threaten, complain, put down, punish, or bribe anyone, including your children, with whom you want to stay close.

In fact, this axiom goes way beyond children. It applies to all relationships and is the core of beginning to use choice theory in your life: *Do not do anything with anyone if it seems to increase the distance between you.* Unsatisfying as it may be, doing less may be the best thing to do. Here again, prevention, which means keeping a failing relationship going, may be much better than anything else you can do. Children grow up, and what was once a poor relationship often gets better. But if there is too much of a split, it may get better but never get to the place either child or parent wants.

To illustrate what I mean, let me show you how I counseled a forty-five-year-old divorced woman. As you read what I did, try to put yourself in the place of the client. Her name is Linda, and I'll start when she sat down in my office.

"You mentioned on the phone you were having some difficulties. Can you tell me a little more about what's going on?"

"Well, actually, my doctor sent me. I've been having these terrible tension headaches, you know, the kind that go up the back of your neck and throb in your forehead. I thought I had a brain tumor."

"I'm sure your doctor gave you a thorough checkup, CAT scan, the whole nine yards."

"That's right, he found nothing physical. So he said I was probably suffering from stress and recommended that I come to see you. If I seem skeptical, it's because I don't think that kind of pain could be caused by stress, whatever that is."

"Well, whatever we do, it has no chance of making things worse, so please go back to see your doctor or to another doctor if what we discuss doesn't help you."

I always say this to people who are sent by a physician for any reason. It reassures them that I don't think they are crazy or that their doctor is necessarily right. I try to come across as someone who will help and, more important, as someone who will listen to what they have to say. Many physicians today, trapped in the demands of managed care, haven't the time to do so.

"The way I look at it, stress is very simple. It occurs when something in your life is not the way you want it to be. From my experience, it is most often attached to an unsatisfying relationship. Is there anyone in particular who isn't doing what you would like him or her to do?"

"Well, for years it was my husband, but four years ago I had the sense to call that marriage quits, so it's not him. I'm very happy with all the people I work with. I had a lousy boss for five years and he drove me up the wall, but my new boss is a doll. If I was going to have stress headaches, I should have had them then. I got rid of that boss and my husband the same year. I sure felt better after that, but these headaches are new, really only for this past year."

"Do you have any children at home, teenagers?"

"Yes, Samantha; she's sixteen going on seventeen, and she's a handful."

"Girls that age can be. How do you and she get along most of the time?"

"Frankly, it's got to the point where I can't stand the sight of her. She's the most irritating, nasty-mouthed human being I've ever encountered in my life. I'm sick of her."

"I think she's worth talking about. Tell me a little more about what's going on with her?"

"Well, she never does anything I tell her. And when I complain about it, she just rolls her eyes and gives me the silent treatment. She spends most of her time in her room with the door locked on the phone or listening to that music. Thank God, it's a solid door, but the vibrations shake the house."

It's Samantha, but what makes it so hard is that Samantha, for all Linda's protests, is still in Linda's quality world and Linda is in hers. Linda didn't get the headaches with the husband or the lousy boss because she was able to take them out. No such luck with Samantha; she's in it for good. And because Samantha is there, Linda hesitated to tell me about her. I had to probe a little more than what I've written here.

"I'm pretty sure that Samantha may be the problem. Are you willing to talk about your relationship with her?"

"Yes, I've got to talk to someone. Do you think you could help me with her? I'd about gotten to the point where I thought it was hopeless. It's only two more years before she goes away to college. Thank God, she's doing well enough in school for that."

"I don't think you're going to be able to last another year like this, and I'm sure I can help you. But I need you to tell me something more specific. It's more than her locking her door and talking on the phone. You could live with that. It's got to be something else, something that brings you more in contact with her and that goes on all the time that you feel is driving you up the wall."

"OK, I'm a fastidious person. I work in a bank where everything has to be just right. I'm damn good at my job, and I make a pretty good salary. And I'm sure you can guess the rest."

"Maybe I could, but it will save time if you tell me."

"I come home from work and I like to have a clean kitchen before I start to get dinner together. All I ask is that she cleans up the kitchen before I get home at five thirty. That's all; it's not that much—ten, twelve minutes—is that too much to ask? I don't mind making dinner; I even set the table because I like it done right. She helps me wash up after dinner, but it's that dirty kitchen, just a few dishes from breakfast and a few things from snacks the night before and after school. She starts snacking as soon as she gets home; it's almost all her mess. I see it when I walk in the door, every goddamned day. Pardon my French, but it drives me crazy."

"That doesn't sound like much to ask. I can't understand why you're having so much trouble with her over this."

"Well, she used to do it, but she was so sloppy I had to do it over myself. I kept telling her, 'If you can't do it right, don't do it at all,' and about two months ago she just stopped. When I come in, she doesn't say anything but she gives me that *It's your house, if you don't like the way I do it, do it yourself* look. See, that's what I have to put up with, her horrible attitude. It's awful."

"Tell me, what do you do or say when you come in after work and see the kitchen's a mess? I gather it's been the same for months."

"Before I even come in the door I start to tense up."

"And your head, does it start to hurt?"

"Not right away, but I know I'm in for one later on. When I

walk in, I get so angry seeing her lounging on the sofa watching her soaps. She has them all recorded. She can do that, but she can't help me. I think I'm beginning to hate my own daughter."

The angering when she comes home prevents the headaches. The headaches come a little later when she realizes that the angering doesn't work, and they prevent her from increasing the angering into rage and violence. The headaches also prevent her from depressing, which would have an adverse affect on the best part of her life, her work.

"Before that, when she was younger, did you get along pretty well with her then?"

"Pretty well, except there was a little trouble when her father left us. She was twelve. He never disciplined her; whatever his darling daughter did and still does is fine with him. I think he enjoys seeing me so frustrated. But I've got to give her some credit. During the divorce, she was a great support to me. Once she saw him for what he was, she took my side and still does."

"Does she see him very often?"

"Every couple of weeks he picks her up and takes her out to eat. The only good thing I'll still say about her is she won't go to his house. She hates the woman he's living with."

"I don't think what's going on has anything to do with her father. I'd like you to tell me what you do when you come in and see her on the sofa watching the soaps. This is important, tell me exactly."

"She's got to learn to be responsible. I know what I'm talking about. I'm successful because I'm a very responsible person. I've got to teach her some responsibility; it's my job as her mother. God knows she'll never learn it from her father."

"So?"

"I yell at her. I threaten her, I've grounded her, I've cut her allowance."

"All over a few dishes?"

"No, it's not just the dishes. Like I told you, it's her nasty attitude. The world owes her a living. It's all about her, nothing for me. The dishes are just a symptom but they're a goddamned annoying symptom. But last week the worst happened. I got so furious with her nasty mouth that I slapped her in the face. And you know what she did? She slapped me back. OK, she said she was sorry and we cried and hugged, but it was awful. She hasn't really spoken to me since. Her hugging me, it was as if she felt sorry for me, can you believe that? That night I had the worst headache I've had yet."

This account confirms what I suspected: Linda is close to rage and violence. She needs the headaches to keep any semblance of control. This is serious, but there's a lot of hope. Samantha wants to get close to her mother, that was obvious in what her mother said, "It's as if she feels sorry for me." But Samantha doesn't know what to do. Linda's doing everything wrong and thinks she is doing everything right. The third belief of external control psychology, *It's my obligation as a mother to do what I'm doing,* is driving her behavior. But the slapping, she knows that was wrong. I'll deal with that.

"That slapping bit, it sounds like you don't want to do it again, do you?"

"No, it was frightening, I was out of control. I guess I do need help. Can you help me?"

"Are you willing to listen very seriously to me? I am going to ask you to do something that you're going to find very hard to do."

"What?"

"If nothing you do when you get home seems to work, I'd like to make a suggestion. Stop doing it, just stop."

"What do you mean just stop? She's the problem, not me."

"She's not the problem, and you're not the problem. The problem is your relationship. Do you understand what I'm trying to tell you?"

"But if she'd just clean up the kitchen, we'd have a good relationship. That's all I ask."

She's having trouble with the relationship concept, but I'll keep working on it.

"OK, fine. What do you think she'd say if she was here and I asked her what was wrong with your relationship? She's not happy with it either."

"She'd say I should get off her back. She says that almost every day. But I can't get off her back; I'm not a stranger, I'm her mother."

"When you work, have you ever had a good customer who was a grade A pain in the neck?"

"What has this got to do with me and my daughter?"

"Well Samantha's a grade A pain in the neck, isn't she?"

When I counsel, I often try to show that being right is not very effective if you don't have the power. Linda doesn't have power over her daughter, but she thinks she has. She knows she doesn't have power over a good customer. That's a difference that may make sense to her.

"What do you do with a customer who's a big pain?"

"The customer is important."

"Is he more important than your daughter?"

"My God, my God, what am I saying, that girl is all I have. . . ."

Linda burst into tears. Most people get kind of a jolt when they realize that the psychology they have been using for years is destroying an important relationship, and that comparison with the customer gave her a jolt. These tears have been a long time coming. They are better than the headaches. That crying is going to do a lot for her headaches.

"When you go home today and step into the room with her, pretend she isn't your daughter; pretend she's a good friend and the kitchen is clean. What would you like to do?"

"I'd like to pour myself a glass of chardonnay, sit down with her and watch the TV. And as Samantha would say, chill out."

"Could you do this today with Samantha?"

"I can't. She . . . "

"Why can't you?"

"Of course I can, but she's going to think I've lost my mind."

"So what? I'm sure she's been hoping for a long time that you'd lose your mind. Today is a good day to do it. The mind you've been holding onto hasn't seemed to have done you much good with her. C'mon Linda, you know what I'm talking about. Part of you has known it for months. Just sit down quietly beside her—no yelling, no criticizing, no complaining—and relax with her."

"How long am I supposed to do this?"

"Could you do it for three days?"

"And just let the dishes go?"

"No, no, you won't let them go; you'll get up and do them just like you always do, but you won't have gone through all you go through now. The house will be quiet, she'll be quiet, you'll be quiet."

"Am I supposed to do this for two years until she leaves home?"

"No, I just said for three days."

"Then what?"

"I don't know. What might you say to her if you and she were sitting quietly together that might be better than what you've been saying?"

"Well, I guess I could ask her how her day went, try to be a little more friendly."

"What if she asks you why you've stopped yelling. What will you tell her? Better yet, what would you like to tell her?"

"I'd like to tell her I've screamed my last scream."

"Would you be willing to tell her that if she doesn't ask?"

"I'd like to tell her it hasn't worked and I'm going to stop doing it forever. But I don't think I'll be able to do that."

"How about for three days?"

"OK, I can handle three days."

"After watching TV for half an hour with her, get up and tell her, 'I'm going to get dinner.' Don't ask her to help. Do the dishes and then start dinner."

"But that's not fair. I do all the work, and she does nothing. What do I get out of it?"

"If life was fair, there'd be no need for counselors. I'm sorry, that's a good question, What do you get out of it? Let me put the question this way, What do you really want with your daughter?"

"I want us to be like we were a few years ago; we were best friends."

"Look, you are a very intelligent woman, and you do a hard job well. I don't think the dishes are what you're really worried about. They are an aggravation, but you're really worried about something a lot more important than dishes."

"She never tells me anything. She stays in her room, talking on the phone to that boy. . . ."

"She has a boyfriend? Are you worried about what she may be doing or thinking of doing with him?"

"I'm worried sick about it."

"Would you be less worried if you were getting along better with her than you are now?"

"Of course. But I'd still be worried."

"Let's get back to the dishes. What if tomorrow or the next day she got up when you got up and helped you? She may, especially if you do what you say you are going to do for three days."

"What if she doesn't?"

"During the three days you're quiet on the sofa with her watching TV, are you willing to do what we talked about a little while ago, tell her you're through yelling for good? I don't think you're stalled on the screaming road."

"If you believe it'll make a difference, I'll tell her."

"If it were you with your mother, do you think it would have made a difference with you? Were you totally different with your mother than your daughter is with you?"

"No, my mother says I got the daughter I deserve. But you're right, it would've made a difference with me."

"If she doesn't make a move to help you, let things go until the fourth day and then say, 'Samantha, how about giving me a hand in the kitchen and then I'll make dinner.' If she doesn't come, don't say anything. Don't say anything for a week. But I think she'll come if you say it in a nice way. Nothing like, 'You should have done this without my asking' or 'It's about time.' You know what I mean, the way you talk to good customers at the bank, friendly, no pressure."

"It's the relationship, isn't it?"

It takes people like Linda a while to realize how important the relationship really is. I'll have to keep finding ways to remind her.

"That's all you've got going for you, but it's a lot. She's desperate to get close to you. Give her a chance; give her some time."

"She hasn't acted like she wants to get close to me. The way she's been, it seems just the opposite."

"But you're going to be different, very different. She'll notice it tonight, you'll see."

"OK, what I've been doing hasn't done much good. I'm willing to let it go. Now what?"

"Now I'd like to get back to her boyfriend. Do you know anything about him?"

"All I know is he's on the basketball team and he comes from a nice family. But she never brings him home."

"And you're worried they might become involved sexually?"

"Yes, I'm worried sick about it. I've preached till I'm blue in the face. She used to tell me everything, and now she won't talk to me."

"Would you like to go out with her and the boy, sit in her ear where he couldn't see you, and give her advice if you think she needed it? I mean be there but be invisible? Only she could hear you?"

"Now you're getting silly. No one could arrange that."

"No one has to arrange it. It's already arranged. You're actually in her head right now, just like she's in yours. The only thing is, she isn't listening to you very much; you know that. If you can get closer to her, she'll listen to you again like she used to."

"I hope it isn't too late."

"I don't think it's too late. It's never too late to get close to a child."

"I've been missing what's most important, haven't I?"

"Come back next week, and let's see what happened. I don't think you've done any real harm; she hasn't been that easy either. But this way may work; let's see. During this week, I want you to think about it. Not only with Samantha but with all the people in your life—your boss, your mother, your ex, everyone you have anything to do with: *Whose behavior can you control?* We'll talk again next week. If you want to talk to me during the week, call me and I'll get back to you."

That session got things well started. I didn't hear from Linda during the week. Samantha did the dishes for a few days and then stopped for a day. Testing. Linda didn't take the bait; she did the dishes herself without saying anything. Samantha has now done them again for two days, and Linda plans never to say anything about the dishes again. Linda and I talked, and I spent some time introducing her to choice theory. She said that she is going to do everything she can to get close to Samantha and she could already see how much closer they were just this week.

About a month later, Linda told me the following. Samantha wanted to talk with Linda about her boyfriend. He is putting pressure on her for sex, and they have come close to doing it. Linda didn't respond with horror. She just asked Samantha calmly if she wanted some birth control pills, but Samantha said no. Samantha told Linda that her boyfriend carries a condom with him and has promised to use it. Linda told her it could be a bad experience at her age unless she is deeply in love, and Samantha said she's not. It's just that a lot of her friends are doing it with their boyfriends and she's curious.

I told Linda that's all she can do, and I complimented her on handling the situation so well. What she said has brought them closer, and that's the best thing for Samantha as she struggles with her own and her boyfriend's hormones. Early sex is part of today's culture. Whatever Samantha does, it is better for her that she and her mother are now talking and that Linda has stopped preaching, criticizing, and controlling.

CHOICE THEORY CHILD REARING

Using this session as a guideline, I would like to try to explain how to rear a child using choice theory. As I look back, I think I learned a great deal about choice theory from my experience with my children. Both my late wife, Naomi, and I did not know any choice theory until our three children finished college. We almost always agreed on what to do with them, so we didn't cast any blame on each other for the lives they have chosen to live. We used very little punishment in our child rearing and never had any of the usual problems with them that many parents have. They were never rebellious, and we all got along well. Our children had many friends who were always welcome at our house, and almost all their friends are successful and productive adults. For a hint of how to use choice theory with children, you might watch how grandparents behave with their grandchildren. We all seem pretty good at that job.

I am well aware that many people will disagree with what I am going to say. Just as there is a great deal of chance in marriage, there is no foolproof way to rear a child or to get along with every member of a family. If you try what I suggest and it seems not to work, I may be wrong. But there is also the possibility that you may be more committed to external control psychology than you realize.

Choice theory is much more effective when it is used to prevent problems than to solve them. If you look honestly at the lives of the people you know who have long-standing relationship problems or at your own, you will see that few of us are able to come up with a good solution to any of these problems. In most instances, the problems drag on and are never really solved. Eventually, we learn to live in unhappy marriages by expecting less and less from the relationships. I believe that we do the same thing with children. We deal with our disappointment not by rejecting them, but by expecting less from them and they from us.

The biggest concern of most parents is the future of their children: Will they lead happy and successful lives? To me, what is equally important is, Will they like to spend time with us and we with them? If they are happy and like spending time with us, as parents we are well satisfied. Most of us do not aspire for our children to be extraordinary; we seem to know enough choice theory to realize that beyond a certain point there is nothing we can do to push our children to the top in any endeavor. We can help and support, but much of what children ultimately become is not within our control.

Following the third belief of external control psychology, *We know what's right for our children*, most of us reward and punish to attempt to get our children to do what we believe is right. We can keep doing so until we have destroyed our relationships with them without succeeding in getting them to where we want them to be. Even if our children become successful and do what we think is right, we may, in our zeal to push them to where we want them to go, lose the closeness that most of us want. Some people say that as long as their children lead the lives they want them to lead, the closeness doesn't matter. I don't accept this belief at all. To be unable to share success is unsatisfying to both parents and children.

I can explain only the basics of choice theory child rearing: a lot of love and no punishment. I have no day-by-day prescription for what you should do if the child is way out of order, but sending a young child who is acting up to her room or a calm-down chair, with a minimum of yelling, is usually effective and does not harm the relationship. When you send her, use the admonition, "When you feel calm, come out. I'd like to talk to you about what happened and see if we can help it from happening again, but if you don't want to talk, that's OK. I'll settle for you just calming down." And when she comes out, do something enjoyable with her that tells her it's over, no hard feelings.

Creativity is at the heart of any good relationship. Do things that are unexpected. With very young children who are carrying on, I fake crying and carrying on. They are so amazed that they start to laugh or come over and comfort me, and I tell them how much I appreciate it. They often forget what they wanted or what they were doing, and I don't remind them. Sometimes when they are about to cry, I teach a little choice theory and say, "You can cry now or a little later, which do you want to do?" They learn that whining and crying is a choice and maybe not such a good choice for them. It does give them something to think about: They can choose not to cry if they want to.

As a choice theory parent, it is helpful if you teach children a little choice theory directly. Explain the needs and the quality world first and total behavior later. Children as young as five years old are now taught this theory in some of our schools that are trying to become quality schools, and it certainly can be done at home. Material to do so is described in the appendix of this book.* Teenagers can read sections of this book and easily learn from it. They will be especially interested if you tell them that much of what you are trying to do with them is taken from this book.

As far as love goes, don't connect love with any specific behavior. Make it clear that you love your children no matter what they do, but be candid that if they are totally out of order, loving them isn't easy. The best way you can communicate that you love your children is always to be open to talking and listening. With this openness, you have a right to express your opinions and should

---

*Many years ago I created a drug abuse prevention program, called the Choice Program, that is suitable for children aged ten to fifteen. It includes a videotape of a cartoon that the children watch and a workbook that they fill out afterward. There is also a parent component in which the child teaches the parent the choice theory he or she is learning. In those days I called the theory control theory, a name I later abandoned because it was misleading. But the material is accurate; all you have to do is explain the name change to the child. This is good material for a school, church, or youth organization. It was used with over 100,000 students and worked very well. I am selling this material at my cost. You get a videotape, two booklets, and a teacher's guide. You can copy all I send you and use it over or share it with anyone you want.

Carleen, my wife, has a booklet, *My Quality World Workbook*, to teach choice theory to children who read at the third-grade level. She also has *The Quality World Activity Set* for teachers and others who work with children who read at the fifth-grade level. All this material and all my books and other materials are available through the William Glasser Institute. See the appendix for information about the institute.

feel free to tell them if you disagree with what they are doing or intend to do. But don't harp on what they are doing over and over. When you disagree, expressing yourself twice is usually enough. Things get much more difficult, however, when your children want you to support what you disagree with.

For example, your daughter wants to change colleges to follow a young man she is in love with. You don't agree. What do you do? There is no good answer. If you have a strong relationship with her, it probably won't make much difference. It is up to you to judge whether what you do or don't do will keep you from separating farther from her. Your obvious disagreement has already precluded your getting closer; what you don't want is to get further apart.

Ask yourself, if I do or say this, will we be closer or farther apart? Tell her that whatever each of you does, you don't want to be farther apart after this incident than you are now. Explain why and ask for her help. This is the child-parent solving circle that is comparable to the circle used in marriage. Teach it to your children as soon as you believe they are ready to learn it. And teach it at a time when you are getting along well, so you can use it later when there is a problem.

In or out of the child-parent circle, the best thing to do with the daughter who wants to change colleges is to lay your cards on the table and tell her why you disagree and tell her you find it difficult to support what she is going to do because you fear she will be hurt. But also tell her that your relationship with her is more important than anything else and ask her how both of you can work out what to do that will keep the good relationship you have. Her chances of doing anything that will ruin her life are much less if you do so. But keep in mind that when romantic love is involved, no one can tell anyone what to do. Choice theory says strongly, *Do what you can to keep close to her. The relationship takes precedence over always being "right."*

When you deal with a child, offering advice is better than barking out instructions. Keeping as close to him as you can without getting deeply involved in his future is probably as good as offering much advice. If you offer advice, don't repeat yourself or nag. It is almost certain he heard you the first time and knew what you wanted him to do before you gave him your advice. Don't rake up the past if what he has done previously has not been successful. What's done is done; to keep this failure alive is divisive.

Going over past successes, however, is an excellent idea. It takes a long time before any of us get tired of hearing that we have done a good job. When the child is very young, try to establish the idea that, in time, most mistakes can be corrected or lived with. Very little is so bad that it can never be corrected or let be. Present yourself as always being ready to help but not ready to do it for him. One serious mistake I made with my oldest son was to intervene too fast and do too much to try to help. Love them, but let them flounder when they are young when floundering doesn't carry the penalties it may later on.

The basis of a choice theory relationship is to establish trust. Parents can't start too early to behave in a way that encourages their children to trust them. Establishing trust means that there is nothing the children can say or do that will persuade you to reject them. Later, when they are teenagers, it gets much more difficult to do, but it is always best never to reject your children. This does not mean you support what you disagree with. There is a big difference between not rejecting and not supporting, and children easily understand that difference and your position if you are close.

As I explained, parents are in their children's quality worlds, which means the children either trust their parents or want to trust them. Children keep parents they do not trust in their quality worlds because there is no one to replace the parents. And as long as parents are there, children want to trust them. When a child no longer wants to trust a parent, it's as if the parent has become an inactive member of his quality world community. You are there, he may even enjoy your company, but he does not trust you. The only way you can regain his trust is to spend some time talking with and listening to him and moving toward each other in the process.

When you are dealing with a child who you do not believe trusts you and you make a mistake, be quick to admit it. You don't expect him to be perfect, and you are not perfect either. The admission that mistakes are possible builds or rebuilds trust. Parents who are the first to admit a mistake are seen by their children as much more trustworthy than are parents who are *always right* and have a hard time admitting they are wrong. Children need to trust their parents. If they can't, they are living on quicksand.

Choice theory parents begin to teach their children by three years of age that they have to be willing to take responsibility for what they choose. But taking responsibility does not mean being punished. Sending them to their rooms is the maximum you should need for control. There is no punishment in a choice theory upbringing. Punishment is external control psychology to the core—an imposed consequence that always increases the distance between parents and children. Almost all punished children spend time and effort to avoid or resist punishment, time and energy that could be spent learning how to expand their lives and satisfy their needs. Punished children tend to contract their lives, to concentrate on evading responsibility rather than accepting it. Children should not be made to suffer any more than the natural consequences of what they chose to do.

For example, if your son is consistently late for dinner, he should still get dinner, but it may be cold and some of it may be gone. He may even have to fix something for himself, but he should not go hungry unless he is too lazy to get some food. If you believe that punishment solves problems, try doing without it. You will see that with a little conversation and guidance, your children will solve their own problems. Or they will accept your solution, not because you can punish but because they trust you. This way you don't risk harming the all-important relationship.

Instead of punishment, the choice theory parent continually sends the message: *I want you to learn from your mistakes. My job, if either of us is dissatisfied with what you chose to do, is to get together and help you to figure out a better way.* There is almost always a better way. I will, however, step in and stop you when I believe you are too young to know what you are getting into, but my focus will not be on stopping you. It will be on letting you learn before you do something that you may regret. Here trust is all-important; if your child trusts you, he will listen to you.

Many parents struggle with their children over bedtime, and up to four years do the best you can without punishment. But when the child is older than four and still doesn't want to go to bed, you can use this situation as an opportunity to teach him a valuable lesson in personal freedom. As soon as you believe that he is safe to leave up around the house, tell him that you trust him to figure out how much sleep he needs. This statement sends the message that you are not rigid or always right and are more than willing to give him a chance to do what he wants as long as he doesn't hurt himself or anyone else.

After the hour that you feel he ought to be in bed, tell him it's bedtime but that he doesn't have to go. He can stay up as late as he wants, but he can't have any more attention from you or anyone else who is up. He is on his own. He can play or, if the television is not in use, watch it with the sound turned down low. When you, the parents, go to bed, close your door and tell him that he can't bother you anymore or anyone else who is up. If he bothers anyone, you will put him to bed even if it takes a big fight. But since he thinks he is getting away with something, there will be few fights. Tell him that you will get him up for school and expect him to go even if he is tired. If he falls asleep in school, don't worry about it; his admission to college is not in danger.

This is the time to begin to teach responsibility, not later when your child is a teenager and there are some real opportunities for him to get hurt. If you struggle over bedtime, you waste a lot of effort that could go into teaching your child that whenever there is a choice in which no one can be harmed, you will give him the freedom to choose. When a child goes to bed harms no one else. If he's too cranky to have fun the next day or to do his schoolwork, he'll learn to go to bed earlier. That you and he are not adversaries makes it possible for you to give him some advice and likely that he'll listen. All through early childhood, look for these opportunities. In most cases, letting him choose his bedtime works out fine. It gives him the chance to take care of himself in a safe situation and not depend on anyone else.

Talk with him about how things are working out now that bedtime is up to him. Ask him if there are other things he could do to take care of himself and tell him that you will try to go along with what he wants. Tell him you hate fighting and arguing and that you appreciate that he is taking care of something you used to argue a lot about. Never tell him, *I told you so* if he tells you that he needs to go to bed early; just say bedtime is up to him, early or late.

This approach changes the relationship. You are not the automatic, *my way or the highway* person many children believe their parents are. Your child learns that you don't impose rules for the sake of rules or because other people do things a certain way. You are his partner as well as his parent, and you want to give him as much freedom to choose what he does that you believe he can handle. But if you don't think he is ready to handle a situation, your way will prevail until you think he's ready. And you are always open to talking it over to try to find out when this is. There are no automatic or nonthinking no's in a choice theory upbringing, and you are not going to fight or argue anymore. That's not the way you want to relate to him.

Now here is an example of when you don't think a child is ready to make a decision; a time when it has to be your way. Your eight-year-old daughter refuses to go to school, and reacts with a great deal of hysteria when you try to get her to go. You have not been a choice theory parent, but up to now there was no reason to worry about her upbringing. She has been given a lot of love, and this school problem comes as a surprise. She had always been a little resistant to school, but this much resistance is new. When you talk with the principal, she tells you just to get your daughter to school and the school will deal with her. The principal has seen this behavior before and believes that the child will calm down as soon as she realizes this situation is not negotiable. Still, you are concerned. The idea of using force does not sit well with you.

But now as you are learning to become a choice theory parent, you tell her that going to school is not a choice. It's what all children, including her, do. You do it with love and concern, but you are careful to do it in a way that the child gets the clear message that this is not a negotiable situation. You are good parents, you love her, and this situation is very difficult; her hysteria seems so genuine. But the longer you allow her to control you with hysteria, the harder it will be to convince her that school attendance is not a choice.

If you had been a choice theory parent, then she would know that you are flexible in many situations. You have, however, gotten along well with her. She knows you love her, and you must be ready to act firmly in this nonnegotiable situation. No matter how much she cries, bodily take her to school, give her a kiss, and drop her off. You will have alerted the school that you are going to do so, and the staff can deal with her in any reasonable way, but you are willing for her to cry all day if she wishes. Once she sees you mean it, she will not cry very long. The trust that you have built will pay off. You may never find out what was wrong or she may tell you, but either way this is the way to handle this problem. Stand firm, without threats and punishment, when you believe it's necessary. Be flexible as often as you can.

Eating is another hang-up for parents who know *what's right* and punish to enforce it. Rather than get stuck in this easily lost battle, this is a good chance to be flexible. Your daughter who is not malnourished eats only a few foods. If it is convenient, give her those foods and say nothing. If it is inconvenient, give her what you are making for everyone else and that's it. Say nothing if she picks out what she wants from her plate and leaves the rest. The clean-plate club is one of our charter external control organizations. If she is willing to prepare her own food, let her do it. That's all. No arguments, no coaxing, no cajoling. No telling her "I told you so" when she eats the food or terrible concern if she doesn't. She is not going to starve. If you make too much of a fuss over food when she is young, you may be setting yourself up for dealing with anorexia later.

Choice theory says that all I can give you in this book is information, and this is what I've done. Nothing I have said takes precedence over you using your own judgment. Enforce what you think is worth enforcing, but try to do so as little as possible. Let the rest go. Don't protect your children from minor problems or try to get them to do it your way when it doesn't really matter. In this way they will learn from experience, one of the world's greatest teachers, what's smart and what's stupid. They will also learn that you are not rigid or overly opinionated, that you don't care very much about many things their friends' parents care a lot about. But they will also learn at an early age that when you do care, you will hold the line no matter how much they protest.

When they were young, you managed fine with giving them control over their bedtime and with what they ate and wore. A little later, things you cared a lot about like school, health, and safety were not negotiable. But by beginning to let them choose many things most children don't get to decide on, you are teaching them the value of negotiation because by the preteen years, much of what they want can only be negotiated. You can't physically control them as you could when they were young. You can ground them, but grounding them is difficult to enforce and you risk weakening your position in their quality worlds if you are too strict. Now, more than ever, you need to have a strong presence in their quality worlds. They can get into a lot of trouble during the hours you can't ground them, such as before and after school.

Whether you like it or not, you have no control over what your children choose to do when they are on their own. Drugs, sex, alcohol, and crime are all available, and the only thing that may keep them from these destructive behaviors is your picture, front and center, in their quality worlds. It is not just being there; you are almost always there. It is how strongly you are there that will have a lot to do with the choices they make on their own. Your willingness to negotiate most of the time, plus the fact that you have done a lot of negotiating during the years you could have been coercive, keeps you and what you believe alive in your children's quality worlds. Start to teach them to negotiate as soon as possible by doing it.

Your son is nine years old and wants a dog. You don't particularly want a dog, but you agree that this is a reasonable request at his age and you don't want to be arbitrary. When he asked at age six, you said that he had to wait until he was nine, and he waited. This shows he respects your judgment. But he will lose this respect if you don't show that you respect his judgment. At nine, he is old enough to learn to negotiate, which means that you will work out how much he is willing to do to take care of the dog. The best way to start this, and all negotiations like it, is to talk to him a lot about the dog and to show enthusiasm for his request. If the request is reasonable, avoid being a wet blanket. If you really don't want a dog in the house, hold the line. It's easier to be firm in the beginning than to vacillate, postpone, and then get tough later.

Discuss the breed, the size, whether it should be a puppy or a housebroken dog and have long hair or short hair, its temperament, and the cost. Encourage him to read a lot about dogs, which is also a good way for him to appreciate how useful reading is. If you are in a large city, go through the classified ads with him, especially those about adopting a good free dog. Take him to visit some dogs. Make a big deal about it; it's a way to get close and sets up the negotiation. As you do so, talk to him about the care of the dog, how much he will do and how much you will do. He is only nine, so you should not expect too much, but walking and feeding the dog are reasonable tasks.

If you are in a city, explain why a pooper scooper is needed and how to use it. I would not ask him to clean up after a puppy inside the house; that may be too much for him, and housebreaking is only a short period anyway. You may both decide that getting a dog that is already trained may be a good idea for a first dog. Try to get him the dog he wants, not the one you want or wanted as a child.

Keep in mind that teenagers need a lot of love. Certainly as much as younger children, who have less potential for trouble than teenagers. We tend to forget that fact and treat them as grown-ups, but they are not grown-ups. It takes a lot of creativity to love teenagers enough so that they will listen to you even if they don't agree and still keep you strongly in their quality worlds. Don't wait for trouble. Anticipate it by talking, laughing, and doing things with your teenagers. All this is a savings account, which you can draw from later when there are serious disagreements.

If a husband and a wife have formed a circle and extended it to the parent-child circle, it is natural to extend it further into a family solving circle. If you look at families who get along well, you see this circle in action. The family joins together as a supportive unit to help each other deal with whatever comes along. Members of external control families tend to blame each other when there is a problem. Each knows what is right for himself or herself but rarely thinks of what's right for the family. Trust keeps the circle strong. As long as you and your children are in that circle, whether you are together or apart, you have the best chance for happiness.

DEALING WITH ABUSED CHILDREN OR ADULTS WHO WERE ABUSED AS CHILDREN

If the abuse is currently going on, we must do all we can to stop it, which usually means taking the child out of the abusive situation. But often, when the abuse is found out, it has already stopped. The child, however, still needs help to deal with what happened. Even more often, the abuse is never reported and stops sometime during childhood but surfaces later as the possible cause of an adult problem. The abuse can be physical, but nonsexual, as when the child is beaten. It can be psychological, such as being reared in a torrent of threats, criticism, and blame alternating with neglect. Or it can be sexual, which is mostly physical but also psychological. Most often it is some combination of all three.

Abused children are usually damaged by one or more of the

people taking care of them. Natural parents, stepparents, grand-parents, uncles, cousins, foster parents, even neighbors, someone the child tends to trust, are most often responsible for this injury. The conventional wisdom is that an abused child, especially a sex-ually abused child, will never be able to deal with what has hap-pened unless he or she is made aware of it and, perhaps, goes so far as to confront the person who did it. It is believed that the abused person cannot deal alone with what happened and needs a psychotherapist to guide him or her through what is called a heal-ing process. Whether they do so purposefully or not, therapists who believe clients are damaged tend to teach them that they are helpless victims and that unless they can revisit what happened in the past through counseling, they will remain victims.

Choice theory looks at past abuse far differently. It teaches that these children, or now adults, can use choice theory to help themselves. They are no longer victims of what happened unless they choose to see themselves that way. Choice theory explains that the current thinking that they must relive, and even confront, the abuse is not only ineffective but can be harmful. In any situa-tion, it is always harmful to imply to people that they are victims and can't help themselves. Countless people in the world who have been abused as children and adults, many horribly, have helped themselves without traditional therapy and with no knowledge of choice theory. They have had bad experiences but still have been able to learn to trust people. They have suffered, but they have not been permanently damaged.

Children or adults who have not dealt effectively with the abuse need good counseling, which should include the choice the-ory explanations both of what happened and how to deal with it. Most important, they must learn that they are not suffering from the abuse itself as much as from the fact that they have lost trust in or may never have learned to trust people. Sexual abuse is one of the most difficult behaviors to deal with because, in many in-stances, the child did trust the abuser when the abuse began.

As I explained when I discussed child rearing, learning to trust is crucial to learning how to satisfy our needs as we deal with the world. From their experience, not trusting people makes sense to abused children. If they have been hurt by people in their quality worlds, how could they possibly trust strangers? What they have to learn is that most people are not abusers and that many, but not all, people can be trusted. And they need to learn how to distinguish those who can be trusted from those who can't and steer clear of those who can't. Basically, they have to be cautious when they meet people and get to know them better before they trust them. They need to be extra cautious to avoid being hurt again and losing what little trust they were beginning to gain.

When the abuse ends, they are like people who were blind for a long time, maybe since birth, and suddenly regain the ability to see. Although they can now see, they are not able to use their vision normally; they literally have to learn or relearn to use their eyes. Abused children or adults have to experience loving and trustworthy people and, literally, learn to trust and then love. But to do so, they have to learn to let go of the idea that they are victims or have been permanently damaged. To be cautious makes sense; to continue to think they are victims makes no sense.

Counseling them with reality therapy and, concurrently, teaching them choice theory can do much more for them than taking them back through the abuse. Revisiting a bad experience does not make you stronger. If you have been starving for a long time, you need food, not an explanation why you weren't fed in the past. Wounds, even severe psychological wounds, can heal, but only through experiencing love and gaining the trust that, with effort on their part, this love can be sustained.

Choice theory explains that all problems are present problems because the needs must be satisfied now. You cannot eat a meal you missed any more than you can eat a future meal. You can store food for the future just as you can make a good friend whom you can enjoy in the future. But enjoying the friend now is the key to enjoying the friend in the future. An abused person, because of an unhappy past, may be less capable but not incapable of dealing with the present. The past, be it abuse, neglect, or rejection, is not the problem. His or her present problem is no different from anyone's present problem—all present problems are relationship problems. We all need a satisfying present relationship with someone we can trust.

Terri, a thirty-three-year-old woman, came to me because she was unable to sustain satisfying sexual relationships. As soon as she began to get close to a man, she chose to behave in ways that destroyed the relationship. What she actually did is unimportant. Let's take a look at how, using reality therapy, I counseled her. I will focus on what I did that got her redirected from the past to the present and helped her to learn to trust. What I did is not the only way to do reality therapy, but it is a good way. Other reality therapists might do it differently, but we would all be going in the same forward direction.

"Terri, tell me your story. Everyone who comes here has a story. I'd like very much to hear yours."

"There is no story. I'm lonely and miserable. Well, I shouldn't really say that. I enjoy my job and the people I work with, but my social life, I always seem to screw it up. A good friend where I work told me about you. I talk to her a lot about my screwed-up love life, and she tries to help me. She said you helped her cousin; she could see her cousin change when she went to see you. Her cousin told her a little about how you worked, but she didn't want to try to tell me because she wasn't sure she understood it. Anyway, I need help. I have a little insurance; I can see you ten times this year. If it's going to take much longer, I'm not sure I can afford it. Between my car and my rent and the few clothes I have to have, there isn't much left. Also, I'm paying off a big dentist bill. Can you help me if this is all I can afford? I've heard therapy takes a long time. I don't want to start and then have to leave in the middle. Now that I've mentioned this, I guess that's my problem with men. I start in OK but I never seem to get much further."

"How long it takes depends on you. A lot can be done in ten sessions if you are willing to make some effort to learn a lot more about yourself than you know now. It's not like going to the dentist. With the dentist, all you had to do was open your mouth, and he fixed your teeth. I can't fix your love life, but I can help *you* to fix it. We work together. It's more like after going to the dentist, when you learn how to take better care of your teeth. The difference is that here you start right in, right this minute, learning how to take better care of your life. That's what my kind of therapy is all about—learning how to take care of yourself. We'll talk, I'll ask you questions, and you'll also help by beginning to take a close look at what you are choosing to do with your life right now. I'll use the word *choosing* a lot because I believe that we choose what we do and that you have to learn to make better choices if you want to be happy. Tell me what's happening; begin anywhere you like."

"It's men, I want a relationship. I meet them easily. A lot of them don't mean much to me, so for a little while we get along and then we just drift apart. But once in a while, one of them does mean a lot to me, and then I screw it up. That's what's happening right now with Tom. He's just like all the others I cared for. We find out we're interested in each other, and then I ruin it."

"Be specific. I need to know as much as you can tell me about all that's going on. Tell me everything; it all helps. How are you ruining it with Tom?"

Being specific is very important. Life is lived specifically; generalities like "I screwed up" are worthless in therapy. It's all the details that count.

"We got off to a good start. With Tom even the sex was good from the start. But then I started making demands. I started criticizing him for a lot of little things. He told me that a woman where he works lives near him and asked him to take her home after work; she gets a ride to work but she needs a ride home. I blew my top and accused him of wanting to go to bed with her. It was off the wall—she's almost old enough to be his mother—but when I blew I was serious. But it can be anything. All of a sudden I don't like his beard, I hate the tattoo on his arm, he didn't call exactly when he said he would. This goes on more and more. It all ends with me accusing him of not loving me. How the hell could he love me? We just met, but I accuse him anyway. I tell him he's just seeing me because I fuck him; I get crude like that and it's awful. The other night he blew up a little himself. He said, 'You're right, I am seeing you because I like to make love to you.' He didn't say fuck; he's not crude like me. He said, 'Of course I like to make love to you; I think that's a marvelous reason to see each other. I can't think of a better one.'"

"And?"

"I went berserk. I told him I don't want to just go to bed; I want something more. I started to scream and cry and beat on his chest. We were in bed; it was before we even made love. The poor guy got up, got dressed, and started to leave. I got up and ran after him and begged him not to go. So he stayed and we made love and it was terrific. It was the fight that made it so good. I was pretty good in the morning, but as I left for work, I'm on the early shift this quarter, I gave him a parting shot. I told him if he ever gets up out of bed like that again, we're through. I didn't need to do that. I was sorry as soon as I said it. There's something wrong with me. It's not him. I decided to see you because this guy is the best yet. He works and doesn't drink. He's divorced, of course; they all are except the married ones. I've tried them, too. I'm fucking up my life and I don't know why."

What's missing is obvious. She doesn't trust him, and I guess she hasn't trusted any of them. I'd better bring it up right now. There's no sense beating around the bush. She seems comfortable with me. Something happened in her life. Maybe she can tell me; I'll see.

"What does the word *trust* mean to you?"

"If you're trying to tell me that I don't trust guys, you're right. I don't, why should I?"

"Maybe because of what you said: He's a pretty nice guy, but you're afraid to get close to him. That's the usual reason, and it's probably right."

"Look, he's divorced, he has two kids, and he's paying child support. Is he going to start in again with a nut like me? What's in it for him? Anyway, why should I trust him? Why should I trust any of them after what I went through?"

I'm not going to ask her. She'll have to tell me. If I ask her, whatever it is, my asking will make it too important. She's got to stop thinking about it, stop depending on it as a way to avoid getting close to men now. She's thinking about whether to tell me. I won't say anything. She went on after a long pause, but she kept looking at me as if to say, *What's wrong with you? Why don't you ask me what happened?*

"I didn't have exactly a great upbringing. If I tell you all I went through as a kid, I'll eat up the whole ten sessions in no time. I've read about lousy childhoods, how they screw you all up. Do you want to hear about mine? I guess you do; that's where it all is, isn't it? My childhood, what happened to me as a child. My mother says she's sorry now but she didn't seem sorry then."

OK, it's out now; I can ask her. She wants to tell me.

"Who was it? Your father, your stepfather, your mother's boyfriend?"

"Not my father. He left when I was six. It was my mother's boyfriends—three of them. It started when I was nine; it didn't end until I left home. I was seventeen. I left home, my mother gave me a little money, I guess she felt guilty. She pretended not to know, but she knew what was going on. I guess she was afraid she'd lose her boyfriends. If you think I'm a wreck, you ought to meet my mother. She knew where I was when I left; we've always kept in touch. For a while I lived with a girlfriend; it was tough, but I was out of there. I got this job in a market. I'm smart. As soon as I was eighteen, I moved up to checker. I'm good at it. It's the one good thing in my life. It's how I meet guys. The market's in a good neighborhood; I meet guys that have some things going for them. The guy I have now works in a sound studio; he makes out OK."

She's pretty up front. She has every right not to trust men, but her genes have no memory; they don't know she was molested. They want love and sex, and they want it now. She has sex. She says she enjoys it, and that's good. But if choice theory is correct, I have to go forward. If I go back through all the abuse, what good will it do? She has a life and she is on some kind of terms with her mother, and that's good. Maybe her mother should have protected her, but she didn't. The men shouldn't have done what they did, but they did it. I can see she expects me to go back through the past. To blame her trouble with men on what happened. But if I do, where is she? Can she do anything to undo what happened? Will it do any good to blame her mother? She sees her mother as helpless, and maybe that's the best way to see her. I'm not going to go in that direction. It's enough that she lived through what happened to her once. She doesn't need to go back through it again. It's obvious she has some strengths. I've got to help her build on them.

"OK, I get the picture. I've counseled women who've been abused, some not as bad, some worse. Tell me, what's good about working in the market? You say you have friends at work?"

"What's good is I get good pay and benefits like seeing you. I like the people I work with and I like the shifts, it's open twenty-four hours. You meet different people on different shifts. I met Tom at four in the morning. There was no one waiting, so I had time to talk. My boss is pretty good. He knows I'm a talker and thinks it's good for business. When it's busy, I'm fast as lightning and I can still talk. I enjoy meeting and getting to know some of the customers. I'm lucky to have this job."

"When you came in, you said you were miserable, but sitting here talking to you, you don't seem so miserable."

"I'm not miserable here with you. It's hard to be miserable when you're talking about yourself. But I was miserable the other night when Tom got up out of bed to leave. I like this guy and I'm going to drive him away. That's why I'm miserable. Last night I held it all in. I didn't say anything when he called me from the studio and told me he was going to be three hours late and then it was four. He didn't get there till almost midnight, but I didn't say anything. He loved it; I could see the scared look on his face when he came in. But I felt like I was all bottled up. It felt like it did when I was young, with those men, all bottled up. We ate and then made love, but it didn't work that good for me. It's like, if I had really let him have it, the sex would have been better. I kept thinking, Here I am being all sweet, and it wasn't as good as when I'm a bitch. You can see why I'm here, can't you?"

I'll take a chance and give her the answer she's looking for but give it in a way that shows I don't think she's been ruined for life. She is a talker, and that's good; she's easy to know and she opened up quickly. She wants happiness; relationships are important to her. She seems comfortable with me, and I feel comfortable with her. I can feel that what I think about what happened is very important to her. I've got to come across to her as someone who doesn't think that what she went through has damaged her permanently.

"You're here because of your childhood. You had bad experiences with men, and your mother didn't protect you. You think that's what I'm looking for—that that's the reason you don't trust men. Well, I agree; I think that's the reason. But it's not the cause. The abuse is over. If you read the pop magazines, you get the message that you're supposed to be messed up for good if you've been sexually abused unless a therapist can fix you. Right now, that's what everyone believes. Do you think you're messed up for good?"

"Well, it must have done something, I've been messed up with men ever since. I came here to get unmessed."

"Suppose I told you that I can't do anything about what happened."

"Then maybe I'd better see someone else."

"You want to go back through all that happened, all that helpless bottled-up feeling again? Wasn't one trip through it enough?"

"I'm just supposed to forget about it, as if it never happened?"

"I'm not saying that. You know it happened. Remember it as long as you like. I'm asking you to forget what you've read that you have to do about it. It was terrible, but it's over. Do you think it's going to happen again? If you think it's going to happen again, then I would advise you to keep thinking about it, to be on your guard."

"It's not going to happen again. But it did happen and it's got me all messed up."

"How? Tell me how it's gotten you all messed up."

"With this guy, the way I act."

"The way you choose to act. Why do you think you choose to act this way?"

"Because of what happened to me. I keep telling you that. Didn't you listen to what I said?"

"What happened to you isn't messing you up with Tom. It's your choosing to keep thinking about it that's messing you up."

"But I can't help thinking about it?"

"I'm not sure of that. You think about it because you're afraid to trust a man, to trust Tom. What good does that do? Is Tom like those other guys? What happened is not permanently stuck in your brain; you choose to think about it. What good will it do you to push Tom away?"

"But that's it; it is stuck in my brain. I can't help it. You're supposed to get it out."

Now she's talking about it, but she's not getting any help from me to keep thinking about it. She can see that it's not as important to me as she thought it would be. That's got her a little puzzled and a little angry. I've got to convince her that she can stop thinking about it only by doing something different with Tom. If she keeps doing the same thing with him that she's done with the others, she'll never get it out of her head. If I go back through all the abuse, all her feelings about the men and her mother, a lot may come up that she doesn't want to deal with. It's not at all what she thinks: get it out and then it goes away. It's the opposite. The past doesn't intrude on the present unless we choose to hold on to it. Later, when she reads some choice theory and I explain it to her, she'll understand. But now I have to teach her to be careful but to take a chance and trust this guy. If she can, she'll find out that her past has not damaged her. It is her thinking about it now and her choice not to trust men that is causing her difficulty and that I can help her to stop. I answer her last request about helping her get it out.

"I think I can if you'll help me. When are you going to see Tom again?"

"Tomorrow night we're going to see a movie. He picks them; I like the ones he picks."

"After the movie, where do you go?"

"My apartment. That's why I'm so broke, I have a nice apartment."

"If you do what you usually choose to do, do you start picking on him at the movie or do you wait till you get home?"

More and more I'm introducing *choose* and *choice*. They are very empowering words that help us all to understand that no matter what happened in the past, we can still make a better choice today. The men who abused her are not waiting around to do it again. They are waiting only in her mind. The idea of choosing can help her choose to get them out.

"We'll go to a late-afternoon show and then come to my place and make dinner together. He's the chef, but I help. I start in after dinner a little; then I really get after him right before we make love. Like I said, the bitching gets me in the mood. He senses that's what I'm doing and appreciates the lovemaking that goes along with it, but I don't think he likes it. It's a little bizarre, and I'll lose him if I don't stop. Nuts like me are fun for a while but not fun enough to get serious with."

"You say the bitching gets you in the mood for sex. But do you like the bitching itself? If you could have good sex without it, how would that be?"

"I don't know. Good sex is important. It's not that easy to have good sex, at least for me it isn't."

"I asked you, do you like the bitching? I know it makes the sex better."

"Of course, I don't like it. I'm going to lose him if I keep it up."

"When you held it in the other night, even though the sex wasn't that good for you, was it OK for him?"

"I guess so. I don't think he noticed that much. I made up my mind to put on a good act. I think a lot of woman are good actresses. When there're no customers at night, I read *Cosmopolitan*. I know all the things to do, and they work."

"Do you want him to change?"

"What do you mean?"

"I mean to like it when you pick on him. To be able to tell you that if it makes the sex good for you, it's OK with him. Is good sex all you want from this guy?"

That question got to the heart of her dilemma. Sex she could handle. That was easy, but she wanted more. She wanted to trust him enough so she could love him without all the testing and game playing. Love was her problem, and I was getting close. I didn't say anything, I just waited.

"Maybe, I don't know."

"Why maybe, why don't you know?"

"Because that's sick; there's something wrong with that. He shouldn't have to put up with that from me. He's never treated me badly."

"Why shouldn't he have to put up with it? Men have treated you like shit. He's just a man. What do you care what he has to put up with if it's better for you?"

"Because he's not just any man. He hasn't treated me like shit. He treats me better than I treat him."

"OK, I'm a therapist. I'll listen to anything you want to say. Do you still want to tell me about the men who abused you? About your mother who should have protected you? About how you dealt with that situation? If you do, I'll listen."

Now she had to think. She had just admitted that this present guy was a good guy. I could see this was quite an admission. Now I was giving her a chance to tell me all about the bad guys, about her mother. What they had done that she could never change. Maybe what she had done that she could never change.

"But don't you have to know what happened?"

"I know what happened. You know what happened. If it will help you, I'll listen. But don't tell me because you think I need to know. You've told me enough; I don't have to hear any more."

There was a long pause. What I said was sinking in.

"Can I see you again?"

"You've got nine more visits."

"You don't think I'm all fucked up."

"It's over. If you keep thinking about it, you're fucking yourself up. You've met a nice guy. Be careful, but give him a chance. You've had your head screwed on backward for fifteen years. It's enough."

"Some very bad things happened."

"I'm sure they did. But is anything very bad happening now that you haven't told me? I mean now with this guy. Have you been holding anything back?"

"No."

"What if he drops you? He might, you know."

"It's not going to happen right away. It's later I'm worried about."

"Do you feel better?"

"I feel a little strange. I think it's better."

"I'll see you next week. This time OK? You can call me anytime."

Terri feels strange because she's getting rid of the way she's been thinking since she was nine years old to deal with the abuse and its aftermath. All this time, she's been convinced that her inability to get along with men is the result of what her abusers did to her. In this first session, I've helped her to become aware that the actual abuse is over. What is keeping it alive is how she is choosing to deal with those memories. It's this new awareness that feels so strange. She'll have some relapses, but if she can keep thinking in this direction, she can begin to gain effective control over a part of her life where she's never had it. She can choose to stop treating all men as if they are potentially abusive. This guy may drop her, but he is unlikely to abuse her. She may have to find someone else, but the next man may get better treatment from the start, and that will help. She has a lot to offer. If she's cautious but learns to trust again, some good guy, maybe Tom, will stick with her.

In future sessions, we'll talk about choice theory and we'll talk about how to use the book. A lot of the next nine sessions will be devoted to how much, even with her childhood, she has already done for herself and how she may go further. Maybe she'll move up into management; she's really into the supermarket business. I'll help her to figure out how to get along better with her mother, whom she has never removed from her quality world and whom she now pities more than blames. Mothers are the first to come and the last to go from our quality worlds.

Suppose she had come to me with the same problem but no recollection of ever being abused. Would I try to dredge up a memory that I suspected she had repressed? I would not for the following reasons. First, I don't believe that we can repress the memories of abuse, neglect, or rejection if it occurred after age three or four, and hers started at nine, especially if she is in a counseling situation where she feels safe. The need to survive would keep those threatening memories accessible. If it had started when she was two and ended at three, it might have been forgotten. Even if I suspected that this is what happened, I would not search for that memory. I would focus on what was going on now because that, not the abuse, is the problem she has to solve. It would be better if the man she is with now is worth loving. But part of what I'll try to teach her is how to recognize the difference between a good man and a creep.

With a client who was having a sexual difficulty but reported no previous abuse, her lack of trust would lead me to look for an abusive man in her life right now or recently. Again, I would focus on what was unsatisfying about her present relationship or relationships and not try to dredge up the past. If her present relationship was abusive, it would come out. If she had been abused in the past but would not admit it to me, it would be up to her to bring it up. If she did, I'd treat her like I treated Terri. If she didn't, I'd treat her like I treated Terri minus the abuse. Therapy should always move forward, never backward. Because Freud did it that way doesn't mean we have to keep doing it. I would still ask the question about trust because no matter what did or didn't happen, that is where she is now.

Regardless of what has happened to us, choice theory does not focus on the past as the cause of our present difficulties. Many clients want to stay in the past. They are afraid to deal with the present problem and are happy to escape into the past to find someone to blame for their present unhappiness. It is the job of the therapist to ferret out this present problem, not to go into the *safe* past. I say *safe* because clients use the past to avoid facing what is really happening in their lives now. Many female clients are unwilling to face the fact that a present male friend or husband is treating them badly and look to the past, his or their own, to avoid dealing with an unpleasant present that they would have to do something about now.

The present problem is much more accessible than trying to recover memories of things that may never have happened. When a person goes to a traditional therapist who is trained to focus on the past and keeps probing for what may have happened that is causing the present problem, the client is often more than willing to help the therapist do so. To blame is much easier than to choose to change. Too many adult clients have been so convinced that they can't deal with their present misery until they can recover a forgotten memory of childhood abuse. Unfortunately, what they do "recover" is a false memory of abuse that never happened. This *memory* has been created by the client's creative system to try to please the therapist and/or to avoid dealing with the present. Neither the client nor anyone else has any way to know that it is not a true memory. To the client, it seems as if it happened. That is how our creative systems work. In my dream, I was really an astronaut.

The false memory may be even more real to the client than if the event had actually happened because it is fresh from the client's creative system and tailored to what he or she wants now. This is why so many clients believe it happened and are so distressed when the memory is proved false. There is no difference between this kind of a memory and a delusion. It was created in an effort to satisfy a need or needs and seems as real to the client as if it had actually happened.

These delusional memories are a common phenomenon in court, when witnesses create perceptions to fit particular cases rather than recall what they actually saw. The witnesses may be trying to satisfy their need to belong or their need for power. We should never rely on any memory that cannot be verified because there is no way to find out if it is real or created. Memories that are elicited under hypnosis or drugs can be equally faulty. There is nothing in hypnosis or drugs that makes a memory more truthful than what is remembered or forgotten without the use of these procedures. At times drugs and hypnosis can actually encourage the person to remember what didn't happen. Just because these exotic procedures are used becomes a powerful suggestion that something must have happened. When the client gives in to that suggestion, it is a short step for his or her creative system to take over and provide what he or she believes must be there. There is also no truth serum; that is another external control fantasy.

Reality therapists are not detectives. We do not set ourselves up to separate the truth from what is false. We know that there are enough real problems in the present, and we look for them. We know that these problems can be dealt with without knowing any more about the past except when the client was in effective control. These strengthening memories, which are usually true or can easily be checked, make therapy more effective. There is no reason to believe that we can't help clients because we don't know much about them besides what they are choosing to do now. This is why the use of reality therapy can substantially shorten the time needed for therapy to be effective. I did not think that Terri's ten-session limit was a block to good treatment. If she needed more, I would have worked out a way for her to pay.

Reading this book can be a good way for many people to handle family relationships that are unsatisfying. If each party in the unhappy relationship can learn choice theory, stop blaming the others in the relationship, get into the solving circle, and subordinate his or her own demands to the needs of the relationship, they all could get along much better than they do now.

CHAPTER 10

Schooling, Education, and Quality Schools

I N THE EARLY 1990S I was invited to Pittsburgh to keynote a
special conference on high schools. The conference organizers
were interested because I had written two books, *The Quality
School* and *The Quality School Teacher*, explaining how choice
theory can be used in schools. Those attending were administrators, teachers, and students from a consortium of about forty
schools that, by all measures of success, were judged the best
high schools in the United States.

Knowing that top students from each school would be in the
audience, I chose to nervous because I was going to start my
speech with the claim that more than half the students in the best
schools do nothing more in class than get by. I was afraid that the
students selected to come to this conference, who might be school
boosters, would resent the claim that their schools were filled

with do-enough-to-get-by students and pay little attention to what I said. It wasn't the teachers and administrators who concerned me. They don't know or want to know as much about the schools as do the students.

The night before I was to deliver my speech, I asked the students if they would be willing to meet with me half an hour before my talk in the morning. I told them I was planning to make a statement about their schools, but I didn't want to say it if they disagreed. Almost all fifty students showed up. I asked for their estimates of how many students in their schools were doing far less than they were capable of. We had a discussion about students' effort, and I told them that I would go along with their criteria but I wanted a number—how many were working hard to learn?

I was surprised at the range of their estimates that 20–45 percent were working hard in class. The students from the 45 percent high school explained that although poor performers in middle school were not admitted, still less then half the students were buckling down. We talked about that low figure, and to make sure they understood what I wanted, I asked, "Are the poor performers incapable of doing good schoolwork?" They said no, but added that some of the most capable students were doing very little in class because they had turned off in middle school. Although in my talk I said that less than half were working, I tend to agree with the students, the actual figure in the best schools is closer to 25 percent, but less than 5 percent in many large inner-city schools.

When I made the claim that this low figure is due to coercive, or boss, management, no one in the audience challenged it. I will describe both boss management and lead management in detail in the next chapter on the workplace. But, in essence, bosses fail because they force and punish, and leaders succeed because, without forcing and punishing, students see it is to their benefit to follow them and do so more because they like them than because of what they teach. If good education is our goal, boss management is costing us at least half of every dollar we spend on this effort.

But even more alarming was what I soon learned while making an all-day presentation on quality schools in Alma, Michigan. The schools were closed for the day; all the school employees and many of the city leaders were in attendance; however, no students were present. As usual, I lectured all morning, but in the afternoon I interviewed high school students. Considering that the town's power structure was there, I knew I was going to get the best students, and I did. Since I had talked on quality schools all morning, I decided to ask, "What is quality?" The students had no trouble answering and defined quality as well as it can be defined: the best you can do, it takes time and lots of effort, it's what we want when we spend our money, and it's usually expensive. I then asked a question they did not expect, "Do you do quality work in school?"

The students were silent, not knowing exactly what to say. I thought maybe these good students did not want to boast. After a pause of at least twenty seconds, a tall young man stood up to address the audience. In the several hundred of these interviews I have conducted, this was the first time a student had ever stood up to make a statement. He said, "I've gone to school here since kindergarten and I've been a good student, all A's, a few B's, no C's. My parents and teachers have been very satisfied. But I want to tell you this. Never once in an academic class have I ever done the best I can do." The audience was stunned to hear this from such a capable young man whom most of them knew. When the interview ended, many from the audience rushed up to talk to him. A few challenged him, but he held his ground.

After the audience was through with him, I asked him what I should have asked during the interview, "If you don't do it in the classroom, where in school do you do your best?" Immediately he said, "On the basketball team. I always do the best I can there." His answer supported my belief that the best work in most schools is done in extracurricular activities for two reasons. First, the students almost always have both the teachers who lead these activities and the activities themselves in their quality worlds. This is by far the most important criterion for good work in school.

Second, there is no *schooling*, a term I will soon explain, in these activities.

What is so disappointing about his answer is that it pinpoints a huge problem in the way we teach. Not only are many poor students doing badly in our coercive schools, many good students are not doing their best either. Although I concern myself mainly with lower achievers, we need quality schools for *all* students. If a future leader like this young man does not choose to do his best, there is little hope for improving education.

Schooling

The main reason so many students are doing badly and even good students are not doing their best is that our schools, firmly supported by school boards, politicians, and parents, all of whom follow external control psychology, adhere rigidly to the idea that what is taught in school is right and that students who won't learn it should be punished. This destructive, false belief is best called *schooling*. It is defined by two practices, both of which are enforced by low grades and failure.

The first practice is trying to make students acquire knowledge or memorize facts in school that have no value for anyone, including students, in the real world. The second practice is forcing students to acquire knowledge that may have value in the real world but nowhere near enough value to try to force every student to learn it. Forcing people to learn has never been successful, yet we continue to do it because we think it is right.

Schooling is what students, even many good students, rebel against in school. If they are failed or given low grades because of this rebellion, many stop working altogether and take not only the schooling but the teachers who school out of their quality worlds. To be fair, many teachers believe that the coercive system that runs the schools forces them to school students and that if they don't, they will be punished. If we are to get rid of schooling, we must stop defining education as acquiring knowledge.

Education is not acquiring knowledge; it is best defined as using knowledge. The dictionary defines knowledge as the fact or awareness of knowing something. I recognize that you have to know something to use it, but except in some television quiz shows or party games, there is little value in merely knowing something. The value is in using what you have learned, and this is where the schools fail to focus.

Much of what students are required to do in school and are punished if they refuse is to memorize information they will never be asked to use except in school. What makes this practice senseless is that in most instances, the school does not require that the students retain the knowledge, just know it for tests. As Linus said in a Peanuts cartoon strip, "The difference between A students and F students is the A students forget it five minutes after the test, the F students, five minutes before."

Education is worth the effort; schooling is not. Education is worth improving; schooling cannot be improved. If you know something, you know it; if you don't, you don't. You can't know it better or worse. Where you can demonstrate your competence is in using knowledge. You want your dentist to be able to spot a cavity when she sees one, but if she doesn't know how to fill it properly, you might be better off if she didn't even see it. We commit a fraud on students when we tell them that because they learn facts like dates, names, and places, they have acquired something worth knowing. The real world does not reward schooling. If needed, the knowledge of where to look up names, dates or places is well worth acquiring. If the popular schooling game Trivial Pursuit had been called Serious Pursuit, it would have been a dud.

Schooling is what the young man from Alma was referring to when he said he did not do his best. He couldn't do his best in temporarily acquiring knowledge. But on the basketball team and in most nonacademic areas, students put in a lot of effort because they not only use what they learn but can improve it. The real excitement attached to learning anything is improving it. When students tell you, "We have a great teacher," what they are saying is that the teacher has taught them to use and improve knowledge, not just acquire it. That is why the best teachers are usually the toughest teachers: They require students to think. For most students in our schooling schools, thinking is new and seen as difficult. But once they see that it's useful, they respect their teachers and are willing to do the work. In or out of school, there is nothing good about knowing something or bad about not knowing something unless you use it or intend to use it.

Most people will agree that much of what they memorized for both school and college was useless. But there is still the argument of the popular educator E. D. Hirsch, who has written a series of books on what children need to know. Hirsch claims that just being aware of a certain amount of knowledge is indispensable if we want to succeed in the culture we live in. If he was talking about using knowledge, I would agree with him. My question to people like Hirsch who define things worth knowing is, *How are we to get this knowledge into the heads of almost all the students if we don't concurrently teach them to use it?*

Since we are a widely diverse culture, in which the gap between the haves and have-nots is widening, the blind forcing of what experts say we all must know will be rejected by many students who do not have homes in which education is valued. They will be failed for this rejection and will "retaliate" by taking schoolwork and then school out of their quality worlds. Many will drop out of school into lives that include violence, crime, prison, drugs, and unloving sex. In a quality school, where students are led instead of bossed, they acquire a lot of knowledge by using what they learn, and they retain it. We need more quality schools if we are to reduce the increasing and costly gap between the haves and have-nots in our society.

This point leads me directly into the second procedure of schooling, where things get more complicated. Some teachers at another conference asked me to role-play how a teacher or a counselor could deal with a capable seventeen-year-old girl who was failing senior English because she had stopped working in class. A teacher volunteered to play the girl. I played the counselor.

"Your teacher sent you to see me. She thinks you have a problem. What's happening in that class?"

"I'm flunking English. I try, but I really don't know what's going on in that class. I don't make any trouble. But I'm going to fail, and without that class I won't graduate. I want to graduate but I don't think I'm going to."

"Is your teacher doing anything to help you?"

"He's trying. On Tuesdays and Wednesdays there is after-school tutoring, but I can't go. I have a job every day after school and I need the money. It's not just for me. I have to help out my mother; there isn't enough for food if I don't help. I have a little sister and brother, they have to eat."

"You seem intelligent, why are you failing?"

"It's *Macbeth,* it's Shakespeare. They're making me take Shakespeare, and I don't understand it. I hate it. I used to try, but I got all mixed up and I flunked the tests so I've just given up. Why do I need Shakespeare? Why can't I graduate if I don't know Shakespeare?"

This is a good question. There is value in knowing Shakespeare, but is there enough value to flunk this hardworking intelligent girl because she doesn't understand *Macbeth*? Even if she graduates, her chances of finding happiness are not that good. If she fails, she has even less chance to do whatever she wants to do with her life. To find happiness, she may have to pursue some more training, and without graduating she'll be sour on school and there is less likelihood she will try to do so. I don't think this girl should be failed, but she will be unless some exception is made. Because I believe that the core of English is to be able to read and write and understand what you have read and written, I asked her, "Would you be willing to read a book, write a report on it, and take a test on it if your teacher would let you?"

"Not if it's Shakespeare. Besides, I don't have time to read books. I have barely enough time to do what I'm doing to pass my other courses. Anyway my teacher wouldn't let me do that. If he let me, the whole class would want to do it. They all hate *Macbeth*."

Here you can see the difficulty with forcing culture. Do we chance ruining a student's life for refusing to learn what may help her to succeed in our culture? I worry a lot more about students learning to read and write well than I do about Shakespeare.

"What do you like?"

"I like animals. I have a cat and I have a book on cats. I read that."

"Would you be willing to read a good book on animals? It was a best-seller, and I have it at home. If I give it to you, would you read it for English and take a test on it? I think you could pass that test and I know you'd like the book."

"What's it called?"

"*All Creatures Great and Small* by James Herriot."

Should we punish a young woman for not understanding Shakespeare in a class filled with students who, like her, are hostile to Shakespeare and angry at being threatened with failure if they don't want to make the effort to understand *Macbeth*? My claim is that she and the culture she lives in would be better off reading Herriot and writing and talking about what they read than they would be even if they managed to pass Shakespeare. I don't say give her an A. Give her a C or if she does a great job a B. But don't fail her. There is no sense in that. Given the conditions that exist in that all-too-typical class, I don't know what else to suggest.

After the role-play, the teachers were divided. Some agreed with me but said they couldn't do it because the administrators would not let them. They realized how destructive failing her and not letting her graduate with her class would be, but their hands were tied. However, other teachers said the girl was correct about one thing: If they made an exception for one student, many more would want the same thing. The fear of failure may be motivating, but it will never be motivating enough to make many of them appreciate Shakespeare. It is pure external control psychology that we should not change the system to accommodate this girl (and many others) who is willing to demonstrate that she can read and write well.

The teachers who wanted to fail her were saying that it would be right to sacrifice her to preserve the coercive system. My concern is that this right is creating a large group of intellectual have-nots who hate the haves and hate to learn in school. This hate makes a large contribution to the flat line of human progress graphed in the first chapter. The choice theory right is to teach students the skills they need to succeed in our culture. Universal education must mean more than forcing students to attend school. It must mean that all are learning because they have school, teachers, schoolwork, and each other in their quality worlds.

At one teacher in-service training program, to kick off the 1995–96 school year, a school district invited me to make a day-long presentation to their K–12 teachers. After my morning presentation, I interviewed four eleventh- and twelfth-grade students. I asked them things about their school that would illustrate some points I made in my morning talk. One question I asked was if they had ever voluntarily read a book on their own that was not assigned in school. I was surprised to hear that not one of them had. When I asked if they thought they ever would, three said they seriously doubted it, and one, an eleventh grader, was adamant that he never would.

The students' answers shocked and puzzled the teachers in the audience, and after the students left I continued our discussion. One of the elementary teachers stood up and sounded heartbroken when she said, "I taught that little boy in the third grade and he loved to read then. What happened?" Schooling is what happened. An important purpose of education is to nurture a love for lifelong learning in all students, not kill it. The system being used in that district, and almost all others across the nation, is killing students' love of learning.

CALCULATION VERSUS MATH: SCHOOLING AT ITS WORST

As much as the two practices of schooling stop useful learning in the nontechnical or soft subjects of school, they save their worst horrors for math. With math, we destroy students' lives by the thousands for no other purpose than to keep the right to school them intact. If you ask some average citizens, who may have taken math in school but do not use it in their lives, What is math? they will give you the schooling answer: Math is calculating. If you ask them for examples, they will say, the times tables.

If you asked all elementary teachers the same question, almost all of them would give you the same answer. If you asked all secondary teachers and college teachers, except those who teach math, as well as captains of industry, politicians, doctors, lawyers, and judges, the same question, almost all of them would agree.

All who believe math is calculation are wrong. Math never was and never will be calculation. Calculation in school, which means to add, subtract, multiply, divide, and do fractions, decimals, and percentages by hand, is exactly what its name says it is, calculation. It is a useful skill to learn, but once learned, it is not useful to repeat over and over as is now done in most schools. Repetitive calculation by hand, something no adult in the real world has done for almost fifty years, has made the lives of millions of children miserable and wasted millions of instructional hours and billions of instructional dollars in a country that desperately needs the more useful skills of reading, writing, speaking, listening, and problem solving, including, of course, mathematical and scientific problem solving.

Recent studies have found that fourth graders do well on math and science tests but that there is a huge drop-off when eighth graders are tested in the same subjects. In chapter 3, I attributed this drop-off to the students taking these subjects out of their quality worlds. But calculation, which makes sense to first through third graders, makes less sense to fourth through eighth graders. Students in these grades in places like Singapore are busy doing real math and science, while our students are stuck senselessly doing repetitive calculations by hand and memorizing science. In an effort to be right, we are dumbing down the curriculum with schooling and then wondering why our students are doing poorly.

The math books are getting better. My sixth-grade grand-daughter's text has a lot of useful math in it but also a lot of useless calculation, which she told me she had learned to do by the third grade. As good as parts of the book are, the authors do not distinguish between this real math and calculation. They could have and they should have.

Math in the real world is only one thing: solving story problems. If you look around you no matter how far you travel, almost everything you see that is human-made had a story problem or problems involved in its making. In a quality school, students learn math starting in kindergarten and continue to learn it until they leave the school. In the early grades, they hand-calculate to get the sense of the processes and to appreciate the power of numbers. But as they get into the third grade and can demonstrate competent hand calculation, they are offered calculators.

Anyone who does math in the real world—anyone who solves a story problem, from totaling a restaurant check to sending a spacecraft to Mars—uses a calculator or computer. Math is getting the problem to where calculation is needed, and that only a human being can do. Calculators can't set up the problems; their only use is to do the calculation at the end.

Calculators are cheap, available, and accurate. If your life depended on an engineer dividing 23,682 by 5,033 and doing it in a hurry, would you rather he did it by hand or used a calculator? If your life depended on that same engineer knowing how to set up the story problem that required that calculation, would you rather he had studied math or spent a lot of time doing long division by hand? Engineers, and I have a degree in chemical engineering, use calculators and computers. We had to study math so we could learn how to get the story problem to the place where we knew what to calculate.

But in most schools, calculation rules the roost in the early grades. It is necessary, but it should not be the priority. Story problems should be introduced immediately, so students can see the relationship between math and calculation. However, by the fourth grade, story problems should predominate and students should be introduced to hard problems that require algebra and calculus and shown how this more powerful math was created to make hard problems easy, not the other way around.

Then by the time they are ready to tackle problems, such as where the trains met or how long it took the boat to go upstream against the current, they will have learned the algebra that makes it easy. If they don't learn the algebra, they cannot do these problems no matter how well they can calculate. If they can do the algebra, the calculations are so simple that most people can do them in their heads. But also remember that even if you couldn't solve these difficult story problems, you still passed algebra. You passed by doing a lot of algebraic exercises and manipulations that, like calculations, have nothing to do with solving story problems.

This avoidance of story problems continues in higher math and even makes up a large part of all college math. Schooling is diminished, but even in the smaller role it plays, it is alive and well in college math. But if you do math in the real world, you don't *school*, you do story problems. The sad part is that most of us ended up both fearing and hating math when most of us didn't even do it. But if we came from homes that supported education, we managed to pass our mandatory schooling in hand calculation and non-problem-solving higher math.

I've worked a lot with students who, because of schooling, took schoolwork and school teachers out of their quality worlds and didn't get through school. And what they were told they had to do, and punished for not doing, were calculations they were told were math. Our prisons are filled with young men, disproportionally African American and Hispanic, who wouldn't memorize useless facts or learn Shakespeare and who certainly wouldn't do repetitive long division, the most punishing and worthless calculation of all. When they flunked school, they were on the fast track to prison. This failure has led to a great deal of violence, drug use, and nonloving sex and has compounded the problems of child neglect and abuse when they father children. It is the children who were themselves abused and neglected who are the most vulnerable to the depredations of schooling.

If we were short of mathematicians to do real work, which we are not, anyone who was forced to learn math would not be anywhere near good enough to do it when it had to be done. Instead of insisting that all students go on to algebra and geometry, we should focus on teaching them to solve the nonalgebraic story problems that most of us run into in the real world. All students can learn this arithmetic if we are patient and do not fail them. But so few of us can even do arithmetic because we were turned off by too much calculation or later by the mysteries of "higher math."

If we stopped the forced schooling represented by the torture of hand calculating and really taught the arithmetic we can all use that few of us know now, many more students would be interested in going further into real math. By spending much less money than we spend now, we could use our present math teachers to teach these voluntary, interested students in small classes, and by the time they finished high school, they would have completed the undergraduate math of most colleges.

In the end, we would have many more and much better-educated mathematicians than we have now. These would be happy classes. The interested students who want to learn real math are harmed by being taught with reluctant students who are forced to be there. The argument that math teaches thinking skills may be correct, but only to the students who want to learn it. It does not teach thinking to many students who are forced to take it. All you get from coercion is resistance, no matter where it is used.

Before I leave this discussion of math and how it is destroyed by schooling, I want to offer an example of a simple, nonalgebraic story problem that I don't believe more than a few people in the country who aren't mathematicians can solve: *Should I buy or lease a car*? Most people who lease cars would be better off to the tune of up to $100 a month if they bought cars. But they can't do the math, so they are prey to car salesmen (most of whom can't do the math either) who have been told to lease cars because the dealers make more money that way. If the dealers make more, lessees lose that money. Read car advertisements, and you will see that the prices of the cars are rarely advertised, only the monthly costs of leasing them. And look for what is called an *acquisition fee*, only a totally nonmath person would ever be gullible enough to go for that scam.

Another example of real-world, useful math that schoolchildren could start learning by the third grade is how much families, especially large families, could save if the students were taught the value of clipping and using grocery store coupons. Teachers could go to the stores and pick up the flyers with the coupons in them and explain where else these coupons are available. The children could take these coupons to the stores with their parents and figure out the savings as they shopped or at the checkout counters. Parents would be impressed with this useful knowledge and might share a little of the savings with the children.

NONMATH PROBLEM SOLVING VERSUS MATH PROBLEM SOLVING

The basics of education-useful learning—not schooling—as taught and practiced in a quality school, are learning to speak, listen, read, and write and to use these skills to solve problems. Once you learn these skills, you can keep practicing and improving them for the rest of your life. After graduation, it is a rare day that you do not use these skills to solve problems. In school, to prepare for life, you should be taught vocabulary by using better words, not by memorizing the meaning of words you don't use.

Problem solving is basic to history and literature, as well as to math and science. It is not who, when, where, or what in history or literature that is important, but the problems the characters, real or fictional, were struggling to solve and whether they succeeded. If they succeed, why? If not, why not? In a quality school, students are asked these questions, the core of using knowledge, from the beginning. These are the questions that are now asked on proficiency tests, and quality school students do well on these measures.

The arts do not ordinarily suffer from the ravages of schooling.

Students enjoy recognizing paintings by studying what the artists were trying to portray. Recognizing the Mona Lisa is only the beginning. One useful discussion about who she was and why Leonardo painted her smiling will lock that enigmatic smile into a student's memory for life. Students are more than willing to memorize music or the lines of a play for performances. The whole basis of art and music is to do it or to appreciate others doing it.

There *is* a place for memorizing in education, but not if students are forced and have no choice in what to memorize. I memorized the last paragraph of Lincoln's second inaugural speech in the eighth grade, and it was so beautiful that I still know it almost sixty years later. But I was asked by my teacher what I wanted to memorize; I had a choice. I was given time to do it and I enjoyed doing it perfectly. The teacher, who knew all the pieces by heart, prompted the students who had difficulty and got them through it. No one was flunked or threatened. The class liked memorizing their chosen pieces, and it was a good experience. A good experience with a good teacher is the key to learning anything well.

Right now if your second and third graders are memorizing and calculating and love doing it because it is new and exciting and they like you, I can't criticize. But when this initial pleasure in acquiring knowledge begins to wear off, as it will, don't force them to continue. Move quickly from schooling into education, and you'll set them on the path to real learning for life.

The Stacys of Our Schools

I use the unisex name Stacy to refer to a large group of students who begin to take schoolwork and teachers out of their quality worlds as early as the second grade. It is that they had so few Stacys that made the high schools that came to the Pittsburgh conference so outstanding. They may have had a lot of students who didn't do much schoolwork, but these students still had their schools, some teachers, and some schoolwork in their quality worlds. Although they may have wanted the school to be better, they had enough support from both their teachers and parents that they didn't put up much of a fight against the coercion they experienced even in their good schools. If there were no coercion, the number of students who worked hard would have been double or triple what the students I met with reported. Many of the students in these good schools, who do enough to get by because school is in their quality worlds, get into college. There, with more choices and much less *schooling*, they may do very well.

The Stacys are a different story. Usually, they don't get much support for education at home, and they frequently don't receive as much love and attention at home as they want. They need to get this support and attention in school if they are even to do enough to get by. Without what they need at home, they are extremely vulnerable to the forcing, schooling, and punishing they encounter early in school and that they resist by taking schoolwork; teachers; and, eventually, the school itself out of their quality worlds. Like almost all students, Stacys start school with teachers and schoolwork in their quality worlds.

Many do quite well in kindergarten and first grade, and the schools, their warm and caring teachers, and the need-satisfying schoolwork become even stronger in their quality worlds than when they began. If their teachers are patient, flexible in their approach to teaching them to read, and read a lot to them from interesting books, they learn to read and write. If their teachers make an effort to talk and listen to them, both individually and in class meetings, the students quickly improve the way they speak and listen.

But by the second grade, teachers begin to add a little coercion and a lot of *schooling* to their approach. Acquiring knowledge, doing calculations, and being assigned homework, accompanied by grades and the threat of failure, begin to intrude on what was mostly love and fun. This change is subtle, but the students who are to become the Stacys begin to detect it and to resist. The students who are not to become Stacys may also rebel a little at this change. The teachers see this behavior as a disciplinary problem and begin to prod them a little. The difference is that when the students who are not to become Stacys are prodded, they choose to work a little harder. The Stacys take some of the schoolwork, usually the *schooling*, out of their quality worlds. When this change occurs, the two groups begin to separate, a separation that will increase markedly when they reach middle school.

Until the two groups separate, there is no way to tell the difference between the Stacys and the other students. More than thirty years ago, when I worked in Watts, a low-income, segregated section of Los Angeles, I saw students who had been eager, involved learners in kindergarten and first grade gradually stop doing schoolwork in the higher grades of elementary school. I was puzzled then, but now that I know choice theory I am no longer puzzled. There was nothing wrong with their brains; it was the coercive system that they rebelled so self-destructively against. As I mentioned, in the beginning, the change is uneven and hard to detect, especially by teachers who don't know about the quality world and how vital it is for the children to keep them and what they teach in it. But as the change continues into the third and fourth grades, it becomes easier to see.

The students who will become Stacys start to pay less attention. They talk and attempt to socialize by forcing themselves on children who are trying to learn and disrupting if they don't get the attention they want. For whatever reason, they need more love and more patience in school than do other students. But as they begin to behave in ways that frustrate their teachers and to force themselves on other students for attention, they fail to get what they want from the teachers and the students. Then they increasingly resist doing what they are told to do by using a lot of behaviors that are labeled disciplinary problems.

The third, fourth, and fifth grades are a vital time. If the potential Stacys continue to take schoolwork, teachers, and good students out of their quality worlds, they are on their way to becoming full-blown Stacys. The process of becoming Stacys can be reversed comparatively easily at this early stage. Many good teachers in our punish-them-if-they-don't-do-what-they-are-told schools are able to recognize this resistance early and immediately stop the punishment. They give them a little more attention, for example, a friendly greeting in the morning, a few pats on the head, an assignment they can do, help them to do it well, and then a little praise for doing it. All of this may reverse this disastrous process.

These students need to form satisfying relationships with loving, patient teachers, who may be the only reliable source of love they have. Good teachers know how to give students what they need, and it doesn't take that much time. In the end, it saves time because the students buckle down and go to work. Having classrooms with only twenty children in the first three grades, as has recently been funded in California, is a wonderful step in the right direction. It frees the teachers to give students the attention they could not otherwise get.

These good teachers also send messages home asking the parents to read to the children or send games home that the parents can play with them. They have enough sense not to blame the families for the children's problems in school. Most parents have enough problems of their own; they don't need more from the school. But knowing enough choice theory to realize what is actually going on is also vital if teachers are to help more children stop choosing to become Stacys.

But many teachers don't recognize what is happening and either phone the parents or send home a barrage of messages telling, almost ordering, the parents to do something about their children's behavior in school. They expect parents, who know little themselves but force, to punish the potential Stacys. Now the lonely children become desperate. Less and less loved both at school and at home, they turn more and more to whomever is available, other Stacys like themselves. Yet most of those potential Stacys are still in their deciding stage in the elementary schools.

The big change comes in middle school where there is an abrupt shift to more schooling and more coercion and much less time for teachers to give students individual attention. The process can still be reversed, but it is much harder now than if it had been noticed and dealt with in elementary school. If a student is a full-blown Stacy and has somehow gotten into high school, it is unlikely that this choice will be reversed. But occasionally it happens. It is really never too late as long as the student comes to school. It just gets progressively harder the longer the student is thinking about giving up and becoming a Stacy.

In middle school, the Stacys do poorly academically, often skipping class. They quickly begin to lose ground and may be less prepared for high school than when they entered middle school. Schoolwork and teachers are no longer in their quality worlds, and now they begin to lose or give up on the few good friends they still have who like school. It is these friends who are the incentive to keep school flickering in their quality worlds.

Now, if they stay in school, the Stacys are attached to one another because of their common interest in disruption, violence, sexual activity, and drugs. They may not drop out for another few years because occasionally there is a teacher whom they can relate to, a subject like art or music that they still enjoy, or athletics. Even if they don't get along well with them, the Stacys rarely give up on their mothers, who continue to tell them to stay in school and try to graduate. But in most cases they are so far behind that their mothers are not enough to help them stay in school.

The Stacys are increasing in number because to succeed in our society, education is more and more necessary, and they have none. They will not succeed in our present one-school-fits-all academic system. Even if these schools are improved, most Stacys have little interest in all-day academics. They need to be offered something that they can do—hands on—at the middle school level. Our present excellent vocational schools take only senior high school students, but for most of the Stacys, that is too late; they have already taken school out of their quality worlds.

We also need to enlarge our vision of what vocational education is and expand apprenticeship programs down to the middle school level. What is already obvious is that when they are in a vocational school setting, Stacys often renew their interest in academics. As we enlarge the opportunities for nonacademic education, we also have to publicize the idea that this is not second-class education. Students should understand that although vocational education is not the direct route to college, that route is still open to students who begin to see themselves going further. All this can be done for far less than we are spending now on the Stacys. But schools will have great difficulty doing so alone; they need community support.

In poor neighborhoods, urban and rural, Stacys make up much of the total school population. Right now, hardly anyone in the nation has the slightest idea what to do with them, in or out of school, beyond punishment, which increases their number. When the male Stacys are in their late teens, many go to prison. Most of their offenses have to do with drugs, from which they obtain both pleasure and money.

A significant number of the male Stacys are incarcerated for what we consider senseless violence. But it is not senseless to them; it is what they are looking for. Putting them in prisons, especially the more punitive ones that the society is now demanding, almost ensures that they will give up totally on happiness and concentrate on what pleasure they can get for the rest of their, often short, lives. These are dangerous people. Violence that would horrify most of us means little to them.

While the Stacys are the visible products of the present system that runs our schools, they themselves are not the problem. What needs to be changed is the system. Almost all the Stacys who go to school would be willing to learn if we would change to a choice theory system, which means changing from schooling to education, from punishment to friendship, and from having to, to not having to make up for past failures. If they are willing to learn the useful skills of reading, writing, and problem solving now, we will forget the past.

Waiving the requirement that they gain the knowledge that they have not acquired will give them hope. Once they have caught up on their skills, then we can worry about requiring knowledge. We have to do what it takes to prevent them from becoming Stacys. No matter how badly they do in school, we can reverse this process if they attend. In most cases, we have several years to reach them, but to do so, we have to change the system.

What we also need to do that is now within our reach is to create model quality elementary schools all over the country. To expand quality education to middle schools is much harder but possible if the students come from quality elementary schools. I think quality high schools are out of our reach until the communities the high schools are in move toward becoming quality communities (I discuss quality communities in chapter 12). In the end, it may turn out to be easier to move an entire community to choice theory, the basis of a quality community, than to move only a high school.

Quality schools would be schools staffed by teachers and principals who practice lead management and teach choice theory to both students and their families. Already more than two hundred schools have banded together to try to do this in the Quality School Consortium. What is stopping other interested schools is the lack of administrative and community support and the few dollars needed for training. The cost of keeping one Stacy in prison for three years would more than pay for the total training of fifty teachers.

Cooperative leadership from both district superintendents and the teachers' union is needed to get things started. There is plenty of room for skeptics and naysayers in the thousands of schools that will not consider this approach; there is no room for any of them in quality schools. Just as all administrators and teachers need certificates to teach and manage, every member of a quality school staff should have additional training that would lead to a specialist's certificate in quality school education.

Our experience so far has been that unless schools are staffed by teachers and principals who hold these certificates, we will never have more than a few quality schools. The William Glasser Institute does the training that is needed and awards these certificates. It is prepared to cooperate with schools of education that want to educate prospective teachers in this specialty. (Further information on how training is done is presented in the appendix.)

We are pushing for drug-free schools. We need to push even harder for coercion-free and failure-free quality schools because it is the alienation caused by coercion and punishment that leads young people to turn seriously to drugs. At the Huntington Woods Elementary School in Wyoming, Michigan, the principal and teachers have all been fully trained in the ideas of this book and my other books. What we have learned from that training has now become the substance of the Quality School Specialist Program offered by the institute.

THE LEARNING DISABLED

Public school teachers who read these paragraphs will recognize immediately that they have some or many wannabe Stacys in their classes. When parents are educated and involved with what their children are doing in their school, it could be that many of the potential Stacys are incorrectly labeled learning disabled.

This label strongly implies that the students have something wrong with their brains that makes it difficult for them to learn. But what makes it difficult for so many of them is not abnormal brains but excessive schooling. Our brains are not set up to memorize information we do not use, and we are certainly not given brains that can even remotely compete with a calculator. What many of these students do is take schooling and with it, a lot of essential schoolwork, such as reading and writing, out of their quality worlds. When they do so, there is no way anyone, through any sort of testing, can tell whether they have chosen not to put what they are told to learn into their quality worlds or their brains are incapable of learning what they are told to learn.

These Stacys often have parents who accepted schooling, did well in school, and see nothing wrong with their children being forced to memorize and calculate. They are puzzled by their children's poor performance and tend to go along with any diagnosis that explains that what's wrong with their children is no one's fault; the children have abnormal brains. The current diagnosis that parents and teachers tend to accept is attention deficit disorder (ADD) or attention deficit hyperactive disorder (ADHD). In terms of what the students actually do, it doesn't make any difference whether they *won't* learn or *can't* learn. They choose the same behaviors: They don't attend, become hyperactive, or display what is called emotional disturbance.

They may even claim they want to learn and are often puzzled themselves when they seem unable to. A child who knows nothing about his quality world can't tell the difference between not having something like reading in his quality world and having something wrong with his brain that makes it difficult for him to learn to read. All he knows is that he is having trouble learning to read. The way to tell if it is a brain dysfunction or if he has taken reading out of his quality world is to observe him closely. This close observation cannot be done by a pediatrician; he or she does not have the time. It must be done cooperatively by the school and the parents, who then report what has been observed to the pediatrician. Diagnosing and labeling a child as learning disabled or handicapped because of an inadequate brain is a serious diagnosis. It can affect the child's future, so it should be accurate. Here is what to look for.

1. Does the child who is labeled ADD or ADHD watch television and understand what he or she is watching? Does the child play games like Nintendo that require close attention? Is the child able to use a computer?

2. Does the child do better for some teachers than for others?

3. Does the child do better in one subject that requires reading and listening than in another subject that requires the same level of reading and listening?

4. Does the child have good friends, who are attentive in school, with whom he or she enjoys playing and who enjoy playing with him or her?

If the answer to *all* the points of the first question is no, the child probably has a learning disability and should be evaluated by a competent pediatrician, and some of the current brain drugs like Ritalin should be considered. If the answers to questions 2 and 3 are no, again you should suspect a learning disability. If the answer to either one is yes, it is unlikely that the child is learning disabled. The brain does not turn off in special situations; the problem is that the teacher or the subject is not in the child's quality world. If the child has good friends who are attentive in school whom he or she enjoys, question 4, I would not suspect a learning disability. If the child has no good friends, then I would suspect that he or she is lonely and too concerned about making friends to pay attention in school. Before that child is diagnosed and labeled as having a learning disability and given medication for it, a serious attempt should be made to help him or her learn social skills and make friends.

It may also be that the child who is not doing well in school is not getting along well enough with someone at home and may be so concerned about this relationship that he or she is not willing to try to concentrate in school. Before a label is put on any child, the parents should pay close attention to the choice theory child rearing I explained earlier. If too much is expected of young children at home and enforced with punishment or rejection, they may rebel by choosing to do little in school or to disrupt. How the child rebels is not predictable. What to watch for is a child who is very good at home but nonattentive or disruptive in school. This child especially needs help with relationships, and the parents may need some counseling, too.

A mentally healthy child is ordinarily sometimes difficult at home but good both in school and away from home. The child behaves this way because he or she feels loved and secure enough to push the limits at home but sees no reason to do so away from home where people will not accept this behavior. But keep in mind that a child who does not accept a school filled with punishment and *schooling* does not necessarily have an inadequate brain or poor relationships at home. It may be that he or she is more sensitive and more discriminating than other children and even more secure. When my grandson was in the fifth grade, he told his mother that he had done his last calculation in school. He would not disrupt; he would draw while his classmates calculated. His mother told the teacher she would not interfere. My grandson scored high on tests with story problems, so his teacher did not press the point.

In Huntington Woods, the few potential Stacys who enroll are taught in the regular program and are not recommended for medication. They quickly become learners, and some have become outstanding students. Obviously, the problem was not with their brains; it was that schoolwork was not in their quality worlds before. What helps most of the students who are diagnosed as learning disabled in coercive schools is that with this label, many of them are put into special classes where they are not coerced or punished and usually not *schooled*. This environment accounts for a lot of the success that trained special education teachers have had with them.

It is interesting that close to half the population who marries—including teachers—have divorced. Of those who have not, many are unhappily married. The reason for this personal unhappiness is the same as the reason for the Stacys: external control psychology.* For example, when you ask a Stacy why he or she does not like school, the answer is: *The teachers. They don't care for me, they don't listen to me, they try to make me do things I don't want to do, they have no interest in what I want, and it's no fun.*

When you ask an unhappily married woman, *Tell me what's wrong with your marriage*, she almost always says: *My husband. He doesn't love me, he doesn't listen to me, he tries to make me do things I don't want to do, he has little interest in what I want to do, and it's no fun.* When teachers learn enough choice theory to put it to work with the people they want to be close to in their

---

*See my article comparing school failure and marriage failure: William Glasser, "A New Look at School Success and School Failure," *Phi Delta Kappan* (April 1997): pp. 597–602.

own lives and see how successful it is, they will be much more inclined to try it in their classrooms than they are now. And they will be much happier in both places when they do.

THE SCHWAB MIDDLE SCHOOL

The Schwab Middle School, a 700-student seventh- and eighth-grade school in the Cincinnati public school system, was a troubled school when my wife, Carleen, and I arrived in the fall of 1994. Carleen worked full time the whole year, and I consulted and spent about seventy days that year in the school. Ninety percent of the students were African American, and many had failed one or more grades. External control was firmly in place. For example, 1,500 students had been suspended for ten days the year before we came—15,000 school days of suspension. The school was like a sinking ship with the crew and the passengers fighting over the few lifeboats that were operational. But we soon discovered that the staff was highly skilled. They had been fighting a losing battle with the fear-driven system that is central office policy in Cincinnati, as it is in most school districts, for so long that they had almost given up hope.

To be fair, the central office was pressured by the school board, and the board operated in fear of the newspaper and the community. What we were dealing with in Schwab was a good staff rendered close to nonfunctional by the threat-and-fear hierarchy that was and is alive and well in Cincinnati. It took us from September to January to convince the teachers that these students were not dedicated Stacys. They were wannabe Stacys who would change their minds if they were treated differently in a better system.

I asked to be invited into the classrooms, and I received a lot of invitations as soon as the teachers found out that I wanted only to help and support, not to criticize, and that I was willing to work with the students. I would go to a classroom for the period before the teacher had a student-free preparation period so we could talk afterward about what went on. I went to the classroom of a young teacher who had no preparation in his own education or in his teacher training for what he had to contend with at Schwab.

There were about twenty students in attendance. When the bell rang, the teacher locked the door—students were locked in or locked out, depending on how you look at it. It was a math class. The teacher gave a ten-minute lesson on how to solve a story problem that asked students to use a map to find the shortest way from home to school. This was a sensible problem, and the teacher taught a good lesson. The only difficulty, and it was a major difficulty at Schwab, was that I was the only one in the class who was listening. The students were talking at their seats or walking around. About four had their heads down on their tables with their hoods pulled up over their heads. They were inert; they may have been sleeping.

The teacher had put four problems on the board. He finished the lesson and told the students to work on the problems. Not one student even looked at the problems; they all just continued socializing or sleeping. They did this all quietly; there was no noise or fighting. This was actually a good class. Some were much worse, and many with more skilled, experienced teachers were much better. But even in the good classes, although students did work, they retained little of what they learned because a lot of what they were asked to learn was *schooling*. The students could see no way that they could use what they were being asked to memorize in their lives. Since nothing was retained, each day was a new day. I, too, had no preparation for what to do, but I thought that since the teacher viewed me as an expert, he expected me to do something, so I thought I'd better start.

The girl sitting next to me had paid no attention to the teacher and no attention to me. She was writing furiously in a spiral notebook, and her writing was legible. She was doing something educational even if it wasn't math. I asked her softly, "Are you going to do the problems?"

She looked at me with surprise. Either she hadn't seen me or she was surprised that I had spoken to her. She said nothing and went back to her writing. In a polite and interested way, I repeated myself, "Are you going to do the problems?"

She then recognized my presence and said, "What problems?"

"The problems over there on the blackboard."

"Where?"

I pointed. "There."

She looked at them, turned to me, and said, "Oh, those problems."

She went back to her writing.

After a moment I persisted, "Are you going to do them?"

She looked at me as if this was a strange, somewhat foolish question and then politely said, "No."

At this point, the teacher was going around the class prodding students, but no one paid any attention to him. In desperation, because my reputation was on the line and the teacher was also watching me, I said to the young woman who continued to write, "How about if you just do one problem."

She looked at me as if this was an interesting suggestion and apparently liked the way I suggested it, not threatening or criticizing, and said, "OK."

She did the problem easily and then went back to her writing. I summoned up my courage and said, "Look, that was easy. Why don't you do the rest, and you'll have done all the work for today."

She paused a moment in thought and then said "OK" again. With a little help from me, she did the other three problems.

I then said, "Good, go back to your writing."

I took her paper with the problems on it, and now I knew what to do. I spent the rest of the class tutoring students one at a time with good results. (And spent the rest of the year at Schwab tutoring students with good results.) The bell rang and the students left. I asked the teacher if he saw what I did. He said he had, and I gave him the papers of the five students I had tutored. I asked him what he did while I was tutoring, and he told me what I had seen him do: He walked around the class trying to prod students into doing the problems. I asked him if he had any success, and he said, "None." I asked him if he would have had more success if he'd done what I did, and then I got the answer that I heard many times from teachers when I suggested tutoring: "But if I sit down to tutor one student, what will the rest of them do?"

I answered as I always answered, not sarcastically but truthfully, "Exactly what they were doing while you were walking around—nothing. If you had tutored another five, half the class would have done the lesson." A small amount of tutoring was the key with many of these kids. They needed the personal attention. But we discovered that we only had to tutor them a few times to get their attention, and then they would begin to work by themselves as long as the work made sense to them. Schooling occasionally worked at Schwab if it was easy. The students loved doing things they could do for a while, but if it continued too long, they got bored and quit. They also liked the math story problems but needed some help to get started. What they really wanted was a lot of personal attention, a little conversation, the feeling the teacher really knew and cared that they were there. Most of the Schwab teachers were able to teach in a way that made a lot of sense and were willing to give the students the personal invitation to get started that they wanted.

But the teachers needed personal attention just as much as the students did. They were laboring in a system in which the only attention they got was criticism from people who had no idea of how hard their jobs were and couldn't do them if their lives depended on it. From the day we walked into that school, Carleen and I expressed appreciation for their efforts. We spent time with them, talked with them, ate meals with them, taught them all we knew, and listened to them. Quickly it became clear that they knew a lot more about what to do than they were doing but did not feel free to do it. It was as if it was wrong to use their skills to teach effectively, to get as personal as the situation warranted, and to give up all but a little schooling—and to stop threatening and punishing.

In addition to her daily sessions with individual teachers and small groups of teachers in her office, Carleen began to meet after school with whomever would come on Tuesday, Wednesday, and Thursday afternoons. First the meetings were gripe sessions and she listened, but gradually she began to ask the teachers what they wanted that they didn't have now, which gave them the message that she would listen seriously. I attended many of those meetings and told them that we couldn't guarantee we could get very much of what they wanted, but that at least they should tell us. In the beginning they began to ask indirectly for something that I thought we could help them with: Could they teach the way they felt was best? They seemed afraid that if they did what they wanted to do, it might be against central office policy or a deviation from the prescribed curriculum. Fear again. There was a lot of it at Schwab.

When we asked them what we could do to get them the permission to teach as they wanted to, they said they wanted someone with authority to come from the central office and tell them they could teach as they wanted. No one from the central office seemed to want to come to Schwab. Finally, I called a vice president at Procter and Gamble—that company has a lot of influence in Cincinnati—whose assignment was to help the schools. I told him I needed someone from the central office to visit the school and reassure the teachers that they could be flexible in what and how they taught.

He got someone important to come and reassure them. But the teachers didn't believe her and told her so; they wanted it in writing. She then sent a letter confirming what she had said, and this was a huge boost for the teachers. This letter was tangible proof that we weren't just talk. But before they would go ahead, they wanted another letter from the State of Ohio Department of Education, and we got that letter, too. Things began to look up.

The next thing we did was very important. Many of the teachers believed that the students, because of so many years of not doing much in school, were unwilling to buckle down and do some useful schoolwork. To deal with that problem, Carleen and I, with the help of the math department, organized a two day tutor-in for math, their worst subject according to the state achievement tests. We divided the students into groups of ten, each group with a staff member. We had enough on our staff to do this if we used everyone in and out of the classroom.

Carleen got on the phone and went into the neighborhood, the teachers helped, and we got a hundred people to volunteer for the two days. With the math department's assistance, we put together a special math book for the tutor-in, starting from the elementary level and working up to eighth-grade story problems. It was a huge undertaking for Schwab, but it was intended to show that with personal attention and sensible subject matter, the students would buckle down and work.

For the tutor-in, there were, besides a staff member, one or two helpers for every ten students. The groups were spread all over the school. The students were told there would be no failure. They should do as much as they could and ask for help if they needed it, which they would get immediately. It was a remarkable success. For a day and a half they did huge amounts of both calculation and then math and did them both reasonably well. This was neither the time nor place to fight the schooling battle; the last third of the book was story problems, and they enjoyed solving them.

The last half day they still worked but not with the gusto of the first day and a half. We should have stopped then, but it didn't hurt the experiment. The students were relaxed and enjoyed the time to chat with their teachers and helpers. What the tutor-in proved to the teachers is that the students were willing to work in a no-failure, lots-of-help, sensible situation. What we had to do was figure out how to get a similar approach going every day. But the groundwork was laid to do something big.

Carleen continued her one-on-one contacts with the teachers during the day and the after-school meetings. More teachers came, and she asked them over and over what they wanted more than anything else. They told her they wanted smaller classes and no disruptive students. The disruptive students were mostly the over-age students—there were 170 of them—some of whom had been in the seventh grade for up to four years. The teachers said that if we could get rid of these students, they could really teach. These students seemed to be the real Stacys of Schwab; they had given up on learning. Yet even these students worked during the tutor-in.

There already was a special program in Schwab for the over-age students, but only 75 of the 170 were enrolled and only about 40 of them regularly attended. I asked the five teachers who were working with these 40 regularly attending overage students if they would take all the rest. I said that if they would do so, we could transform the school. I was asking them to quadruple their teaching load for no more money, but they were willing to discuss it.

There was a lot of discussion. They said that they needed two more teachers. Two teachers from the regular staff volunteered. They needed a place. I thought that an old wood shop that was being used as a classroom in the present overage program would be ideal for creating the environment we wanted for the students in the new program. Without their asking, the teachers were given total control over the program; there would be no interference from the principal or the central office. The central office had no problem with this request and was supportive of the program from the start. When I explained the program to the principal, he agreed wholeheartedly.

The old shop needed total cleaning, carpeting, painting, and furnishing. There was $22,000 left in an Ohio State Venture Capital Grant awarded to Schwab to be used for our quality school program. Used sofas, dinette sets, and computers were installed. The room was painted and carpeted. It was furnished this way because I believed the room would not work if it looked like a classroom; these students did not have classrooms in their quality worlds.

Now we were able to tell the regular teachers that what they wanted was going to happen. They were going to get smaller classes, on average five fewer students per teacher, and no overage students. At first, they were both pleased and worried. But the fear of the new was a momentary thing. The seven teachers who volunteered to teach the new program interviewed all the overage students and told them what was going to happen. The students were interested. They wanted to graduate and go on to high school but all had given up on the idea that they ever would.

The teachers, with our support, were free to be creative. They worked day and night preparing a new curriculum based totally on the district's required competencies that every student needed to get into high school. Their approach with the students was, Forget all the failure of the past; just show us you have the skills and the knowledge needed for high school. This was to be no free ride.

The program was supposed to start in January but it didn't actually start until the second Tuesday in February 1995. It was called the Cambridge Program, patterned after the university in England. The large room was to become the commons; five adjacent classrooms were used for tutorials in math, science, social studies, career education, and remedial language arts. The main language arts were to be in the commons.

The first day looked chaotic. All 170 students showed up, but no one knew exactly what to do. In all the seeming chaos, I sat in the center of the room at a table tutoring some students in math. The second day was less hectic; I continued to tutor, now in English. The staff were discouraged, but I was encouraged. It seemed a lot more organized than I thought it was going to be. The students were loud, but I noticed no hostility. Everyone was pleasant, and we never lost that pleasant mood.

The third day there was an act of God. It snowed and the yellow buses didn't run. Only eighty students showed up in the whole school that day—forty who could walk to school and were in the regular program, and forty from the Cambridge program, all of whom normally rode the bus, who somehow got there on their own. Those forty had seven teachers and one teacher's aide all to themselves. They did a lot of work that day and loved it. After that day, we were over the hump.

There were no traditional seat-time classes. It was all tutorial, and the students had the choice of what tutorial to go to and when. We said they had to be fair about it, and they were. Before long they had their own schedules worked out. It was the first time any of them had this much choice in school, and they were thrilled. They could change their schedule every day if they wished. Their job was to show us they could do what was required to move to high school.

Individual tests were given, but no one failed because the students were told just to keep working until they could show the teachers they could do the lessons that the teachers were continuing to work day and night to create. As soon as a student finished an assignment by showing the staff personally what he or she had done and it was accepted, the student went on to the next lesson and then the next. There were a lot of competencies, and the students worked harder than they had ever worked in school. As soon as they completed all that was needed for a subject, they were finished with that subject.

These students were now in business for themselves. They knew what to do, they knew they could do it, and it was their choice to do it. If they didn't do it, they understood they would continue on next year until they did. It soon became apparent that we would need a summer school program to allow most of them to finish. We got permission to extend our Cambridge Program into summer school, and many students finished their requirements. With these students out of the regular classes, the school was quiet and orderly. Our students became polite, even though no one spoke to them about manners. There was no vandalism, no graffiti, and not one hole was poked in the upholstered furniture.

The six security assistants for the 700-student school who were busy the first semester had less and less to do, but they made a great contribution by socializing with the students. The students needed socializing with happy people who cared about them more than anything if they were to get the idea that they, too, could be happy without drugs and violence. By the end of summer school, 148 of the 170 students enrolled in the Cambridge Program went on to high school. The predicted number for this group when the school year began was close to zero.

As much as possible, we got rid of the failure that is so disastrous in school, especially when there is little support for school in the home. Even more important, we got rid of it for the staff as well. I don't want anyone to think that we did more than we did. What we did is show it could be done and at a cost of $22,000 plus some training money left over from the previous year. Carleen's salary was paid by the district. Since Carleen is a senior instructor in the William Glasser Institute, she was able to do all the training continuously throughout the year. The staff we inherited was capable but demoralized. It was how they were treated that helped them to do what they did. What we practiced was *lead management* based on choice theory. What they were used to was boss management based on external control psychology.

What we began at Schwab has been accomplished at Huntington Woods. At Huntington, they have created a happy school. Their happiness is based on good relationships, on everyone in the school putting each other into their quality worlds: teachers, students, administrators, and parents. This is the key to any successful organization or relationship, such as marriage and the family. When the students at Schwab were asked why they were working and getting along, they always said, *This is a good school; you care about us.* It's so simple to say, but in our coercive world, so hard to do.

School Discipline

When we got to Schwab, the school was almost nonfunctional. Few of the students were in order, and even fewer were learning. The halls between classes were filled with yelling, screaming, pushing students. Every forty-three minutes when the bell rang, it looked like a scene from a rock concert where no one could find a seat. All the teachers could think about was discipline, and the main procedures were segregation into time-out rooms and suspension. What we did was to show the teachers that discipline is never the problem. The problem is sensible education–no schooling, no failure, a lot of care, a lot of patience, and an opportunity to start over if you are far behind. At the end of the year, a lot more education was still needed, but disorder was no longer a problem. We had made a strong beginning toward changing from a punitive bossing system to a satisfying, choice theory leading system.

For years, schools all over the country have been buying discipline programs that promise to get students in order in a coercive system. Such programs provide fertile ground for problems to occur. I developed one myself in the 1970s, the Ten-Step Discipline Program based on reality therapy, and unfortunately it is still in use. But by the time I began to understand choice theory, I realized that rebellion or resistance to being forced to do what you don't want to do is the natural, even the sensible, choice. Discipline programs, even those that are *kindly coercive*, do not work on potential Stacys who are the real problem. They work only on the students who have teachers and schoolwork in their quality worlds. But, of course, these students don't need these programs. They need a little attention, a little patience, and a lot of useful education.

The school administrators believe in these programs because they think the programs would have worked on them when they were students, and it is probably true. These people had, and still have, teachers and schoolwork in their quality worlds and were rarely out of order. It is analogous to the parents who show up at Parent-Teachers Association meetings and school functions. It's good to have them, but they're not the ones who need to be there; their children do well in our schools as they are.

Examples of the programs that are now in vogue besides my ten-step program are assertive discipline (pure but mild coercion) and restitution, a program that claims to follow my ideas. But because it focuses on the student, not on changing the system, it is not following the quality school concepts I clearly spelled out in *The Quality School* and *The Quality School Teacher*. Any program that focuses on changing the student instead of the system is not a choice theory program. What we started at Schwab, and what has been put into place at Huntington Woods, is a complete change of the system. In a choice theory system there are disciplinary incidents but rarely problems. Each incident is treated individually; programmatic approaches to discipline will not work. There is no happiness in coercion and punishment.

HUNTINGTON WOODS

This small elementary school in Wyoming, Michigan, is completely based on choice theory, and the teachers, students, principal, and parents have each other in their quality worlds. It was started by a dedicated and charismatic principal, Kaye Mentley. Everything described in my two books on quality schools can be seen in operation in this school, as well as the class meetings that are so crucial to the success of any school program, which are explained in my *Schools Without Failure*. But the entire staff has created, and continues to create, far more than I could even imagine when I wrote those books. It is the kind of school that I would want my grandchildren to attend and your children and grandchildren, too. Although I will describe it and urge you to visit it, it should not be copied. It is, as is Schwab, a school to be understood. Once you understand it, you can also create a quality school, but one that you tailor to the needs of your staff, students, and community.

Kaye Mentley read *The Quality School* and immediately had a dream, *I want one*. She was then the principal of a good elementary school in Wyoming and she began to start to realize her dream in that school. But it was difficult; some of the staff wanted to learn choice theory and others did not. As Abraham Lincoln might have said, a school divided against itself will never become a quality school. Even Huntington Woods could not have accomplished all it has unless it started with an undivided staff. To start with a highly divided staff and students who have been threatened and punished for years, as we did at Schwab, makes the job much harder. However, Schwab had one advantage over an easier school: The staff was not complacent; most of the teachers were desperate for change.

With strong parental support for what they have accomplished, Huntington Woods could expand into a middle school and high school if it had the room. Expanding from an elementary school is one way to create secondary quality schools. To do what we did at Schwab with so many turned-off students to begin with is much harder. The sensible thing to do in Cincinnati would have been to use Schwab as the middle school model and create a K–12 track focusing on what was being done at Schwab. Whatever money any school, whose students come from homes that are not highly supportive of education, spends that continues to use coercion and punishment will either be wasted or, more likely, make things worse.

The superintendent of the Wyoming Schools saw the problem Kaye was facing and believed in Kaye's ability to lead a school to become a quality school. He had an old, unused elementary building and offered it to her. She could take the teachers she wanted from her present school and hire other teachers who believed in the ideas and were willing to do the training. Now her entire staff has had training, and most have finished the institute's training program and have been certified in the use of choice theory ideas. It is this kind of dedication that has made Huntington Woods one of the top elementary schools in the nation.

What you see at Huntington Woods is happiness. There is joy on the students' faces, and the teachers are obviously very happy doing what they are doing. The school is a beehive of activity; children inside and outside the classrooms are busy learning. There is no schooling. Children are learning by themselves or in a variety of group situations. The classes are all double, fifty students and two teachers. Each class is made up of students in one of two age groups. Kindergarten and grades one and two are in the lower grouping; grades three, four, and five are in the upper grouping. By the time the children get ready to move to the upper level, many are already doing upper-level work.

There is no failure; no sense of I'm ahead of you or behind you in school; and no attempt to keep the students apart in the classes by any measure, including age. The teachers share the instruction, and because two are in each double classroom, one can tutor while the other teaches if that seems the thing to do. The children also help each other, and the upper level will send students to the lower level to tutor or help. The competition is more with oneself than with others. There are no bells and no formal recess. The teachers can take the children outside to play or to learn any time they want to for as long as they want.

The teachers and children eat together in the room, and this is a time for relaxing and socializing. The emphasis is always on getting along with each other and enjoying each other's company. The teachers are treated as professionals. They decide what goes on in their classroom. The principal's job is to see that they are able to do it. She is on call anytime a teacher wants her for anything, including taking over all fifty students if that is what's needed.

All the children are taught choice theory, and by the time they are in the school a year, most of them know it quite well. They know they are in a quality school and why. There are signs all over the school saying, "Whenever we have a problem, we talk it over with the people who are involved and work out a solution with no one threatening or hurting anyone else." Because problems are worked out, there are no ongoing problems or problem children. All the teachers and the principal are trained to counsel, so while there are occasional disciplinary incidents, they are worked out as soon as they occur. There is no punishment or time out.

There is absolutely no need for a discipline program; taking care of problems individually, not through an inflexible program, is the ongoing practice. But even though all the teachers have been trained to counsel using choice theory, the main reason there are no problems is that the quality school program prevents problems. Schools with the kind of teacher-student relationships that are the norm at Huntington Woods have no difficult problems.

There is no programmatic focus on learning disabilities. The staff recognizes that children learn differently, and the program is adjusted to take care of these normal differences. Some children have been diagnosed as suffering from some sort of learning disability, but so far they have been handled easily by the program. A few of the children are on medication for behavioral or learning problems, but this is at the parents' request. The school never requests this.

To give you the flavor of this school, here is one of the many letters I get from Kaye Mentley:

How are things with you? I hope terrific; they sure are that way with me! We had a new fifth-grade student enroll three weeks ago. He is a foster child with one of our families. When I talked to him, he told me he hated all schools, all teachers, and everything about school! I told him, OK, he could hate us, too, and I was glad he was here. I wish you could see the difference in his face from three weeks ago to now. He is smiling, loves his teachers, is doing ALL his work, and even told a visitor last week that he loves this school. We also got a new second-grade student two weeks ago. She said that this school is much better than her old school because the students are all nice to each other and the teachers don't yell at her. She says she is learning a lot more than at her old school.

Since Kaye is a firm believer in our economic system, visitors have to get on a waiting list and pay $50 for the privilege. She pays for almost all the training with this money, and the more she raises the price, the more people want to come. The students show visitors the whole program; it's part of their education. Even cleaning the school and replacing the towels and the toilet paper are a part of their education. The students know how much everything in the school costs and how much work is needed to keep the school functioning. They do not waste supplies, time, or money, since they have learned the value of what they are asked to do. They are paid for their work in school money, but they have to use that money to rent their desks and to buy their supplies. There is no free ride at this quality school. In this program, school mirrors life.

COMPETENCE, OR TLC, AND TESTING IN A QUALITY SCHOOL

In a quality school, to get credit, all students must do competent work—the equivalent of B in a traditional grading system. There are no lower grades than B. This situation again mirrors the real world, in which competence is the minimum requirement to succeed. Besides, even though it is not required, all are encouraged to do some quality work or the equivalent of what would be A or better in all other schools. This level of competence has been achieved at Huntington Woods. The worst flaw in the punitive schools we have is that they use low grades not only for punishment but to give students credit for incompetent work. In any place work is done, you cannot accept anything less than competence if you want high quality. In a quality school, we call that level TLC, for "total learning competency." That TLC is also the acronym for "tender loving care" is a lucky coincidence.

The students, however, are urged to improve any of their good work until they and their teachers agree that it is now quality work. One of the ways in which quality work is accomplished is through using tests, but not so much to measure students' progress as to increase the quality of their work. To understand what I mean, let me suggest a way to increase our knowledge of the rules of the road by improving the written test we take now when we get or renew our driver's licenses.

Recently I had my driver's license renewed in California. I studied the booklet, but when I took the test I had difficulty with a lot of the questions and I had to guess. I barely passed. I missed six (out of thirty-five) questions, the limit you can miss and still pass. They kept my test so I had no chance to learn what I missed, and I left feeling that the test did not accomplish what it set out to do. There are important rules of the road I don't know, and the next time I will even think about learning them will be four years from now. This, like most of the tests we take in school, was not a learning experience.

Even though all the licensed drivers on the road eventually passed this test, many, like me, don't know and perhaps will never know the answers to the questions they missed. And since the test does not cover more than half the questions in the booklet they give you to study for the test, I think it is safe to say that most drivers do not know more that three-quarters of what they should know. This is a perfect example of a nonlearning or *schooling* test. I suggest that California use a longer test with a question covering every point in the study booklet, maybe as long as sixty questions. To pass, you would have to get every question correct.

Under the present system, it would be impossible to institute these requirements because very few would pass. As in the schools, what needs to be changed is the system. The change could be simple, like making it an open-booklet test. There would be no excuse for not passing; people would just sit there and keep studying the booklet until they answered all the questions correctly. To check if what I am suggesting is valid, two things could be done. One, give the applicants the choice of the old way, in which they could fail, or the new way, in which they couldn't fail. My guess is that most of the applicants would opt for the longer open-booklet version. Two, give an oral test six months later to two randomly selected groups, those who took the short version and those who took the long version, and check which group knows more. I'd bet heavily on those who took the long version.

This is the kind of learning test that is used in a quality school, where children are always tested for their ability to use knowledge. There is no schooling in a quality school, so there are no schooling questions on the tests and all tests are open book. These tests require the students to do much more than remember; they require the students to think. However, most tests are short and are given frequently. A test in math, science, history, or English literature might have one question, but the answer would have to demonstrate competence. No credit is given for anything less than a competent answer.

To demonstrate competence, the answer usually has to be written, but beyond that, at the teacher's or student's request, the student would be asked or given the opportunity to explain to the teacher or a teacher's assistant why she chose to answer a certain way. By doing so, the students get ongoing practice in speaking, listening, and thinking about what they write, and the teacher checks students personally to make sure they understand what they have answered. The skills of speaking and listening have the largest payoff of all we learn, and the present schooling schools do next to nothing to teach this important skill.

For example, a history question might be, "Why did George Washington turn down the offer to become king after we won the War of Independence, and how do you think his decision has helped our country?" A science question might be, "Why are scientists worried about Earth warming?" A math problem might be, "Your father is painting the house. He tells you to go to the store and get enough paint for the first coat. You have to figure out how much paint to buy." In English literature, a question might be, "What problems did each character in the story have, and how would you have solved them?" For each question, the student would have to write a competent answer or solve the problem.

If the work is competent, the student is finished. If the work is not competent, the student is told, "Keep working until we are both sure you are competent." The teacher may ask competent students to continue and improve what they did to the point of quality. The students may also do so on their own, and this is what good students usually do. But no student would be coerced to try for quality.

If there is a sure way not to get quality, it is to use coercion. Therefore, in a quality school such as Huntington Woods, there is no enforced competition, but there are many incentives for students to do their personal best. The students can compare what they did with what other students did, but what other students do cannot affect anyone's grade. The teacher not only checks the work but encourages and gives thoughtful feedback so the student can get a better grasp of what he or she is learning. This need-satisfying intellectual interaction creates a powerful learning climate. The students are busy thinking, speaking, listening, and solving problems at Huntington Woods.

In our present schooling schools, students memorize enough to pass or to do well, but there is no competence or quality in memorizing. When the usual test is finished, it's over, whether the student did well, barely passed, or even failed. The students rarely learn the basics of quality, which is continual improvement based on feedback. They settle for good enough, as the young man from Alma, Michigan, did. It was good-enough A work, but he recognized it was far from the best he could do and always did on the basketball team. In a quality school, students compete against themselves. They can never lose and often help each other because what they do for someone else has no effect on their grades. This is much closer to the way the real world works; no business can survive unless the workers are competent, cooperative, and moving toward quality. Our present schools are filled with students doing C and D work, cooperation is rare, and quality is an endangered idea bordering on extinction. We owe our students more.

People ask, "What if the students never do competent work?" The answer is that they never get credit. They are helped, encouraged, and allowed to take the tests home. But to get credit, no matter how long it takes, they have to do a good job. If this approach is started in kindergarten, there is no problem. Students like to do good work, and given time, they all do it easily. Although we started later at Schwab Middle School, most of the students caught on and did the work to get into high school. The ones who refused were held back to try next year. But 148 out of 170 did more work than they had done in years, maybe more than they had ever done in school. The old system of one shot at a test and failure if you don't pass had led to their giving up in school. Think of this: If you were a student, would you like to be given a longer time to do good work with no schooling or would you like to be flunked quickly if you did poor work and given no chance to improve? Students are no different from you.

Another question is, "I have thirty students in my class. Where can I find the time to go over all their work?" In practice, since they are all working, there is usually time. You go around and spend a little time with individuals as they do the work. You can quickly find out who needs you and who doesn't. You have no disciplinary problems to contend with. Discipline became much less of a problem at Schwab when the students buckled down and did what was needed for entering high school.

In a quality school, the proficient students are offered jobs as teacher's assistants, and they love to do them. If TAs are routinely accepted in college, why not in public schools? The TAs do quality work on the tests and then help the teacher check what other students are doing. They learn more in the process than they could possibly learn by just doing a good job on the tests. One of the teacher's jobs is to help the TAs when they get stuck. In this quality system, in which there is no failure but all must be competent, to get credit is so motivating that teachers are free to teach; they no longer have to police.

Another question is, "The problem with this system is they all do good work. How do we rank them?" The answer is, you don't. The present ranking based on schooling is phony. If principals tell the colleges what is required at their schools, I assure you that any student who had a record of being a TA would be looked at closely even by competitive colleges. The students who memorize and calculate well now rank high, but if you follow them to college and out into the real world, they don't do nearly as well as students who are asked to think and use knowledge. Anyone who thinks that the real world is like school doesn't know the real world. Using knowledge cooperatively is the only payoff in the real world. A quality school prepares students for the real world, in which you get paid only for good work. You usually get more pay for quality work and a pink slip for poor work.

We do not pay students in schooling schools, but we accept low-quality work and do not insist on good work. We do expel students, but rarely for poor work. In a quality school, unless the students do enough competent work to pass a course, nothing is recorded on their transcripts. This is what the real world does; for example, a bank does not keep a record of the money you don't have. There may be students who don't do enough work to graduate, but this system graduates many more students than the present system and the students who graduate are competent. The present Cs and Ds produce incompetent students, many of whom think they are competent because they got credit. To give credit for incompetence is phony, and the students are cheated. What makes the quality system work, as it has begun to do at Schwab, is that students know exactly where they stand. They are in control of their own destiny, which means they can blame only themselves if they don't choose to do competent work, and there is no way to cheat.

The final question is, "How do we cover all we have to cover if we have to wait for slow students to do competent work?" The question I have to ask in return is, "When you cover more ground, are all the students with you?" You know that the faster you go, the more students you leave behind. It doesn't matter how much or how fast you teach. The true measure is how much students have learned. Would you rather be operated on by a slow, competent surgeon or a fast, incompetent one? The way our schools work now, a lot of students don't get anywhere, they don't know what's going on, they often don't even know where they are supposed to go. Many don't get there, and many C and D students who think they are there don't even know where *there* is.

One essential requirement in a quality school is writing, and learning to write takes time. Every year, all year long, the teachers work with students to improve their writing. Since almost all the short tests are written—a few are oral—they continually teach writing and the grammar that is needed to express ideas clearly. This is always actual context teaching and is always useful. By the end of the year, all the students have to demonstrate high-quality writing or improvement in their writing from the beginning of the year.

They can demonstrate that they have improved in any way they see fit. Some use their improved tests, the ones they followed through to quality, to demonstrate that they can write well. Others embark on a writing project like writing a book. Others use the writing they do for extracurricular activities like the school newspaper. Anytime during the year, they can ask their teachers to check them off if they believe they are writing well. It is up to them to evaluate their writing, go to their teachers with it, and ask if the teachers agree.

All students in a quality school also do a special project of their own choosing, which may or may not be based on what they are assigned to study. Anything the students suggest that they can justify as useful before beginning, is eligible. A science project, a book, a song or a video, a community service project, anything the students figure out that can be recognized as quality is fine. The students make informal monthly progress reports, so the projects are not left to the last minute. No prize is given for the best project unless the students want to be competitive. It is up to the students to figure out the best way to show their work to the school and to others. Students love this opportunity to use their creativity, and doing these projects gets the idea of quality across to them better than anything else they can do. The projects are theirs. When we own something, we put our best efforts into it.

COMPETENCE OR PROFICIENCY TESTING

I used to think that the state proficiency tests were unfair and inaccurate, but I don't think so anymore as long as the students are allowed plenty of time and the tests are not focused on memorizing and calculation. There are at least two reasons why many students do badly on these tests now. *First, they don't read the questions very well. Second, they haven't enough experience taking these kinds of tests.*

To read the questions well, students have to learn to read better than most do now, and the way to help them do so is to give them more experience with writing. Writing is the best preparation for good reading. That is why there are few objective tests in a quality school. Writing, problem solving, and explaining are the best preparation for these tests. But the main reason that students don't do well has to do with the myth that learning can be transferred. It may a little, but for most students it does not transfer as much as most educators think.

If you want to do well on the basketball court, you don't play baseball or football; you play basketball. If you want students to test well on multiple-choice tests, they need to practice on these exact tests. You can't assume that the teacher-constructed tests they are given in most classes will prepare them adequately for the state tests. Practice tests are available, and they should be used.

No students will complain if you ask them to answer one question a day and teach them how to answer it if they have difficulty. Start in the fall, and by Christmas every student should be able to answer correctly all the questions on one seventy-five-question state test and understand why the answers are correct.

It takes time to prepare students for these tests (though not much), but it is time well spent. I think teachers could devote half the fourth grade to this endeavor because schools are so heavily judged by their fourth-grade students' performance on these tests. The fourth graders would learn a lot by spending time on these tests and really learning why the answers are correct. Don't think that the time is wasted. These tests are devised by experts; what they ask is worth knowing, and using this procedure gets results. It is not cheating; the tests are there to be used in any way you want. Besides knowing the material, there is a skill to taking tests that can be learned only with practice. For example, studies have shown that reading the answer choices before reading the question substantially increases the scores. Teachers could check that research out in their classes as a game. Whatever you do, don't give the students the real test cold. That's unfair.

The Huntington Woods School gets good scores on the Michigan state tests—at the eighty-fifth percentile or higher—without what I am advising here. That is a tribute to the teachers' competence in teaching. But I still think that for most schools, a little practice is in order. If schools are not teaching for competence and quality, I advise a lot of practice. Look at all the practice that goes into taking the SAT or the ACT and the money it makes for test-preparation companies. Preparation must pay off, or these companies would not be in business.

What I have suggested about quality schools is my ideal. In actual practice, some schools that are trying to become quality schools will not slavishly follow my suggestions. The kind of people who are involved in quality schools are creative thinkers and implementers. The teachers at Huntington Woods know what they are doing and have added to many of my ideas and gone much further than if they depended more on me. But what is behind everything they do is choice theory. Good relationships are the key. Beyond that, schools are limited only by their own experience and creativity.

The Criteria for a Quality School

At a minimum, there are six criteria for a quality school:

1. All disciplinary problems, not incidents, will be eliminated in two years. A significant drop should occur in year one.

2. At the time the school becomes a quality school, achievement scores on state assessment tests should be improved over what was achieved in the past.

3. TLC means that all grades below competence, or what is now a B, will be eliminated. Students will have to demonstrate competence to their teachers or to designated teacher's assistants to get credit for the grades or courses. All schooling will be eliminated and replaced by useful education.

4. All students will do some quality work each year—that is, work that is significantly beyond competence. All such work will receive an A or higher grade. This criterion will give hardworking students a chance to show that they can excel.

5. All staff and students will be taught to use choice theory in their lives and in their work in school. Parents will be encouraged to participate in study groups to become familiar with choice theory. A few of these groups will be led by teachers to start, but parent volunteers will be asked to take the groups over once they get started.

6. It will be obvious by the end of the first year that this is a joyful school.

CHAPTER 11

Choice Theory in the Workplace

IN 1942, WHEN my late wife was sixteen years old, she worked part time in the office of a large paint factory. The owner, a wealthy man in his eighties, enjoyed bringing her into his office to tell her stories about how cleverly he had run the factory. His favorite story started in 1932 during the height of the Great Depression. At that time his office staff, about forty people, was managed by a woman who had been with him for years. One day he told the manager he wanted her to start work at eight instead of the usual eight thirty and would pay her for the extra half hour. But she was not to tell anyone she was being paid for the extra time.

In 1932, jobs were scarce; there were ten people ready to step in immediately if there was an opening. Six days a week—they regularly worked Saturday morning—forty employees saw the manager hard at work when they came in. A few came earlier and then a few more. They were afraid to say anything to her, and of course she said nothing. Fearing for their jobs, they began to come in earlier and earlier until, in a few months, they were all coming in at eight and going right to work. When he told my wife the story, the old man laughed and slapped his leg saying, "A half hour free work, twenty hours a day, six days a week out of forty people for nine years." Then the war started, jobs were plentiful, and the scam was over.

Boss Management

The power of bosses like that old man has now been curtailed somewhat by better times, but boss management, my designation for external control psychology in the workplace, is still very much the norm. Although many school administrators boss teachers and do untold harm to education, they have nowhere near the power that most private-sector bosses have to send the message: I am someone to fear. But if high-quality work is what the manager is trying to achieve, fear is the worst strategy. The core idea of the leader of the world's move to quality, W. Edwards Deming, is *Drive out fear*.

For most of us, work is the defining component of our lives. What do you do? is often the first question asked when you meet someone. If you are doing very little, this is a painful question. Unhappiness, not so much with the job itself, but with the person you work for or the people you work with, is a leading cause of low-quality work.

Just as a test, when I began to write this chapter, I looked in the newspaper for an example of this unhappiness, and there it was. A man, thinking he was being taunted and ridiculed at work, killed two fellow workers and wounded three others. Two days later, I couldn't miss a front-page story about low-level managers being asked to work overtime, up to forty hours a week, or be fired. The old man at the paint company is not as out of date as I thought. Being treated well at work by both supervisors and each other is in all our quality worlds. When a worker, at any level, is discontented, low-quality work is the result.

Although a top manager who bosses sets the norm for the whole organization, in today's managerial climate blatant bossing does not usually occur at the top. But because it is still a fixture in most workers' minds, it pervades the whole organization unless the top manager has taken some obvious steps toward lead management. Even if these steps have been taken, it takes several years for this fact to register in the minds of lower-level managers who have known nothing but bossing. The longer a lower-level manager has been exposed to bossing, the more he or she uses it, no matter what is occurring at the top. In practice, this means that the lowest-level managers tend to use bossing the most and are the hardest to reach when an organization is trying to change to leading. In a small company of one manager and two workers, even the senior worker tends to boss the other.

The specific harm of boss management is that it prevents anyone who is bossed, which means most managers and almost all workers, from putting the people above them into their quality worlds. But it goes further than this, creating a dog-eat-dog climate in which trust is the dog that always gets eaten. Low quality and high cost are the prices we pay for all this unnecessary distrust and fear. If we are to have any chance of ridding the world of work from the depredations of boss management, the people at the top need to become aware of its effects and then take active steps to replace it with lead management based on choice theory. As they do, they have to be prepared for a struggle. Lower-level bosses like to boss, and workers don't mind it too much because it gives them the excuse to play the ancient workplace game: do as little as you can get away with and blame the boss for the low quality of the work.

Boss management is not complicated. Reduced to its essentials, it contains four elements:

1. At all levels, the boss sets the task and the standards for how well the work is to be done and rarely consults workers in this process. The boss does not compromise; the workers have to

adjust to their jobs as the boss defines them or suffer the consequences, including losing their jobs when there is no union or contractual protection against this power. The boss fights long and hard for the right to boss without interference. The more he or she bosses, however, the lower the quality of the work.

2. The boss usually tells, rather than shows, the workers how the job is to be done and rarely asks for their input as to how the job could be done better.

3. The boss, or someone the boss designates, inspects the work. Because the workers are not involved in this evaluation, most do only enough to get by and inspectors are continually under pressure to pass low-quality work. This is a deadly quality-destroying combination. Furthermore, in a boss-driven environment, workers who do more than they have to are ostracized by their coworkers. Since the work itself is never in the workers' quality worlds, the idea of doing quality work rarely crosses their minds. They laugh at the slogans about quality that are a fixture of many modern boss-managed workplaces.

4. When the workers resist the boss, as they almost always do in a variety of ways that compromise quality, the boss uses threats and punishment to try to make them do what he or she wants. In so doing, the boss creates a workplace in which, from top to bottom, the managers and workers are adversaries and fear rules. The boss thinks this adversarial relationship is the way things should be; cooperation with workers is a subversive idea.

In this present era of high employment, it may seem as if I am making too much of an issue of how people are managed. There are plenty of jobs, and the country is prosperous. The major factors that have led to this prosperity are low inflation, stable prices, workers who are not demanding more than small wage increases, and technology that has led to increased productivity at the same or lower cost. Competition has also kept prices and wages in check, and the Federal Reserve Board seems able to adjust interest rates to keep inflationary pressures low. There doesn't seem to be any popular demand for greatly lower taxes and no wars are in sight, both of which tend to restrain interest rates and keep a lid on inflation. All this has been coupled with a slow but steady deflationary decrease in the deficit.

What we have done, and no one seems sure of how we have accomplished it, is to achieve a good balance of all the factors needed for prosperity. But this balance is delicate. It depends on restraining something that has never in human history been restrained very long, something endemic to business and politics that has destroyed prosperity in every modern society the world has ever known: *human greed*.

There are plenty of greedy people who, thinking only of themselves, do not even try to understand how fragile prosperity is. Some are demanding lower taxes, others higher wages. Some say there should be more military spending, others less. A popular rallying cry is cut big government, while others say there is a limit, that we must maintain a safety net. If any single group gets as much as it wants, the fragile balance we seem to have fallen into may be destroyed. History will repeat itself: The stock market will falter, and prosperity will be threatened.

The Federal Reserve Board can regulate interest rates, but it can't regulate the potential for greed that is written into our genes. Coupling a variation of the third false belief of external control psychology—It is right for me to have much more than others—with the genetic need for power, *greedy people picture themselves in their quality worlds as deserving a lot more than other people*. Historically, the prosperity pictures in the quality worlds of powerful people have never been successfully frustrated.

If these pictures raise their ugly heads too high, the present years of low inflation and high employment will come to a screeching halt. We will then have to repeat the painful process of getting all the prosperity factors back into balance. It took almost twenty years and a war to do so the last time, and the stock market is rolling along with as much or more power as in 1929.

In defense of what seems to be their greed, the people who want a lot for themselves use the *I deserve it* argument and claim it is their skills that keep their companies competitive. Without these skills, there would be much less job security for their employees than there is now. I can't fault this argument; look at all the jobs and wealth Bill Gates has created. Who can say that Gates does not deserve the billions he's made for what he has done? Unfortunately, the main cause of greed has little to do with what anyone deserves. It is the product of the intense need for power in the genes of greedy, successful people. These people, like all of us, are driven by what they feel, and the stronger the need, the better it feels to satisfy it, no matter what others may suffer.

Within reason, taxing seems to be a way to limit greed that most Americans, the greedy are an exception, have accepted. Our rate of tax compliance is among the highest in the world, strong evidence that we are not a greedy people. But it is also well known that the greedy in all societies throughout history have been creative in evading taxes, so taxation has never been as successful a balancing factor as it might be. Political systems with no free elections work badly because there is no way to restrain greed without the ability to pick who governs.

As much as our American system is criticized, we may be among the least greedy people with wealth and power the world has ever known. Europe did not ask for the Marshall Plan after World War II. General George Marshall, a man who seemed to have no greed at all, offered it, and the American people supported it. This leads to the question I would like to try to answer: *Will we always have so many greedy people that there is no way to ensure much longer periods of prosperity than we have had?*

The answer to that question would be yes if all successful, wealthy people with strong power needs also had very weak needs for love and belonging. People with that profile never restrain their desire for more, no matter how much they have. What prosperity we have had has been due to the fact that besides their strong need for power, most people who have become successful also have a strong need for love and belonging. They built a lot of their success on good relationships with the people they do business with and with the people who work for them.

When some successful people become greedy, it may be that their love and belonging behaviors, which might be strong enough to moderate their greed in a choice theory society, are difficult to express in our external control world. They tend to distrust people who are not their friends and, especially, people who are less fortunate than they are. If the people who are in charge of others, almost all of whom have normal or even above normal needs for love and belonging, made an effort to learn choice theory—and use it successfully in their personal lives—they might attempt to make more friendly contact with the people they manage.

Once you give up external control psychology for choice theory, it is almost impossible for you to come into contact with people who work for you and not think about how much better it would be if we all got along well. If these contacts are satisfying, it feels good, and you will tend to want even better relationships; that's how our genes work. If Scrooge was able to give up being greedy, there is still a little hope for the world, but something more than ghosts and spirits is needed. We will never make a dent in greed with the psychology we are now using.

We have hardly scratched the surface of the prosperity we could have if we changed from bossing to leading in the workplace. Southwest Airlines is successful because its satisfied employees work hard for a CEO who is not greedy, who does not downsize when other, more greedy, managers would. I am not so naive as to claim that people will not work hard for bosses. Many will because they see themselves as hard workers, no matter how they are treated. They will give their hands and, even, their brains to a boss. But they will give their hearts only to a leader, and the feeling we experience when that happens is something a boss will never know.

LEAD MANAGEMENT

Lead management is to boss management as choice theory is to external control psychology. While it is effective anywhere it is used to manage people, it is much easier to practice in the workplace than in schools because there are few on-the-job equivalents of schooling. Some things you are asked to do on the job may not be pleasant, but everything you are asked to do has some value in the real world. Also, you are paid to work, and on most jobs, although you can be fired, there is no failure in the sense that you are failed in school for refusing to do what makes little sense to you. What makes work more difficult than school is that, unlike school, almost all jobs depend on people working together. Even if you want to do your best at work, you may be frustrated because others you depend on are not doing their share. But when others are doing their share, working hard together for a good manager can be one of life's most satisfying experiences.

What makes boss management so destructive is that it focuses on individuals and pits them against each other, as was done in the paint factory. What makes lead management so successful is that it focuses on creating a cooperative system and on the belief that if you treat people well and explain what you want them to do, you can trust them to do a good job. In the following four elements of lead management, you will continually see that the message, *We care about you,* is central to this effort. Lead managers know that caring costs nothing and has a huge return. Lead managers keep asking themselves the core choice theory question: If I do this, will I get closer to the people who work for me or further away? If the answer, which is usually obvious, is further away, they don't do it.

Lead managers also know choice theory and use it in a way that is apparent. But as it is being used, it is extremely effective to teach the workers choice theory so they understand that this is something that can be both learned and used. A good way to do this is to offer to teach choice theory to the workers and their spouses at a company-sponsored seminar. This way they all see that it is not just another company gimmick but a genuine attempt to help them succeed not only at work but also with their partners and children.

Lead managers know that the core of quality is managing workers so they put the manager; each other; the work; the customers; and, in private industry, the stockholders into their quality worlds. That is, all who are involved must get close and stay close. As in every other area discussed in this book, good relationships are the key in the workplace. There are four elements of lead management that parallel what I described as boss management:

1. Lead managers engage all workers in an ongoing honest discussion of both the quality and the cost of the work that is needed for the company to be successful. They not only listen but continually encourage the workers to offer them any suggestions that will improve quality and lower costs.

2. The lead manager, or someone designated by him or her, models the jobs so the workers can see exactly what the manager expects. Even as the lead manager is doing so, the workers are encouraged to give input into how their jobs may be done better. In this way, the manager works to increase the workers' control over their jobs.

3. The workers are responsible for inspecting their own work with the understanding that they know best what high-quality work is and how to produce it at the lowest possible cost. But the manager makes it clear that quality takes precedence over cost. In practice, when the workers are given this assurance, quality goes up and costs go down. High quality depends on a level of trust between workers and managers that cannot be achieved by bossing.

4. The lead manager uses every chance he or she has to teach that the essence of quality is continual improvement. Unlike schooling, everything that is done in any job can be improved or done more economically. The managers make it clear that their task is to facilitate improvement by providing the workers with the tools, training, and a friendly place to do the work. When the company is making higher profits because of increased quality, the lead manager sets up a compensation system in which the workers share some of what their efforts have made possible.

The strongest argument for lead management in the workplace is that because it is both more productive and leads to higher-quality work, it saves money. This is money that boss-managed companies must spend. There is no difference in the actual cost of labor and material between competitive companies. Ford and General Motors pay similar wages and buy steel and tires at the same price. It is the other costs, beyond the actual cost of labor and materials, that are so much lower in a lead-managed workplace than in a boss-managed workplace. Many of these costs are tangible. Bossing leads to increased worker's compensation claims and to more theft, absenteeism, abuse of sick leave, lateness, difficulties with unions, violence, and harassment, sexual and otherwise. But even more costly are the intangibles, such as obstruction, that are common to boss management.

OBSTRUCTION

Whether it is within the company or in how the company deals with the people it does business with, including, unfortunately, its customers, obstruction is a huge but intangible cost. The more workers are bossed, or in many instances even when they are not bossed but are so used to being bossed that they perceive every request as bossing, the more they enjoy using what little power they may have to obstruct. You can hardly go through a day at work without meeting someone whose mission in life seems to be saying, *I'm sorry, I can't do that; it's against company policy; I don't have the authority; You'll have to wait;* and, often, just plain *no.*

Playing it safe and enjoying it while the company grinds to a halt is the goal of obstruction. Workers in many modern boss-managed companies are told to use their initiative and make decisions—it's become the thing to tell them—but no one knows the choice theory that explains *why* it is the thing to tell them. As soon as workers at any level in a boss-managed operation take the initiative in an effort to keep the machinery going smoothly and something goes wrong, they are punished. This has to happen only once for the word to get around that it's safer to do nothing or to say no. Let the boss figure it out; that's what he's being paid for guides the worker no matter how it hurts what the company is trying to do. I had the following conversation with an airlines counter woman a few years ago.

"Here're my thousand-mile upgrade certificates. How many will I need?"

"You'll need three, but you're OK; there are three here."

"Wow, three. How far is it?

"It's a little over two thousand miles."

"Do you give me change? I mean, can you at least give me a five-hundred-mile certificate back? You sell those."

"No, you can buy a five-hundred-mile certificate and use it now to save the miles, but that's the best we can do."

"Does that seem fair to you?"

"It's company policy; there's nothing I can do."

"Do other customers complain, or am I unusual?"

"They complain all the time."

"I'll bet your company has meetings to get input from the staff. Do you have these meetings? Most big companies do nowadays."

"Oh yes, sure; we have them."

"If there are a lot of dissatisfied customers, would you bring this issue up? I think the policy makers ought to have some feedback, don't you?"

"I'm not concerned about the policy makers. I'm not going to bring it up, not a chance. I keep my mouth shut unless they ask me a question."

"Why?"

"I'll be marked down as a troublemaker, not a team player. They are always laying off; I'd be the next one to go. I'm sorry, it isn't worth it."

This woman's attitude is an example of the boss-management use of what could be a good procedure in a company that is trying to improve the way it manages. The woman won't open her mouth at those meetings if it could be construed by anyone above her that she was criticizing company policy. The company is getting nothing more from her than the use of her hands. Her brain is not on board, and her heart, which is what the company in that competitive business needs so desperately, will never be the company's.

But the habit of saying no extends far beyond what happens inside the boss-managed company. Workers often say no even when they are asked to do something they are paid to do as long as there is no way to check up on them. Since there are many instances in which it is hard to check up on them, customers can be very frustrated.

In dealing with their customers, many hotel employees delight in saying no. No is always safe, and they use it a lot. Some variation of what I am going to describe happens to me in hotels several times each year; it is only June, and it has already happened three times this year. The cost of this obstruction must be staggering. Keep in mind that if it happens with customers, it must also happen with coworkers who are as much the victims of this obstruction as are customers.

I was giving some seminars with my colleague, Dr. Chester Karrass, and we were working at a huge New York hotel. Karrass's office had shipped three boxes of supplies to the hotel, and when I checked in, I wanted to get the supplies in hand. I had learned enough about this problem not to wait until the last minute. At the convention center in the hotel, a woman told me that the supplies were in a receiving room; all I had to do was call the clerk and he would bring them to my room. I asked the woman to stay with me for the next few minutes while I called in case there was any difficulty.

"Hello, this is Dr. Glasser. Three boxes marked *Karrass Negotiation Seminars* have been sent to the hotel. I'd like them brought to my room."

"Sure, Doc, tell me again what they're marked. And are they large or small?"

"They are about ten inches high, a foot wide, and about eighteen inches long. They are marked with a stencil: KARRASS NEGOTIATION SEMINARS, BOX 1 of 3, 2 of 3, and 3 of 3."

The man was gone about three minutes; when he came back on the phone, he said cheerfully, "Sorry Doc, they're not here. If they come in, I'll get right in touch with you."

On the basis of a lot of experience, I said, "OK, that was your first look. I'd like you to take another look; this time, look all over the room. Could you tell me what you are looking for so I'm sure you understand what I want?"

"Sure, Doc, three boxes marked with some kind of a seminar, Karrass, is that it?"

"Yes, KARRASS. Please take another look. They were sent over a week ago from Los Angeles."

This time he was gone almost five minutes and then he said, still cheerfully, as if humoring a child, "Sorry, Doc; they're just not here."

I said, "I still think they may be in the room. Would you mind taking one more look? I really need to locate them."

The young woman who was still with me looked at me as if I were crazy. The man had looked twice, what more did I want? This time he was gone only about twenty seconds; when he got back on the phone, he said, still cheerfully and with no apology, in a tone of voice that sent the message that he was happy for me that he had taken another look, "Yeah, Doc; they're here. The damn things were right under my desk. Where do you want them?"

I told the young woman that she should keep this incident in mind and tell customers to be persistent. She was amazed, but not amazed enough to ask me how I knew to do what I did or anything about what happened. I could see that getting boxes for her customers from the receiving room was not really her concern and that she was certainly not going to do anything to improve the situation. Both the man and the woman had *no* part of their jobs in their quality worlds. The way that hotel is managed, they never will.

This incident, and the thousands like it that occur day after day all over the world, is typical of a boss-managed workplace. No one had ever sat down with that man and explained to him what his job was and worked with him supportively to help him understand it and do it better. By the time I talked with him, that kind of an intervention might have been too late. He would take any intervention as criticism and might do less than the little he was doing. Because of the pleasant way this man dealt with his inadequacy, I think he was not being too severely boss managed—managed by neglect may be the more accurate description—and his manager might be quite open to making this change. Still for lead management to work its way into a workplace will require a lot of effort. Putting a whole new psychology and the skill to use it into place is a big step. But if that step was taken, the hotel would make a lot more money than it is making now.

WORKER'S COMPENSATION

Although most of the tangible workplace problems could be substantially reduced by a change to lead management, the problem of how to deal with pain, weakness, or the more obvious psychological complaints that accompany or follow an injury on the job is more complicated. The better the relationship the workers have with their managers, the less these complaints will surface or persist, but good relationships will not prevent all injuries. When an injury occurs, there is always the problem of how to tell if the complaint is actually part of the physical injury or is the worker's way of restraining the anger at being injured. Or the way the worker is asking for more help or more compensation than he or she is being offered. Or if the worker is using the complaint to avoid having to go back to a job he or she hated and/or feared.

The present way to deal with these complaints is adversarial. The insurance company tries to settle the complaint with no further treatment or to fight it if it is seen as excessive. The worker tries to get better treatment or more compensation for his or her injury. I spent nine years early in my career treating these situations, and I can say that the adversarial way they were and are still handled does not serve the injured worker very well. The worker's physicians, lawyers, and psychiatrists do battle with the insurance company's equivalents. In my experience, the worker's interests are often subordinated to those of his defenders and their opponents.

While I worked for insurance companies, I kept the workers' interests in mind. I told the companies it would cost them less if they would allow me to work honestly with the injured workers, arrive at some conclusion about the cases, and then back me up. Some did, and I was able to do a lot with those workers using reality therapy and trying to persuade each one to look beyond immediate compensation to what was best for him or her in the long run. But whether or not the insurance company agreed, I was always honest and I was still able to help many of them.

One man who had injured his back on the job had been hospitalized for a while but still suffered pain and was not able to return to work as a laborer. He didn't have much education and had a hard time grasping what was going on. He was especially confused by the adversarial system he was immersed in. I was called in by the insurance company to try to get him to go back to work. But I was also allowed to work with him to think about settling, although I never negotiated an actual settlement.

I first saw him during one of his many hospitalizations. I worked with him for about six weeks, talking to him once a week. He was about forty-five years old, divorced, and living alone. He had worked as a laborer for a construction company and had injured his back picking up some heavy concrete forms. He had not worked since the injury a year before and was struggling to live on his temporary compensation. This was his fifth or sixth hospitalization. There was not enough X-ray or physical evidence to consider back surgery.

"John, I'm Dr. Glasser. I'm the psychiatrist here, and your insurance company asked me to see you. I'd like to hear your story."

I made no effort to hide the fact that I worked for the insurance company, but I also did not ask him how he felt. He did not seem to be in any acute pain. He was able to walk into my office from his room in the hospital, and I did not want to suggest, by asking that common question, that I expected him to tell me how much it was hurting. I also told him I wanted to hear his story. In most of the cases I dealt with, the lawyers sent these people to physicians who tended immediately to focus on the pain and, by this focus, emphasize the patient's inability to work. I was going to be different. He said, "You're another psychiatrist. Why do you have to see me? I hurt my back, I'm not crazy."

"I see people who have been injured and are also very unhappy. Pain is usually a part of that unhappiness. But I want to hear the whole story. I want to know what you think about all that's happened, not just where it hurts. And I want to hear what you want. It can't hurt you to tell me."

"Are you trying to take away my money?"

"That's not up to me. I'm trying to find out if I can help you. If you tell me your story, maybe I can."

He was reassured by my telling him I could not take away his money. He was also reassured by the fact that I wanted to listen to his whole story. In the area of workers' injuries, for workers of his educational level, my offer was unusual, and I was sure that he wanted to tell it to somebody. His story was simple. He had bent over to pick up the concrete form and as he started to lift it, he heard a "snap" and the pain started. That was the last day he worked. That story, including the "snap," was the typical story of a man living alone who had only a few friends to have a beer or two with. He had no money, a minimal apartment, an old car, and no family. He had not liked his job that much but he did miss going to work.

"If your back didn't hurt, would you like to go back to work?"

"Not on that job. It was too hard. I'm getting too old to do that kind of work."

"OK, not on that job. What kind of job would you like?"

"I can't work; it's my back, it hurts too much."

"I'm not talking about what you can't do. I'm talking about what you'd like to do. Do you ever want to work again?"

"Of course I want to work. I grew up on a farm; I've been

working since I was a kid. I wasn't good in school but I always did a good job where I worked."

"I can see that. You look like a working man."

That was the truth. He just told me that he had always worked and that he'd done a good job. Most of the laborers who were injured told me a similar story. This persistent back pain puzzled him, but there was still a picture of him working in his quality world. I then went through his positive past with him and asked him to tell me when he had worked hard and felt good about himself and was convinced he had done a lot of good work. I thought that there might be someone on this job whom he had not gotten along with and that this relationship might have something to do with his injury. It was a common element in these cases.

"I am a working man, that's it. I'm going nuts sitting around. My lawyer says I should be real careful, to get a lot of rest. That's all I get is rest."

"On this last job, the one where you got hurt, tell me about the guy you worked for. What kind of a guy was he?"

"He was OK. He didn't talk to me much. There was always work, and I did it. Sometimes I needed some help; some of those forms were real heavy. When I asked for help, he said, I'll see, but nothing ever happened. The funny thing is that the day I got hurt I wasn't lifting that much; it just went *snap*."

Another common story. Lonely, not much help from the boss—just a pair of hands doing a hard, lonely job. That snap is something that back-injured people talk a lot about. I heard about many *snaps* when I dealt with them. It seems to be more a sign of psychological than physical involvement.

"Anyone else get hurt on that job?"

"Yeah, a few weeks before I got hurt, a guy fell when some scaffolding collapsed. Not far but he got hurt. He hasn't been back. Kind of like me; I haven't been back either."

All the pieces are in place. Lonely, no help, no interest from the boss, a guy got hurt. He knew about injuries and compensation, not much, but it could all add up. He's probably not too hurt to do some kind of work, but since he doesn't think he'll find anything, he needs the injury; it's all that allows him to keep the picture of himself as a man who has worked and still wants to work in his quality world. And he's also tired of doing hard, lonely work. Unless he can see himself doing something else, this will be his last job. I won't talk about this laboring job anymore. There's nothing there for him. There may be nothing anywhere for him.

Staying in the hospital was costing five hundred dollars a day. There was no reason for him to stay longer except to talk to me, so I agreed to see him as an outpatient. He could drive in, and I arranged for the insurance company to give him twenty-five dollars to drive himself in and back. He could use the little money he would have left over. Each week he talked a little more about what he would like to do and less about his back pain. He liked seeing me, but he couldn't see me too much longer. I couldn't help him as long as his case was pending. It was costing money that might be better used in the settlement, but insurance companies do not look at it this way. I also got the feeling that he was ready to make some kind of a settlement, but the case had to go to a hearing and one was scheduled. We had a good relationship, and he was happy I was going to testify at the hearing. I told him that I was going to recommend that he was able to do some kind of light work but I didn't know what. I asked him if that was OK.

He said, "It's OK. You do what you have to do."

"The other doctor is going to say that you can't work. He may be right. None of us knows. You know we don't know. If you could be helped by any one of us, we wouldn't be talking."

There was no anger in the man. He was totally confused and tired of the whole thing. I believed that what I did was good for him, but I thought that if he could get out from under the whole thing, he'd be better off, both psychologically and physically. I decided to recommend that the insurance company give him enough money so he could stay out of the hospital for a while. The hospital was costly and bad for him, but each time he ran out of money, his pain got worse and he was readmitted.

Two weeks later I went to the hearing. When John was put on the stand, his attorney questioned him about how he was doing.

He said that his back still hurt. His attorney then asked if he thought he needed more medical care. John's response threw the room in an uproar. He pointed to me and said, "I don't need any more doctors. They can't help. That doctor, Dr. Glasser, he's the only one who cares about me. He says he can't help, but if I see anyone, he's the only one I want to see."

The hearing officer told John to keep quiet and get down from the chair. John again pointed to me, repeated what he had said, and then got down. His attorney told him to keep quiet and looked at me as if I had done something terrible. The insurance attorney suggested that a settlement should be worked out, and the two attorneys went to work on it. The insurance attorney told me I would not have to testify. John got up, thanked me, and shook my hand. He told me again I was the only one who cared.

I didn't feel very good. I was worried that I had screwed up his case. But the insurance attorney said what I did wouldn't affect the settlement. I would talk to these men in a caring way and suggest that they could do something more than they were doing. My care was not phony, I was not protecting the insurance company. These men were the victims of an external control adversarial system that does not care about injured people. The more adversarial it gets, the worse it is for the patients. I have no suggestions except that the sooner I see people like him, the more effective I can be. The man was injured, and by the time I saw him, he was choosing paining. That the pain was psychological does not make it hurt any less.

John's boss was not a cruel man. He did what he had always done with the people he hired. He had no idea how important half a minute of attention a week could be to this lonely man. That job was the only picture in John's quality world that he had a chance of satisfying, but he still needed a little attention if he was to satisfy it and hang on successfully to that hard job. Is it too much to ask that people who manage workers learn enough choice theory to give them this small amount of attention? A few minutes a day doesn't cost anything.

When John got injured, his boss had to spend more time on this claim and going over the site with the safety engineer than the minute or two that might have prevented or shortened the pain. The lawyers and doctors who made a living fighting over his pain were of no value to him or to anyone else. Greed was very much alive on all but his side in this case. John was not greedy. He deserved better than what he got at work and after his injury. The whole procedure has been distorted to the point that it no longer does what it was designed to do. But as long as external control is the psychology of the workplace, it is all we will have.

FROM ANNUAL PERFORMANCE REVIEWS TO SOLVING CIRCLE DISCUSSIONS

Deming is supposed to have said, *No human being should ever evaluate another human being.* I totally ascribe to this belief. He meant that no person with some power should ever make a formal evaluation of a subordinate. Obviously, no one can stop any of us from doing so informally; we do it all day long. We'd be much better off if we didn't, but that is not what I am trying to explain here.

No matter how much a manager tries to lead manage when he gives the usual annual revue to a subordinate, he is cast into the role of boss manager. This yearly obligatory task that many companies, private and public, large and small, insist that a manager perform may undo a great deal else that the manager has been trying to do all year. All workers hate these evaluations, as do most managers. Only unthinking bosses like to do evaluations; it gives them the feeling of power that means so much to them, especially since they can disguise their real motives under the pretense: *I'm trying to help you.*

Workers hate this pretense because they are well aware that their managers have no real way to know what they are doing and tend to try to make a few points, bad or even good, that may have nothing to do with the workers' actual performance. Even if the managers say something good, the workers know that they could just as well have said something bad; they had no accurate information either way. What the workers do is protect themselves as much as possible, no matter what effect it has on the company. This procedure perpetuates a climate of distrust in the workplace. If a worker believes the review was inaccurate, as many do, he or she and the manager will be separated and never trust each other. Companies lose a lot of money because of this phony procedure that has nothing good going for it. It is one of the few things we routinely do in industry that is completely ineffective.

What is needed instead is for the company to provide a yearly opportunity for each employee to talk to his or her manager about how they both could do something to improve the company. Instead of performance evaluations, these yearly discussions might be called company solving circles, the workplace equivalent of marriage and family solving circles.

In a lead-managed company, the manager would call the employee in and say, "I'd like you to tell me what you think you might do to improve things around here and what you think I might do to help. It's not important that we come up with anything great, but this is the time for us to level with each other and talk about what you want and how I might help. It's not the time for each of us to talk about what anyone else is doing, that we can talk about when we get together at our monthly meetings." Obviously, once this type of meeting became routine, this long-winded preface would be unnecessary.

The following is an imaginary dialogue with the airline desk clerk who wouldn't say anything about my mileage problem to anyone in the company. This dialogue assumes that the company has been moving in the direction of lead management and that the level of fear in the company is much lower than when I initially talked to this woman. I'll call the clerk Nancy and the manager, Susan. In a lead-managed company, workers and managers are on a first-name basis.

"Nancy, this is the time for us to get in the circle again. What's on your mind?"

"I'm taking a chance when I tell you this, but the way things have been going, I think I can do it."

"That's the purpose of what we've been trying to do. Get rid of all the fear that was killing things around here. I'd very much like to hear what's on your mind."

"OK, Susan, this is it. I want more say about what goes on when a customer makes a complaint or asks for something that's out of the ordinary. I feel like a fool saying it's company policy over and over when that's the last thing customers want to hear. This is a fast-moving business. The plane is leaving in a few minutes, and the customer has a gripe. I know my job. You know I know my job. I've been behind that counter for eleven years. I might make little mistakes, I'm not perfect, but right now I think I'm making mistakes all day long because I see dissatisfied customers walking away from the counter. Even if it gets fixed later, that customer is going to remember his dissatisfaction much longer than the once in a while we fix something."

"Give me an example."

"OK, it's that mileage thing. We give out thousand-mile upgrades, and the customer is traveling eleven hundred miles. It takes two upgrades. He has to spend two thousand miles to use eleven hundred. I'd like to tell him, 'We don't have hundred-mile refunds, but I can give you back a five-hundred upgrade in change.' Susan, we still make four hundred on the deal. I'd like to be able to make that decision. I might not make it for everyone, but there are times when I'd like to do it and I can't, and I feel like a flunky."

"That's a few steps above me. I can't give you that permission."

"You see, that's it exactly—you're in the same boat I'm in. But you could do something. When you get in the circle with John [Susan's manager], will you tell him what I'm asking? Not just for this but for a lot of things. If you'll do this much, I'm willing to write out a list and give it to you. But first I want to find out how the land lies. Don't leave me hanging. Tell me what happened so I know this solving circle is working. And if you don't tell John who's making this request, that's fine with me."

The higher the request has to go, the more fear there will be in asking for it, but what Nancy is really asking for is some feedback, that something real is happening, that the solving circle is not just some management consultant's daydream that no one at the top is taking seriously.

Susan said, "I think you're on to something. But if we give you more power to make decisions, how will we know what you are doing, how far you are going to go?"

"I've thought about that. I'll make up a lavender form so you can see it real easy. Then, whenever I make a decision that I couldn't make before, I'll write it down. I'll do it when I'm not busy or at home. I don't think it will be very often, but it's the idea that I can't, that I'm a little child who has to ask the teacher to go to the bathroom, that's what I'm talking about. Do you understand? This has been on my mind for five years. It feels good to tell it to you."

"I'm glad you did. I'll talk to John."

"Susan, level with me, I need this job. Do you see what I just said as out of line? Am I now a troublemaker in your book?"

"Nancy, I'm going to give you a letter confirming this conversation, saying you did just what we want employees to do. It'll be just between you and me. Is that OK?"

"It's more than OK. I just wonder why you have to keep it between you and me."

"Nancy, these things take time; it's the best I can do. When I give you that letter, I have to trust you, too. You see that, don't you?"

"It's a tough world, isn't it? You'd think that all of us would be on the same side, but it isn't that way, is it? If all we had to worry about is our competitors, we'd have a much easier job, wouldn't we?"

"Isn't that the truth?"

I am always amazed at the amount of fear in the world. External control confirms what Pogo said so clearly, "We have met the enemy and they is us!"

PART III
The Application

CHAPTER 12
The Quality Community

ALL OF US HAVE experienced kindness and caring from total strangers. Whenever a community is hard hit by a flood, tornado, hurricane, earthquake, or explosion, people from the whole country rally to their support. Even the news of a single person trapped in a cave or on the side of a mountain arouses the concern of people everywhere. When we help strangers, because we know it's only for a short time, we don't ask them to do anything but accept our help. The only picture of them in our quality worlds is to help them. Because we have no expectations of strangers, external control is rarely part of any of these helping transactions. But when we are with our wives, husbands, children and parents, students, or employees, expectations are very much a part of all we do, and external control is the way we attempt to do it.

This book focuses on individuals, on learning choice theory, and on getting along much better with each other. It is my hope that many individuals will make this choice, but they will still encounter many more who don't, who use external control to deal with them. Although it benefits you to use choice theory even if your spouse, parent, principal, or boss won't, it would help you a lot more if they did.

In many places in this book I alluded to how much better it would be if we moved as a society from external control to choice theory. I have envisioned the idea of a quality community, an entire community that has made the commitment to change to choice theory—a community in which you wouldn't have to be concerned that the people you encountered would be trying to make you do what you didn't want to do and in which the people all around you would think, before they did anything, Will this bring me closer to the others in the community or will it tend to move us further apart? In such a community, when you would use choice theory to deal with others, you could count on others doing the same.

It was this ideal that has encouraged me to try to persuade an entire community to think about learning choice theory. If I could show as well as tell a significant number of people in a community, including some influential ones, that these ideas are valuable and worth learning, the community would not have to spend a great deal of time and money learning how to use it; that part would take care of itself. And once this choice theory community got started, there would be a good chance that word of mouth would keep it going. But how do you show a whole community the value of these ideas and then persuade them to read a book that tells them to consider changing the way they live their personal lives?

I vividly remember how much my dad hated to shovel coal when coal furnaces were all there were. Then, in the fall of 1932, two well-dressed men came to our house three nights in a row and talked to my dad. I listened (he liked me to be with him when he did things) and, although I didn't understand much of what they were talking about, the men paid me a lot of compliments and I liked their attention.

These men worked for the gas company and were trying to persuade my dad to put a gas-conversion burner into our furnace. The burner would be free; all he would have to do was buy the gas. He agreed, and they installed a thermostat on the wall. The neighbors were very skeptical: "Now they have you; your furnace is wrecked, and you'll freeze. Besides, even if it works, it'll cost you an arm and a leg for gas." But you know the end of the story; my dad was right. No one has ever fought progress and won. If this book is able to persuade you that choice theory is progress, there may be a chance. What I have to do if I want to sell choice theory to a community is to put on my good suit, sit down with the people in the community, and explain the benefits of a quality community based on choice theory. I also have to remember to show how it could help their children; the gas company men didn't forget about me.

In late winter 1997, I was scheduled to present my quality school ideas to the Corning, New York, school district. I asked if Carleen and I could also give a free presentation the night before to the entire community on applying choice theory to an unhappy marriage. Then I asked my contact person if it would be all right if I went beyond the presentation on marriage and offered the idea of teaching choice theory to the community, especially, if the presentation on marriage went well. We learned that the room would be packed with over six hundred people. I remembered those men from the gas company and didn't take any chances. I put on my good suit and my best tie.

To begin, I explained the use of choice theory in marriage, citing the fact that a happy, lifelong marriage is an endangered species in our society. But I soon saw that this big crowd wanted more than a lecture, so I decided to demonstrate what I was talking about. I got the superintendent of schools, Vince Coppola, to play an unhappy husband and Carleen to play his angry, disgruntled wife. I played the counselor and demonstrated the structured reality therapy that I use in marital problems. Vince and Carleen gave Academy Award performances; the audience laughed their heads off. I didn't have to spell out what I meant. I could tell that in this short demonstration, the audience saw the value of learning choice theory.

While I had their attention, I offered Corning the possibility of pioneering the teaching of this new concept to all the people in the community, who could then use it in many parts of their personal lives. After the talk, I could feel the audience's interest as they buzzed and hung around. People came up and talked separately both to me and Carleen. I had a word with the chief of police, who recognized that choice theory might help reduce domestic violence, one of the most feared situations his officers have to deal with.

The next day at lunch about thirty community leaders met with Carleen and me to discuss this idea further. They were concerned about committing time and money to something they did not fully understand. After I explained the theory in more detail, they seemed interested but cautious. They said they would get back to me.

I kept thinking about their concerns. I knew these community leaders were also worried about something that they had not brought up—that skeptical neighbors would be only too happy to tell them that they'd made fools of themselves. But here the stakes were much higher than with my dad agreeing to convert to gas. If they agreed to this deal, they might make fools of the neighbors, too. I was asking them to agree to go beyond what my dad had agreed to, to put gas in all their furnaces, not just one.

In an attempt to deal with their concern, I wrote the following letter to Marjorie VanVleet, our contact person, to share with the small informal committee that was formed after our lunch meeting.

An Invitation to the City of Corning, New York
from
William and Carleen Glasser

As a follow-up to our recent invitation to your city to become the first quality community based on choice theory, we would like to put the following thoughts in writing.

When we were there, I asked the city to sign a contract

with the William Glasser Institute and I offered some sense of what it would cost to teach and train a whole city in these ideas. Since then I have decided that you need more substantive information to make this decision.

Before you consider signing any contract, Carleen and I would like to follow up on what we did in March by making an in-depth weekend presentation to a much larger group but similar in makeup to the group that met with us at the high school on March 12. We would like to do that at the end of January because by that time, my new book, *Choice Theory, A New Psychology of Personal Freedom*, will be available. That book will not only explain choice theory but also will describe, in great detail, how a whole community can implement this theory.

During those two days, we will present and demonstrate the ideas and give you a chance to break into small groups and discuss what was presented. Then, based on what you have read and heard, you will have the data to decide. By that time, we will have thought enough of this through so that we can give you some clear estimates of what it would cost.

What we need now is a commitment to go as far as the weekend in late January. That group could be as large as you like, but all who come should have read the book. Since the power of the program is improving all relationships, especially family relationships, family attendance at this presentation would model the program and give families a chance to give their input. Also we would want grassroots support. What we offer will not work if it is seen as elitist or as a "we know what's good for you" program.

It is also very important for this program not to be seen as a moneymaking venture for Carleen, myself or the William Glasser Institute. Our hearts are in these ideas; the community approach is the only way we can move the flat line of human progress upward.

The world needs more than words and books; it needs a model community to show the way. I hope Corning can provide this model. We can assure you we will not stint in our efforts to help you to succeed.

APRIL 1, 1997

The people in Corning were cautiously enthusiastic. They agreed to go ahead as far as getting a hundred people, who are representative of the community, to read the book, which could be in their hands by January 1, 1998. Then the hundred, plus any others who read it, will meet with Carleen and me for two days in late January. In this meeting, we will decide where to go from there. Since they are willing to make this pioneering commitment, we will charge nothing but our travel expenses as long as this project takes. So far, people in the community have offered to put us up in their homes so there will be no hotel expenses.

For me, this could be an incredible learning experience. I did not charge the Schwab Middle School in Cincinnati for the seventy days I spent learning and teaching there. If I had not spent that time in Schwab, I could not have learned much of what I have written here about education. As I did at Schwab, I have no intention of asking for money or any formal contract from Corning. But what we did at Schwab worked, and although Corning is a larger project, it may be easier, at least in the beginning. The rest of this chapter describes my vision of a quality community and what I believe may be done in Corning until we meet in January 1998.

THE HISTORY OF THE VISION

Although I was not aware of it, the vision of a quality community based on choice theory started in the early 1960s, well before I began thinking about what has now become choice theory. From 1956 to 1967, I was the psychiatrist for what was then called the Ventura School for Girls, which was run as a prison school by the California Youth Authority. A new school was built in 1962 that housed 400 adolescent delinquent girls. What I describe here happened in that new school.

I now realize that we created a quality community. We were the mothers, fathers, counselors, and teachers of those girls whose whole world was enclosed by a high fence and barbed wire. Without knowing it, we practiced choice theory. All we did was tested by the core idea of that theory: *Would what we do bring the girls and us closer together or further apart?*

These girls had a lot of experience with external control psychology and were about as far apart from us when they came in as anyone could be. They had committed a variety of crimes, had almost uniformly been sexually abused, and almost all were involved with drugs. The girls were used to running the streets freely and were hostile to the idea of being locked up. When they left our school, usually after about ten months, some had to be put into straitjackets to get them into the car to go home. They didn't want to leave what for many was the first place in years where they felt cared for.

Many stayed out of trouble; the success rate for them on parole was very high. If they could have left to go to a quality community, where improving relationships was a major concern, we would have had a much higher success rate. But if they had grown up in such a community and had gone to a quality school, most would never have been sent to Ventura.

The scene that I describe next depicts the very essence of a quality community. It graphically illustrates what could be duplicated in every aspect of a community that was willing to learn and use choice theory. If you agree that what we did was effective and can conceive of trying to do the same in your own life, as an individual, you are ready to make the move. Get a hundred people, including some of the community leaders, to agree that it works, and you'll have the beginning of a choice theory–based quality community.

At Ventura, the girls had individual rooms with their own keys, but for security, they were locked in at night. In the morning all the doors were open, and the house mother walked up and down the two wings to do what she could to help fifty girls get started for the day. If you have one adolescent girl at home, you can appreciate her job. The girls called her Ma and thought of her as their mother. The cottage was their home. Occasionally, we had trouble, but not for long because of what we did, which is well illustrated in the following incident.

A big, tough-looking girl named Tracy, who was hostile and threatening, had come to the cottage the day before. After the staff and the girls did what they could, she seemed a little more accepting of where she was when she went to bed. But the following morning, instead of getting her room ready, Tracy sat on her unmade bed, waiting. When she didn't show up for breakfast, the house mother went down to her room and asked, "Do you need some help?"

The house mother was immediately barraged with a series of curses and threats from Tracy, who had been planning to let her have it when she showed up. She tried to comfort Tracy, asked her politely to make her bed, and told her come to breakfast and that they would talk more after she ate. She also told Tracy that if she was still upset, she didn't have to go to school that day.

"It's not *my* bed; if you want the fucking bed made, make it yourself," Tracy shouted. "You're lucky I haven't torn this room apart. I didn't ask to come here. Why don't you just get off my back. Leave me alone. I'll come out there when I feel like it."

"All the girls make their beds. I'm not asking you to do anything different. C'mon, just do it and let's go eat. The girls have been asking about you; they hope you'll be happy here."

Notice that the house mother paid no attention to the threats and curses, returning hostility with kindness. She had a lot of experience dealing with angry new arrivals.

"OK, I'll come to breakfast, but I'm not going to make the bed."

This was the crucial point. The rule was that everyone made her own bed, so it was important that Tracy make her bed. But it was also important that in the process, we didn't separate ourselves any further from this already alienated girl. The house mother knew what to do. Stop here and take a moment to see if you can figure out how she dealt with this situation, so that the bed got made and she got closer to Tracy. If you know choice theory, this is what you will almost always be able to figure out. If everyone in a community knew choice theory, all could handle situations like this at home, in school, and in the community much better than most do now. In time, the community could be transformed.

If you are still an external control person, and I know it will take more than one reading of this book to convince you to change to choice theory, every fiber of your being is crying out, *I wouldn't take that from her. If she gets away with it, this whole cottage will fall apart. No matter what it takes, I've got to show her who's in charge here and make her follow the rules.*

Here is what the house mother did. It was pure choice theory and achieved the goal of helping Tracy get over her hostility and accept her new life in the cottage. If Tracy gave the school any further trouble, something like this statement would be repeated.

"How about if I ask one of the girls who was wondering about how you were doing to come down here and help you make the bed."

"Fine with me, except she's going to have to make it. I don't make beds for nobody."

Tracy's hostility was already simmering down. Tracy didn't curse any more because the house mother didn't show any concern for her language or her threats. All the house mother offered was help, but she didn't back down on getting the bed made. She also didn't say, "I'm the boss and you'd better make that bed," which would have led to more trouble and to Tracy moving further away from everyone than she already was. The house mother left, and a girl came down to the room.

She said, "I see your name is Tracy. I'm Jill. I hear you're unhappy. Can I help?"

"I hate it here. I hated Juvy [juvenile hall], but I never thought I'd end up here. I'm really pissed. How can you stand this fucking place?"

"I felt just like you when I came in. But I'll tell you, it's not so bad. It's a lot better than Juvy and the reception center." All the girls went to a reception center after juvenile hall and were sent to Ventura from that center.

"Do they make you go to school? I hate school."

"They don't make you do anything, but we all do it. It's really weird, but we do."

"You mean, they won't make me make this bed, and they don't make you go to school and you go? Are you kidding me?"

"Sure I go. It's a lot better than sitting in the cottage all day. I like the school; they have a neat setup where they teach us cosmetology. I could do your hair if you wanted."

Girls helping each other is a powerful technique. We always tried that first at Ventura. It is so much more effective than what many schools and institutions do: have staff members use external control, which makes things worse. But we helped the girls to learn choice theory as we do at Huntington Woods and are beginning to do at Schwab.

"Well, I don't know."

"What don't you know?"

"This fucking bed, I still don't want to make it."

"Then sit here and I'll make it for you. It's no big deal. Or we could make it together. C'mon, I'm getting hungry. If we don't get there soon, they'll eat up all the food."

The girls made the bed together and went to breakfast. The house mother didn't say anything except to welcome Tracy with a cup of coffee and ask her if she needed a cigarette. In those days, all the girls and most of the staff smoked, and a cigarette was allowed after meals and at other times—eight cigarettes a day for both the staff and girls. There were no special staff privileges at Ventura. Keep this scene in mind as you think about choice theory. If almost everyone in a community can understand and agree with what we did at Ventura, at least enough to try to use some choice theory in these common difficult situations, the rest of what has to be done to create a quality community will be easy.

What Would a Quality Community Be Like?

We've all lived so long with external control psychology that it's difficult to conceive of what it would be like to live without it.

Just look back to the girl in the Ventura School. By the end of that day, Tracy was part of the group. No one needed to threaten or punish her; it was all over. We could go for months with the toughest girls in California and not have a serious incident, much less an ongoing problem. But if you visited the school, you wouldn't see what we accomplished. You would see a lot of happy, teenage girls and wonder out loud, as my sister-in-law did when she visited, "Where are the delinquent girls?" If you walked around a quality community, you might wonder, What's so good about this? Even if you lived in one, you might wonder, What's different?

The change would be subtle, but you would see it. The streets would be cleaner and the people more friendly. It would take a while, but the fear that is always present, even in small communities like Corning, would be reduced. A person coming from another small town might see it more quickly than you and remark on what he or she saw. The people in the community would be looking for change, and the newspapers would send out reporters to inquire about change. I believe the changes would take time, but if the people began to use choice theory in any substantial way, they would see change.

If the schools made the choice to work toward becoming quality schools, the students, teachers, and parents would notice it. If you talk to a teacher in a quality school, he or she will say: "Everyone's happier and the students are working harder. Teaching's a lot more fun than it used to be." The visitors would say, as they do at Huntington Woods, "Why can't other schools be like this?" If Wyoming, Michigan, was moving toward a quality community and the teachers in the other schools were learning choice theory, not as part of an in-service training program but as part of a community program, it would be natural for them to think about having their schools work toward becoming quality schools. Huntington Woods has been a quality school for three years. It is visited by people from all over the world, but none of the other schools in the community has attempted to go in that direction. This is why a quality community is needed.

In a quality community, domestic violence would also decrease. When it occurred, there would be something tangible that could be done for it, similar to what the First Step Program, in Fostoria, Ohio, mentioned in chapter 8, does. But a quality community would go beyond the efforts of that program as good as it is, since the First Step Program operates after violence has occurred. In a quality community, where many wives and husbands would be learning choice theory and the solving circle, a great deal of spousal disagreements that later escalate to violence would be prevented.

But if the domestic violence reached such a level that the police were involved, the couple would be advised to enter the First Step Program, and the judge, at his or her discretion, could offer this program as an alternative to imprisonment or fines. The key to dealing with all violence is early intervention before much harm is done or before jail becomes the only choice the judge has. This nonpunitive, educational intervention is ideal. The couple does not have to be taught how to use choice theory; all they have to do is learn it together. To use it then becomes obvious, and how they are using it becomes part of the learning experience.

In a quality community as soon as anyone found out that a child was being mistreated at home or was not getting along at school or in the community, *this information would be considered a community emergency.* Most of the adolescents who were in serious trouble would be known to the community long before they did anything criminal. Early help saves individuals a lot of suffering and the community a great deal of money. My vision is that as soon as a substantial number of people in the community, both professional and nonprofessional, learned choice theory and were speaking a common language, some kind of a community effort would be created to deal with these children as soon as they were discovered. Both Carleen and I would like to offer ongoing consultation to this vital effort. What communities do now is punish or neglect; neither works, and things get worse.

I cannot suggest specific strategies. The best things to do would grow out of the choice theory that everyone involved with a particular maltreated child would know. The child's parent or parents would be asked to learn choice theory, or if the case was brought to court, the judge might order them to do so. But since the wife abusers in Fostoria welcome this intervention, the parents would probably welcome it, too. When trouble occurs, people who know choice theory can figure out how to deal with it. In our external control society, with all good intentions, we fail to help many of these children and actually harm some. Also in a quality community, as the tide of choice theory rose and carried the schools and homes with it, there would be fewer of these children, so it would be more feasible to deal intensively with them.

Lower medical costs would slowly become apparent as members of the community began to use choice theory in their lives. A large percentage of the people who seek medical care for aches, pains, fatigue, and chronic illnesses are suffering from the ravages of external control psychology, specifically, more from the unsatisfying relationships caused by the use of this psychology than by pure medical problems. In a quality community, people who were recognized as not needing medical help would be offered the chance to learn choice theory. The savings would far outweigh the few dollars that this opportunity would cost, since there would be fewer visits to the doctor and less medication would be prescribed.

Nurses; counselors; and, occasionally, general practitioners could be trained to run study groups that might be able to accommodate up to fifteen people (the ideal number could only be worked out in practice). This would be a specific, but inexpensive, extra provided by the health plan to augment whatever these chronic sufferers were involved with in the ongoing community program. I must stress that this offer would never replace medical treatment or one-on-one counseling, but it would substantially reduce the need for both and the waiting lists endemic to them. It would especially reduce the use of expensive procedures like

MRIs and CAT scans that are so often used with unhappy, chronic patients.

Right now, we pay a huge price for treating lonely people as if they are sick. Teaching these people choice theory could reduce that price and give many of them far more help than they get now. As they got help they would become the biggest boosters of the program. If an HMO wanted to be competitive, it would allow the physicians to give the time they would save to patients with diseases, such as cancer and heart disease, who could benefit from more ongoing attention from physicians and nurses. A physician who spends five extra minutes with a patient in intensive care and is perceived as caring can prevent the patient and his or her family from making demands that many, who feel neglected, make now. The best part of such a community program would be that it would not single these people out; what they would be offered would differ little from what the community as a whole was learning.

In a quality community, it would be essential to offer all police and correctional officers an opportunity to learn these ideas, so they could apply them in their work and teach them to those they worked with. For example, a DARE officer could add choice theory to his or her talks with students about staying clear of drugs. In a quality community, the probation and parole officers would teach their clients choice theory, and once the clients learned it, they would have something positive to talk and think about. Probationers and parolees individually, or in small groups led by parole or probation officers, would be asked to read this book. A community volunteer, skilled in the ideas of this book, might also work with the officers because it would be good for the parolees and probationers to meet a person from the community who showed that he or she cared by trying to help them learn these ideas.

Married parolees and probationers would be asked to read this book with their spouses and bring them to the discussion groups. It wouldn't matter if they did so sincerely or tried to use the book and the groups as a con; the effect would be the same. Some of the girls at Ventura used to tell me, "I'm just going along with the program; you're never really going to change me." I would say, "That's fine. Con me by doing well; it's all the same to me." Then several months later, they would laugh and say, "You knew it would happen, didn't you?" I would ask, "What happened?" And we'd laugh together.

The judges in a quality community would find that they had a new sentencing option, a new way to divert first-time nonviolent offenders so they could escape being sucked into the correctional abyss that not only does not correct but usually makes things worse. Judges could offer these offenders a simple assignment—to read the book and then write a report describing how they would use these ideas in their lives if they were given probation. It might get them thinking in a new direction. We have nothing now but external control, which is jamming our jails to almost inhuman capacity.

Inmates serving time in community jails and juvenile halls could be offered a chance to read the book and enter discussion groups as part of the usual time off for good behavior. If they couldn't read or read well, they could listen to someone else read the material or listen to audiotapes. Many of them would welcome a chance to break the monotony of incarceration. Like all others invited to participate, the inmates of the jails would know that this effort was going on in the community—that they were not being singled out for something special. This knowledge could help them decide to be more accepting of getting involved. Also, if some of these people were counseled, the fact that they knew choice theory would make the counseling much more effective.

The best-trained laypeople in choice theory I have ever met are a group of about fifteen prisoners doing long stretches in an Oklahoma penitentiary. They did not consider learning these ideas a chore at all. They loved doing so and said it was very helpful in the stressful place where some of them were going to spend the rest of their lives. Again, all that needs to be done is to teach choice theory and ask how people are using it.

In a quality community, the following might be a conversation during a routine first visit between a parole officer and a twenty-two-year-old man who was released from prison after twenty-six months for purse snatching and possession of drugs. If he repeated this behavior and was caught, he would face a much longer sentence. With his four or five juvenile offenses plus the time he was shot in a gang fight and had to be operated on, the community had spent more than $75,000 on him (not including the cost of his time in state prison), and he has yet to make a monetary contribution other than occasionally paying sales taxes. His chances of going back to prison would be very high if something different wasn't offered. The parole officer would start by saying, "Do you understand what is expected of you?"

"Yeah, no drugs, no booze, report on time, stay away from my old friends, and go to work. Oh, and come here on time."

"And be prepared to give a urine sample anytime we call you in. And bring a list of the places you looked for work."

"No sweat. I'm clean. I wanna work."

"Well, we still have a few more minutes. How do you think I can help you? I want to do what I can to see you stay out of trouble."

"You don't have to worry about me, man, I'm cool."

"I don't have to, but I do. I'm worried about you right now."

"What are you worried about? I told you, I'm cool."

"I'm worried about what you think about."

"Think about? I don't think about anything. Don't bother yourself about my thinking. I'm cool."

"Have you ever read a book and talked about it?"

"A book, are you kidding? I never read a book in my life. I never got through the ninth grade. It was all those books that killed me. What are you talking about?"

"I'm talking about we have nothing to talk about. Telling me you're cool is the same as telling me nothing. You can read, can't you?"

"Of course I can read. But if you're thinking about sending me to college, forget it. I'm trying to tell you I'm just not the kind of dude that reads books."

"You're also not the kind of dude that stays out of jail very long. People who never read books spend a lot of time in prison."

"What are you talking about? A lot of guys in there read all the time, and some of them are never going to get out. What good did books do them?"

"They didn't read until they got the time. If you go back, you may start reading, too. I want you to start now. Do something you've never done before."

"You're the boss. You got a book, I'll read it. I'm cool."

"No, I don't have a book; I have a book group. I want you to go to a book group. They'll talk about a book that a lot of people in this town are reading. It's not just for guys who've been in prison; it's for everybody."

"A group of dudes like me in a book group, you got to be kidding. Is this a joke?"

"No, it's not a joke. It's going on around here all the time. I think you'll find it more interesting than talking to me. It's all about you. It really is."

"What do you mean about me?"

"You'll find out as soon as you go to the group. I'm getting a group together now. Call me in a week, and I'll tell you where to go."

"I gotta do it?"

"You gotta do it."

"Or you'll bust me?"

"Put it this way. I'll be a lot easier to get along with if you do. The group meets once a week for two hours. They'll take attendance. Go four times and then if you want to quit, I'll listen to you. How about that?"

This could be a real addition to what the officer could do. Again, the men and women involved would appreciate that they were not being singled out for special treatment.

GETTING STARTED—THE INITIAL STEPS

Since developing a quality community based on choice theory has never been done before, exactly what we will do together in Corning will have to be worked out at the time. Those who participate in the initial group are very important. If they are community leaders, they will be asked a lot of questions by the media. If their answers demonstrate strong support for this program, we will have a good chance to succeed. The committee agreed to try to persuade at least a hundred people, most of them leaders in the community, to read this book initially. This is the group that will meet with Carleen and me.

Between now and then, the best way to convince the people we need to get started is to begin with whoever has regular contact with people in the community. In this initial phase, the committee may approach ministers who could communicate this need to their congregations. The message—bringing the community together—would be especially appropriate for church groups. I can also see the committee approaching community service groups and even the host of a radio talk show. Any place in the community where people routinely get together is a good place to explain the process and how interested people may get involved in the initial group. But I think the top people need to be approached personally by other leaders whom they know.

Two women in Corning, who already have some training in choice theory, have agreed to make themselves available to explain the program to interested groups and, if there is time, to interested individuals. For other interested communities, we have people trained in the use of choice theory all over the United States and Canada, as well as in a dozen other countries. I am sure these people would be glad to help any community get started.

For the first group, it would be wise for them to read this book with someone else and talk about it with that person as they go along. A husband and a wife would be the easiest, but any two people who will discuss it would be fine as long as one or both agree to attend the first meeting (to ensure that there are at least one hundred people at the planning meeting). But anyone else who has read the book, I hope including those from the media, should be made welcome at the first meeting. I will leave the composition of the first group up to the committee, but I believe the following people should be considered:

1. those who are part of the political power structure: the mayor, members of the city council, the city manager, local state and federal officeholders, and political party leaders

2. those who are part of the business and labor administrative structure, for example, representatives of Corning Glass, labor unions, utility companies, private businesses, banks, insurance companies, realtors, and booksellers

3. newspaper, radio, and television executives and reporters

4. religious leaders

5. judges of the juvenile, adult, and family courts and correctional officers

6. representatives of social service, welfare, and charitable institutions, charitable foundations, the department of parks, and recreational people

7. educational leaders at all levels, from preschools to colleges, public and private, as well as some student leaders who are juniors and seniors in high school

8. the medical and counseling community, including administrators of managed care organizations or HMOs, physicians, nurses, physical and occupational therapists, counselors, psychologists, and social workers, both public and private

9. representatives of the police and fire departments

10. interested citizens who have been involved in community work, including the arts; garden and environmental activists; and advocates of civil liberties

11. representatives of women's groups, civil rights groups, racial and ethnic groups, senior citizens' groups and such organizations as the YMCA and YWCA

12. representatives of service clubs like the Rotary, Kiwanis, Lions, Elks, American Association of University Women

13. some of the traditional skeptics, curmudgeons, naysayers, wet blankets, and obstructionists who read the book

14. anyone else you can think of.

If Corning gets off to a good start, I would advise any group who wants to start this process in their community to come to Corning and talk to the people who were part of this initial effort. In the first meeting in Corning, we will try to generate a plan to persuade a large group of people in the community to read the book. I believe that the intellectual interest is there. The good reading weather of a cold Corning winter will also be on our side.

Readers' Groups—The Ongoing Educational Phase

Given that there will be community support from the hundred or more leaders and others who read the book for the initial conference, a good way to get the rest of the community reading is to form readers' groups from volunteers at the first meeting. The more these people are known and respected in the community, the more they will be able to help the program. For example, it would be powerful if the chief of police was involved and then agreed to lead a group. It would also make it easier for the chief to ask his officers to get involved. But there should be no arm twisting. External control is not the way to a quality community.

The initial leaders of the reading groups do not have to be experts. All they will need is a good sense of humor and some people skills. Many of the people with the ability to lead these groups will be found among the retired. Nothing ages a retired person with a good brain faster than not using it, and this could be an exciting way to use it. If we can get ten group leaders from the initial planning group of a hundred each to fill their groups with about ten people who have some interest in becoming future leaders, we will be off to a good start. Even before the first meeting, the people from the initial group, who are already interested in leading reading groups, should start to get their groups together.

Natural leaders will arise in the initial group and in all subsequent groups, and the ideas will spread the ideas through a ripple effect. The readers' groups will decide how long they want to meet as they go along; there will probably be a great deal of variation, depending on the makeup of the groups. Even while the readers' groups are meeting, people in the groups who would like to lead groups themselves may get such groups together. I can see people in the group inviting others who may be interested to meetings so they can see for themselves what is going on.

Once these meetings get going, there will have to be an information and coordination office with a phone and a computer to register people who want to be in reading groups, make up groups, assign leaders, and keep track of everything. Some information about the people who register can be used to form compatible groups, but how to do so, or if it is wise, will be learned during the process. In the beginning, there may be many diverse groups and then, as the leaders arise, the groups may become more homogeneous.

High school students should be involved, perhaps as part of their English or social studies classes or as part of their community service, but all students should be offered the chance to learn these ideas. If they wish, juniors and seniors can be assigned to adult groups so they feel as if they are being treated as equals in this process. However, no student should be asked to read this book without parental permission.

The bookstores in which the book is sold should be encouraged to make up displays that tell what is going on in Corning, and pamphlets discussing the project should be available to all who are interested, especially, to those who buy the book. Bookstores might be anxious to cooperate with the committee to host discussions about the book. These sessions would be a good place to recruit people for the readers' groups. Some groups can be made up of people who have read the book and want to keep meeting, and others can be for new people. Large and small planning meetings should be scheduled periodically with Carleen and me during the first two years so we can both contribute as well as learn.

THE IMPLEMENTATION PHASE

The major implementation will be the nonspecific readers' groups in which each person is learning choice theory to use in his or her life. Then there will be specific readers' groups, such as school groups, made up of students, teachers, and parents who are learning choice theory separately or together but as part of a school working to become a quality school. Other typical groups would be those composed of police officers, corrections officers, politicians, governmental administrators, health professionals, recreational workers, social service workers, and the judiciary and trial attorneys; the list is long.

I can even envision a group of homeless people getting together for dinner and a discussion of the book. What these groups will have in common is that they will not be therapy groups; their aim will be to introduce their members to choice theory and encourage them to learn it by using it in their lives and, where applicable, their work. Almost all the nonspecific groups will be led by volunteers. The specific groups will be led mainly by professionals, with volunteers helping if necessary.

The other part of the implementation will be to introduce helping professionals, including psychiatrists, psychologists, social workers, marriage and family counselors, counselors of employee assistance plans, substance abuse counselors, and pastoral counselors, who are interested in using choice theory in their work but who have not yet been involved in readers' groups, nonspecific or specific. In Corning, I will offer to get involved with these professionals who have read the book to explain how choice theory is combined with reality therapy in the work I do. After this explanation and demonstration, if they want further training, they can contact the William Glasser Institute, which provides this training all over the world.

With the exception of professional training, which would be optional, the cost of implementing this program in any community would be minimal because the specific readers' groups, the heart of the program, would be led by volunteer employees from the organizations that are involved. Thus, whatever costs there were would be to set up and administer the nonspecific readers' groups. Moreover, every dollar the community spends on what I am suggesting will be reimbursed tenfold by what is saved, plus untold amounts of reduced human misery.

By far the greatest effect of the program would be on everyone's life. Each individual and family who learns the choice theory has a much better chance than they have now of finding more happiness, and there are research instruments to measure these savings. But the reductions in the more obvious problems—illness, family violence, school failure, juvenile and adult crime, family separations and divorces, unrest in the workplace, and drug abuse—can definitely be measured. Some of those statistics are being gathered now.

To avoid guesswork and speculation, the Corning committee has agreed to apply for a grant to hire a researcher to find out what has been good for the community and what money has been saved by this effort. This would be a wonderful project for a social science doctoral student under the supervision of professors who have expertise in this kind of research. There is a lot to be done, but Carleen and I are thankful for this opportunity and will do all we can to help. This is a pilot project. Our goal is to show other communities that working together, we can successfully challenge the flat line on the graph of human progress. It's time to move that line up.

As of October 1, 1998, the Quality Community Project in Corning, New York, is well under way. It is called the Choice Project and has been set up as a five-year effort with a director, funding, and a business plan. Currently two researchers have expressed interest in following the project.

CHAPTER 13

Redefining
Your Personal Freedom

THROUGHOUT THE BOOK, I have stressed how much more personal freedom we have if we are willing to replace external control psychology with choice theory in our lives. Now I focus on what I call the ten axioms of choice theory. It is through these axioms that we are able both to define and redefine our personal freedom.

THE TEN AXIOMS OF CHOICE THEORY

1. The only person whose behavior we can control is our own. In practice, if we are willing to suffer the alternative—almost always severe punishment or death—no one can make us do anything we don't want to do. When we are threatened with punishment, whatever we do we rarely do well.

When we actually begin to realize that we can control only our own behavior, we immediately start to redefine our personal freedom and find, in many instances, that we have much more freedom than we realize. If we don't do what we are told, we can decide how much personal freedom we are willing to give up. For example, when a wife says to her husband, *Unless you treat me better I am going to leave you,* she is in the process of redefining her freedom. It is always her choice to leave; what she has to choose now is how much freedom she is willing to give up if she stays. In terms of taking control of our own lives, which is always possible, we have to continually decide how important freedom is to us.

Think of how much time you spend trying to get others to do what they don't want to do and how much of your time is spent resisting others who are trying to get you to do what you don't want to do. Think of Tina, wasting time trying to get Kevin to propose, time she learned to spend on contributing to the happiness of their relationship. When she learned that she could control only her own behavior, she had more freedom to do what was best for the relationship.

2. All we can give or get from other people is information. How we deal with that information is our or their choice.

Think again of Tina. When she finally accepted that all she could give Kevin was information but that she had total control over what information she gave him, she had the freedom to stop nagging and say what got them closer together. She had much more freedom when she gave up worrying about what she couldn't do: control Kevin. A teacher can give a student information and help him or her use the information, but the teacher can't do the work for the student. When you get out of that trap, you regain a lot of freedom that you voluntarily gave up when you felt responsible for students who chose not to work.

3. All long-lasting psychological problems are relationship problems. A partial cause of many other problems, such as pain, fatigue, weakness, and some chronic diseases—commonly called autoimmune diseases—is relationship problems.

There is no sense wasting time looking at all aspects of our lives for why we are choosing misery. The cause of the misery is always our way of dealing with an important relationship that is not working out the way we want it to. Until we face that fact, we have no freedom; we locked ourselves into an endless, impossible task. There is no guarantee that we can solve this problem, but there is an absolute guarantee that if we don't face it, we will never solve it.

4. The problem relationship is always part of our present lives.

We don't have to look far for the relationship. It is not a past or future relationship; it is always a current one. It is here that we have to redefine freedom. We can be free of many things, but we are never free to live happily without at least one satisfying personal relationship. To get the most freedom in the relationship is a task that I covered over and over in this book, but it can never be a totally free choice. What the other person wants must always be considered, so in a relationship such as marriage, the freedom we can have must be continually redefined as the relationship changes over time. The solving circle is a good vehicle for two people who know choice theory to use in redefining their freedom.

5. What happened in the past that was painful has a great deal to do with what we are today, but revisiting this painful past can contribute little or nothing to what we need to do now: improve an important, present relationship.

Here we have a chance to free ourselves of the idea that it is important to know our past before we can deal with our present. It is good to revisit the parts of our past that were satisfying but leave what was unhappy alone. Most of the time we actually know what happened, but sometimes, if it was very traumatic, our creative systems have stepped in and erased those miserable memories. The argument that if we don't know our past, we are doomed to repeat it is incorrect. Our task is to do what we can to correct our present relationship. We are not doomed to repeat our past unless we choose to do so. Using choice theory we can correct our present unsatisfying relationships with behaviors that are satisfying to both parties. If we believe we cannot function in the present until we understand our past, then we have chosen to be the prisoners of what is over. This is hardly a way to feel more free.

6. We are driven by five genetic needs: survival, love and belonging, power, freedom, and fun.

These needs have to be satisfied. They can be delayed but not denied. Only we can decide when they are satisfied. No one else can tell us. We can help others, but we can never satisfy anyone else's needs, only our own. If we attempt to satisfy other people's needs, we lock ourselves into an impossible task. In locking ourselves into anything, we lose freedom.

7. We can satisfy these needs only by satisfying a picture or pictures in our quality worlds. Of all we know, what we choose to put into our quality worlds is the most important.

The most freedom we ever experience is when we are able to satisfy a picture or pictures in our quality worlds. If we put pictures into our quality worlds that we cannot satisfy, we are giving up freedom.

8. All we can do from birth to death is behave. All behavior is total behavior and is made up of four inseparable components: acting, thinking, feeling, and physiology.

9. All total behavior is designated by verbs, usually infinitives and gerunds, and named by the component that is most recognizable. For example, I am choosing to depress or I am depressing instead of I am suffering from depression or I am depressed.

Accepting this axiom is uncomfortable for external control believers. But failing to understand it takes away a lot of freedom. To choose to stop depressing is a wonderful freedom that external control people will never have. These people think the miserable feeling is happening to them or is caused by what someone else does. As soon as we say, *I'm choosing to depress* or *I am depressing*, we are immediately aware it is a choice, and we have gained personal freedom. This is why designating these choices by verbs is so important.

10. All total behavior is chosen, but we have direct control over only the acting and thinking components. We can, however, control our feelings and physiology indirectly through how we choose to act and think.

Understanding that we cannot directly control our feelings and our physiology, only our actions and thoughts free us to avoid what we cannot control. It is not easy to change our actions and thoughts, but it is all we can do. If we succeed in coming up with more satisfying actions and thoughts, we gain a great deal of personal freedom in the process.

Whenever you feel as if you don't have the freedom you want in a relationship, it is because you, your partner, or both of you are unwilling to accept the choice theory axiom: *You can only control your own life.* Until you learn this axiom, you will not be able to use any of the choice theory ideas such as the basic needs, the quality world, and total behavior. But once you learn it, all of the choice theory becomes accessible to you. You can then freely choose to move closer to the people you want to be close with no matter how they behave. But the more they, too, learn choice theory, the better you will get along with them. Choice theory supports the golden rule. To gain the freedom to use it is the purpose of this book.

The William Glasser Institute

I N 1967, I FOUNDED the Institute for Reality Therapy for the purpose of teaching that therapy. The institute is a nonprofit, charitable foundation. Neither my wife, Carleen, nor I take any salary for our work at the institute. Since its inception, I have greatly expanded my thinking with the addition of choice theory and have applied that theory to almost every aspect of reality therapy. I have also extended the use of choice theory into the schools, as exemplified by the quality school, and into managing for quality in all other areas in which people are managed. In this book I have taken the further step of trying to apply choice theory to an entire community.

With all these expansions and applications, I have gone so far beyond reality therapy that, for accuracy, I was encouraged to change the name of the institute to the William Glasser Institute. I made the change so anyone who is interested in any of my ideas or my applications of these ideas can easily contact us. Over the years, as our teaching and training have expanded, satellite institutes have been set up in many countries around the world.

The institute serves the public through its membership and benefits its members in many ways. Membership is an acknowledgment of a commitment to the principles and practices of reality therapy, lead management, and choice theory psychology. The institute coordinates and monitors all training programs and serves as an information clearing house. My latest thinking is often made available through audiotapes, videotapes, and publications to the members. As a networking center, people can exchange ideas through the institute's newsletter and connect through international conventions and regional meetings. The institute lends support to its members in their work with individuals, agencies, and communities. The *Journal of Reality Therapy* is a vehicle through which members can publish their works on new ways of using and teaching reality therapy. The institute also provides a voice for the membership through regional representatives and international liaisons.

The basic effort of the William Glasser Institute centers on an intensive three-week training program for individual professionals who want to use reality therapy in every area of counseling. (I use the terms *counselor* and *therapist* interchangeably.) There are five parts to this training, which takes a minimum of eighteen months to complete. First, we offer a Basic Intensive Week, which is available to small groups, with no more than thirteen participants per instructor. After this first week, those who wish to go on may enroll in the Basic Practicum group for a minimum of thirty hours. After they successfully finishing the Basic Practicum, they may enroll in the Advanced Intensive Week with a different instructor and, following that, the Advanced Practicum.

Finally, at the recommendation of the supervisor of the Advanced Practicum, a trainee is invited to a Certification Week in which the trainee demonstrates what he or she has learned. For this demonstration, we give a certificate of completion. This certificate is not a professional, legal license to practice, but the training is often used for college credit and continuing education units. Right now there are more than 5,000 certificate holders worldwide.

After obtaining their certificates, some trainees opt to go on with training and become instructors in our organization. There are four levels of instructors: the basic-practicum supervisor, who can teach a Basic Practicum; the advanced-practicum supervisor, who can teach both Basic and Advanced Practica; the basic-week instructor, who can teach both practica, as well as the Basic Intensive Week; and the advanced-week instructor, who can teach all four phases. Fees for the various phases of training vary. For the Basic and Advanced Intensive Weeks, the fees are dependent on whether the group members have contracted individually for the week or have contracted as a group.

For schools that are interested in becoming recognized as quality schools, such as Huntington Woods, the institute has a new program based on almost ten years of experience with this process. Contact the institute for the details. At the completion of this program, each staff member receives a specialist certificate stating that he or she has demonstrated competence as a quality school classroom teacher. The principal receives a similar specialist certificate stating that he or she has demonstrated competence as a quality school administrator. Their school is then recognized as a quality school. Before starting, the principals are strongly encouraged to take a one-week Administrator's Program offered by the institute with instructors who have had a great deal of experience teaching the quality school ideas.

Fees for this training are paid by the schools, but schools that don't have the funding usually apply and get funding from a variety of sources. Since a quality school is a drug-free school, federal and state grants may be available through drug-prevention funds. If a committed school puts effort into it, the funding can usually be obtained. Each phase is funded separately, so the initial outlay may be within the training budget of many schools. This book is the foundation of all we teach. Reading and discussing it is a requirement for phase one.

All our instruction in both programs is by explanation and demonstration. These are *hands-on* programs. It is our hope that people will contact the William Glasser Institute and find out how we can help anyone, any group, any school, or any community to pursue these ideas.

For people who live in southern California and are interested in these ideas, I present them at the institute in Chatsworth (when I am in town) on the last Sunday of every month from 4:30 to 6:30 P.M. There is no charge, and we welcome all who are interested. We give some priority to counselors, since I mostly teach counseling during these sessions, but if you wish to come, call, fax, or E-mail the institute to reserve a place.

The institute employs user-friendly, choice-theory-trained people, so if you contact us, you can be sure of a courteous response. It is my vision to teach choice theory to the world. I invite you to join me in this effort.

Address:

The William Glasser Institute
22024 Lassen Street, Suite 118
Chatsworth, CA 91311–3600
U.S.A.

Phone: (818)700–8000
Fax: (818)700–0555
E-mail: wginst@earthlink.net
Web site: http://www.wglasserinst.com

INDEX

acquisition fee, 247
activity, 4
  creativity and, 135, 136
  in total behavior, 72–76, 78–79,
    80, 83, 85, 87, 146
  of the workless, 112
African Americans, 245, 259
alcohol, 22, 87, 88, 216
Alcoholics Anonymous (AA), 23
alcoholism, alcoholics, 22, 23, 30,
  45, 87
  workless compared with, 108
All Creatures Great and Small
  (Herriot), 241
Alma, Mich., 236, 238
Anatomy of an Illness, An
  (Cousins), 138
anger, 22, 25, 26, 52, 67, 77, 181,
  200
  restraining, 79–81, 83, 145, 146,
    150, 151, 155
animals, needs of, 28, 32, 37, 41
anorexia, 32, 51, 52

anxietying (anxiety neurosis),
  76–77, 79, 137, 146–47,
  154–55
arthritis, rheumatoid, 79, 137–39,
  141–42, 145–46, 152–53
arts, 247–48
aspirin, 141
asthma, 140, 142–45
attention deficit disorder (ADD;
  attention deficit hyperactive disorder; ADHD),
  256
autistic children, 91–92
autoimmune diseases, 137–46,
  152–53
avoidance behavior, 82–83

backaching, 137, 146
bedtime, 213–14
behavior:
  choice of, 71
  defined, 72
  see also total behavior